MW00445527

ABRAHAM
The Friend of God

Jerald F. Dirks
M.Div., Psy.D.

amana publications

First Edition
(1423AH/2002AC)

© Copyright 1423AH/2002AC
amana publications
10710 Tucker Street
Beltsville, Maryland 20705-2223 USA
Tel: (301) 595-5777 / Fax: (301) 595-5888
E-mail: amana@igprinting.com
Website: www.amana-publications.com

Library of Congress Cataloging-in-Publications Data

Dirks, Jerald.
Abraham : the friend of God / Jerald F. Dirks.
p. cm.
Includes bibliographical references.
ISBN 1-59008-009-2
1.   Abraham (Biblical patriarch) in the Koran.   2.   Prophets,
Pre-Islamic.   3.   Abraham (Biblical patriarch) 4.   Patriarchs
(Bible) --Biography.   I.   Title.
BP133.7.A27 D57 2002
297.2' 463--dc21   2002008428

Printed in the United States of America by
International Graphics
10710 Tucker Street
Beltsville, Maryland 20705-2223 USA
Tel: (301) 595-5999 Fax: (301) 595-5888
Website: igprinting.com
E-mail: ig@igprinting.com

Table of Contents

All quotations of the English translation of the meaning of the *Qur'an* are taken from *The Meaning of the Holy Qur'an,* translated by 'Abdullah Yusuf 'Ali, copyright 1989, Amana Publications, Maryland 20705, U.S.A.

With regard to all Biblical quotations appearing in the text, unless specifically identified as being from another source, the following statement is noted in conformance with the request of the copyright holder.

"The Scripture quotations contained herein are from the *New Revised Standard Version Bible,* copyright 1989, by the Division of Christian Education of the National Council of the Churches of Christ in the USA. Used by permission. All rights reserved."

Preface

In the name of Allah, Most Gracious, Most Merciful

All praise and thanks are due to Allah, glorified and exalted is He. It is Allah, Who is the creator and maintainer of the universe, and of all that resides therein. It is to Allah, and only to Allah, to Whom we turn for help and for guidance. It is in Allah, and only in Allah, in Whom we seek our comfort and refuge. I bear witness that there is no god but Allah, the One, Who has no partners. Further, I bear witness that Muhammad, peace be upon him, was the slave and messenger of Allah.

In presenting this modest biography on the life of Prophet Abraham, peace be upon him, I thank Allah for the time and gifts to complete this book. I readily acknowledge the limited and finite nature of my own knowledge about the subject in question, and I pray that I have not inadvertently presented information, which might cause someone to doubt or question the true revelation of Allah. Any errors in this undertaking are mine and mine alone. Despite my own limitations, and despite any errors, which may exist within this book, I pray that Allah will guide the reader to a better understanding, and that this work may serve some humble purpose for the sake of Allah.

The following biography of Abraham represents an attempted synthesis of Islamic (*Qur'an* and *Sahih Ahadith*) and Judaeo-Christian (Biblical and pseudepigraphical) information. Given this approach, the reader may well wonder about my qualifications to attempt such a synthesis. In that regard, my educational history is as follows: A. B., cum laude in philosophy, Harvard College, Harvard University, 1971; M.Div., cum laude in department of the church, Harvard Divinity School, Harvard University, 1974; M.A. in child clinical psychology, University of Denver, 1976; and Psy.D. in clinical psychology, School of Professional Psychology, University of Denver, 1978. Likewise, my religious history is as follows: I was born into and raised within a Christian home; License to Preach, United Methodist Church, 1969; Ordained Deacon, United Methodist Church, 1972; and reverted to Islam in 1993.

Given my educational and professional background as a former ordained minister, I have attempted to share with the reader certain background information about the *Bible* and about Biblical criticism, in an effort to demonstrate how the *Bible* can be mined for nuggets of historical truth. In a number of such specific cases, the end result of Biblical criticism is a welcome support for traditional Islamic positions and beliefs. Unfortunately, the process of deriving much of this information is rather technical, so I have elected to include most of this processing in a series of appendices to this book. The reader, who is interested in the process, can read about it in the appendices. The reader, who would rather just get on with the story of Abraham's life, without too much concern for how I arrived at my conclusions, can simply read through the main body of this book.

With my educational and professional background as a clinical psychologist, I have been unable to resist the occasional urge to speculate about the emotions and motivations of the primary actors in Abraham's life. However, the reader will not find any "psychohistory" of Abraham within the confines of these pages. In writing this book, it is not my intent, nor my interest, to hunt through any recessed corners in anyone's psyche. In my own view, such attempts at "psychohistory" typically reveal more about the author, than about the subject of the author's inquiry. In my occasional application of clinical psychology as a framework for understanding the individuals discussed in this book, the reader will, Allah willing, find that the process has been gentle, and has done nothing more than subtly enrich the reader's understanding and appreciation of the individual in question.

Despite the fact that all errors in this manuscript have to be attributed only to my own shortcomings and failures, there are a number of people who deserve credit and recognition for their contributions to this book. These contributions have variously included proofing and editing, assistance with the Arabic language, reference search, the stimulation of give-and-take arguments and discussion, etc. In that regard, my special thanks are due to: *Hajah* Um Yahya Debra L. Dirks, my wife of 30 years; *Haji* Abu Wa'el Hasan b. Muhammad Al-'Awad; Abu Hasan Wa'el b. Hasan Al-'Awad; Um Hasan Suha bt. Ribhee Al-Khateeb; and *Haji* Abu 'Umar Ribhee b. Mahmoud Al-Khateeb.

In closing this preface, I again acknowledge the probabilistic nature of some of the conclusions drawn in this biography of Prophet Abraham. As to all truth, Allah knows best.

November 6, 1999   *Haji* Abu Yahya Jerald F. Dirks, Psy.D
                                                            Abu 'Alenda,
                                           Hashemite Kingdom of Jordan

Chapter 1
Introduction

The Friend of God

Abraham, peace be upon him[1], is a central and pivotal figure in the history of Judaism, Christianity, and Islam. In the Judaic tradition, he is the original recipient of the covenant between the Hebrew people and God (hereinafter, Allah).[2] In the Christian tradition, he is a famed patriarch, and the recipient of the first covenant with Allah, which was later refined as the Mosaic covenant, whereas the second covenant is seen as being ushered in with Jesus, peace be upon him. In the Islamic tradition, he is a heralded example of unwavering faith and steadfast monotheism[3], a prophet and messenger[4], and the recipient of one of the original books of revelation bestowed upon mankind by Allah.[5] Across all three religious traditions, Abraham is specifically noted to be the friend of Allah. As for the Judaeo-Christian traditions, three Biblical passages make clear this special relationship between Abraham and Allah.

> But you, Israel, my servant, Jacob, whom I have chosen, the off-spring of Abraham, my friend...[6]

> Did you not, O our God, drive out the inhabitants of this land before your people Israel, and give it forever to the descendants of your friend Abraham?[7]

> Thus the scripture was fulfilled that says, "Abraham believed God, and it was reckoned to him as righteousness," and he was called the friend of God.[8]

In the *Qur'an*, Abraham is also designated as the friend of Allah.

> Who can be better in religion than one who submits his whole self to Allah, does good, and follows the way of Abraham the true in faith? For Allah did take Abraham for a friend.[9]

Despite the pivotal role claimed for Abraham by Judaism, Christianity, and Islam, there are those that claim that there can be no accurate and historically-based biography of Abraham. Some would claim that all of the patriarchal stories were written too many centuries after the fact to be of any historical value. Others assert that the patriarchs were not individuals at all, but were the mythical personification of ancient clans and tribes. Against such a backdrop of skepticism, some Biblical scholars have raised serious questions about the actual historicity of Abraham.

In the face of such skepticism, it is not surprising that there have been few attempts to provide a thorough biographical sketch of Abraham. However, even when such attempts have been made: they have often failed to integrate Islamic and Judaeo-Christian information; or they have often been riddled with unsubstantiated "miracle stories", that do more to detract from, than to add to, an understanding of the historical Abraham of antiquity. Such "miracle stories" appear to be primarily derived from a type of Judaic literature known as *aggadic* (*haggadic*) tales.[10] Although more reminiscent of fairy tales and folklore than of history, these *aggadic* tales were sometimes repeated later by Arab and Muslim writers. Unfortunately, these *aggadic* tales so thoroughly mythologize the historical reality of Abraham, that they tend to obscure, rather than to illuminate the Abraham of history.

Against this backdrop of the polar extremes of skepticism and mythology, the present book attempts to provide a thorough biographical sketch of the historical Abraham.

Approaching Abraham: The Risks and Benefits of Synthesis

As alluded to earlier, most attempts to deal with the life of Abraham fail to make any viable effort to integrate Islamic and Judaeo-Christian information on the life of Abraham. As each informational source has its own detailed accounts and narratives concerning Abraham, the end result of the failure to integrate these two sources of information is a less than complete rendition of the life and personality of Abraham. For example, the Judaeo-Christian tradition is basically silent about Abraham's life in Ur and in Makkah. In contrast, Islamic information provides a rich account of these two portions of Abraham's life. However, Islamic information is often lacking details about Abraham's life in Palestine, while the Judaeo-Christian tradition tends to focus on this particular part of Abraham's life. Where information about Abraham from the Islamic and Judaeo-Christian traditions overlap, the two traditions frequently complement each other, with the narrative material of each tradition providing some additional context and understanding.

Nonetheless, at times, it is the case that the two traditions appear to disagree fundamentally about some particular aspect of Abraham's life. A noticeable case in point would be the separation of Hagar and Ismael, peace be upon him, from Abraham. In this particular case, the two traditions disagree about the age of Ismael at the time of separation, about the manner of the separation, and about the final destination of Hagar and Ismael. However, the student of these traditions is not merely forced to chose between the two narratives. Rather, there are often internal clues within a particular narrative that can guide the student to the correct modification of that narrative, as explored in some depth in Appendix IV–Sequential Events in Abraham's Life.

Therefore, what is needed in constructing a biographical sketch of Abraham is a willingness: to examine both Islamic and Judaeo-Christian information; to give each religious tradition's information serious weight; to synthesize across the different religious traditions, wherever possible; and where direct synthesis is not possible, to perform a sensitive and intellectually honest, internal examination of each tradition's narrative. In this way one correctly modifies the narrative which seems to be internally inconsistent or which appears to be a confabulated merging of two different stories. In short, when it comes to the life of Abraham, it is the author's sincere, if possibly mistaken, opinion that there is a real and genuine need to integrate the received traditions and literature of the three so-called monotheistic religions, i.e., Judaism, Christianity, and Islam, where such integration and synthesis is theologically possible. The fact that the *Qur'an* and the received *Bible* are in disagreement concerning various points of theological doctrine and dogma should not obscure the fact that there is far more agreement to be found between the two sets of scripture than there is disagreement, especially when it comes to historical material, as opposed to theological doctrine. It should also not obscure the fact that, when it comes to historical material, the two sources of information often complement each other, one filling in detail and narrative which the other has not provided. As such, the present book is an attempt to construct a biography of the historical Abraham through the synthesis of information found within the Judaeo-Christian and Islamic traditions.

In making this appeal for synthesis of the narrative material across the different monotheistic traditions, one can readily anticipate the objections that will be made. Some Christians and Jews are likely to object to any reliance on the *Qur'an* and on Islamic traditions, claiming that the *Qur'an* is not scripture at all, and was written only in the seventh century CE. However, what these Christians and Jews fail to acknowledge is that the *Qur'an* does not have to be regarded as sacred scripture in order to provide important historical information about Abraham. If one wishes to reject the *Qur'an* as divine revelation, one must then still deal with the incontrovertible historical fact that the historical information within the *Qur'an* was readily accepted by a wide mass of people in the seventh century CE. This would then suggest that, at the very least, the *Qur'an* contained a wealth of stories and historical information, with which the listeners to and readers of the *Qur'an* were already somewhat familiar. In short, the rejecters of the *Qur'an* must then acknowledge that the *Qur'an* contains historical information from earlier sources, whether oral or written, whether from an independent Arab tradition or from Jewish *Midrashic* sources, etc.

Likewise, some Muslims may strenuously object to any reliance on Biblical information. These objections are likely to be based on the Islamic position that the received *Bible* has been so contaminated over the centuries, that it can no longer be considered the original revelation of Allah. In short, their position is that the *Bible* has been contaminated and altered, and that it therefore should not be utilized in constructing a biography of Abraham. This objection is, however, as myopic as the prior objection from Jews and Christians. Quite simply, historians and biographers are constantly working with documents that are distorted, altered, and contaminated. In fact, it is difficult to find historical documents and records that are not written from a biased viewpoint, and that do not reflect a particular set of influences or interests. The responsible historian or biographer does not simply discard such sources of information, but diligently combs through them, looking for grains or kernels of truth that lie hidden in such documentation. Specific examples of this nature can be found in Appendix IV (Sequential Events in Abraham's Life), especially with regard to the handling of three narrations from the *E* strand of *Genesis*, one of which appears to be a simple confabulated merging of two different stories from the *J* strand of *Genesis*, the second of which appears to be a confabulated merging of a *J* strand narration with information reported in *Sahih Ahadith*, and the third of which can be shown to be contaminated by its internal inconsistencies. Nonetheless, once these confabulations and contaminations have been identified, and the appropriate modifications accomplished, the remaining *E* strand information of these stories is useful and instructive.

As a further reassurance to the Muslim reader regarding the use of Judaeo-Christian writings as a source of historical information, one notes the words of Prophet Muhammad, peace be upon him, as preserved in an *Hadith* narrated by 'Abd Allah b. 'Amr and recorded by *Al-Bukhari*.

> Convey (my teachings) to the people even if it were a single sentence, and tell others the stories of Bani Israel...for it is not sinful to do so.[11]

Having hopefully dealt with the objections that are likely to be raised regarding the synthesis of historical information from the Islamic and Judaeo-Chrisitian traditions, it is imperative that the author clearly states that in no way is he attempting a synthesis of the Islamic, Jewish, and Christian religions or of their theological doctrines and dogma.

Abraham in Context

There often appears to be a fundamental need in the collective psyche of mankind to portray history in terms of the "great man" syndrome. Taken to its extremes, this syndrome defines history in terms of a succession of great men or of great leaders, who apparently live, work, and accomplish monumental deeds in a contextual vacuum devoid of socio-economic considerations, geopolitical factors, climatic constraints, and prevailing intellectual, philosophical, and religious beliefs and practices. However, great men do not live, strive, and accomplish in a vacuum, and their monumental deeds can only be properly and fully understood within the broad context of their times.

With this in view, the author has attempted to provide relevant context, in which to surround the life of Abraham. However, as the geographical setting of Abraham's life changed from time to time, variously including prolonged stays in lower Mesopotamia, upper Mesopotamia, Palestine, and Egypt, this necessitated constructing a variety of different contexts for the life of Abraham. These various contextual settings are individually presented at the start of Chapters 3, 4, 5, and 6. It is hoped that these brief digressions from the specifics of the life of Abraham will provide the reader a deeper appreciation and understanding of Abraham's life and actions.

There is, however, one specific, contextual issue involving Abraham's life, which needs special mention at this juncture. Both the Islamic and the Judaeo-Christian literature is quite consistent in portraying the ages of individuals at the time of Abraham as being far greater than the average life span of today. This issue is discussed in some more detail in Chapter 6 (Abraham in Egypt: Postscript to Abraham in Egypt).

Considering the Miraculous

As already noted above, the "great man" presentation of history tends to minimize the historical context, in which any great man lived and operated. Moreover, the "great man" presentation of history tends to invite succeeding generations to create continuing elaboration about the deeds and actions of the great man, thus gently, but firmly, pushing the great man out of the world of historical reality, and into the world of legend. When that great man's primary legacy is one of a religious nature, the world of legend quickly gives way to the world of mythology. This mythologizing of the great man is usually accomplished by the creation of elaborate miracle stories, most of which tend to be missing in the earliest historical sources about the great man, but which can be seen to become ever more prevalent over the following centuries.

This later fabrication of miracle stories is no doubt meant to add stature and status to the life of the great religious leader, and to provide his religious mission with an apparently divine stamp of authenticity. However, as one miracle story piles up upon another miracle story, the cumulative effect promotes an opposite reaction than what was originally intended. The miraculous becomes an every day occurrence, the miracle becomes mundane, and the stamp of divine authenticity degenerates into the world of the fairy tale and myth. In short, the miracle ceases to be at all miraculous.

In considering the life of Abraham, one is constantly exposed to miracle stories that are not recounted in the earliest traditions. These miracle stories are seen in the narratives of later generations, and typically focus on Abraham's birth, his infancy, and the specific details of his escape from a fiery furnace. These miracle stories do nothing to illuminate Abraham's life and the historical reality of his religious mission, and they add nothing to one's understanding of or appreciation of Abraham. They merely transform the Abraham of history into the Abraham of myth. By their sheer exaggeration, they reduce Abraham to comic book proportions, and portray the prophet of Allah as nothing more than a "miracle man".

However, the above in no way means that while discussing religious leaders, one should by default discount all stories dealing with miraculous events. Such an approach would be nothing short of a denial of the divine. Certainly, in the case of Abraham, authentic Islamic and Judaeo-Christian literature document specific miracles, which are recounted in the succeeding pages of this book on Abraham's life. However, the author has gone to great pains to exclude unsubstantiated miracle stories as narrated in the *aggadic* literature, and has made every attempt to avoid portraying Abraham as just another "miracle man".

Sources of Information

To synthesize the historical information relevant to the life of Abraham, five general types of sources of information have been used in this book to construct a biography of Abraham. These are: (1) the *Qur'an* and *Sahih Ahadith*; (2) the *Torah*; (3) other canonical Jewish scripture besides the *Torah*; (4) non-canonical, pseudepigraphical writings in the Judaeo-Christian tradition; and (5) writings in archaeology and ancient Middle Eastern history. In utilizing these sources of information, the author has employed three general rules. First, as a Muslim, the author accepts the information contained within the *Qur'an* as the direct revelation of Allah and as fact. As such, priority is always given to the information contained within the *Qur'an*. Second, without violating the first rule, the second rule has been to attempt to synthesize all other relevant information with the information presented in the *Qur'an*. Third, unsubstantiated miracle tales, such as found in the *aggadic* literature, have not been considered.

For a much, more in-depth treatment of the sources of information used in constructing the present biography of Abraham, the reader may look up Appendix I (Sources of Information). A thorough reading of Appendix I is especially important, in order to enable the reader to comprehend the system and dating utilized throughout this book in referencing the different books from the Judaeo-Chrisitian literature. It is also important in providing a framework for understanding the structure and nature of the literary strands (*J, E, P,* and *D*), from which the books of the *Torah* were subsequently constructed. For those readers who elect not to read Appendix I at this time, it is briefly noted that *Genesis*: is one of the five books of the *Torah*; provides almost all of the information regarding Abraham to be found in the *Bible*; came into being as a literary product about 400 BCE; and was compiled from earlier literary strands in a "cut-and-paste" manner. These earlier literary strands of *Genesis* are known as *J, E,* and *P.* (In addition, *Genesis* includes some passages that predate *Genesis* itself, but that cannot be associated with any given literary strand.) Each of these literary strands has its own date of origin, site of origin, and historical context. In every case in which a specific passage in *Genesis* is cited in a footnote, the appropriate literary strand contributing to that portion of *Genesis* is noted. Further, the specific literary strand is noted in the text if the identification of the literary strand is important for the point being considered, e.g., where two strands disagree.

In addition, Appendix I provides a more detailed accounting of the priority of sources used in this biography of Abraham.

Caution about Anachronisms

This book frequently makes use of geographical anachronisms, e.g., referring to places during the time of Abraham as Iraq, Iran, Turkey, Syria, Ethiopia, Greece, etc., even though those nationalistic or geographical names did not exist until possibly several millennia after Abraham. These anachronisms have been used deliberately, in order to help readers place geographical areas with which they might otherwise be unfamiliar. However, the readers are cautioned not to be misled by or to draw unwarranted conclusions from the use of these anachronisms, and to bear in mind that they are being used solely for the convenience of the readers.

Sequential Events in the life of Abraham

Determining the sequence of events in the life of Abraham is at times rather obvious. Such easily dated events can serve as major markers around which the life of Abraham can be structured. However, there are many events, for which there are no clear guidelines differentiating order and sequence. In such cases, the biographer of Abraham is called upon to offer some sort of chronological sequence, which is based upon what few clues exist in the historical record, and which are occasionally based upon nothing more than informed, albeit speculative, reason. While the use of speculation and of reason is unavoidable, it is incumbent upon the biographer to differentiate clearly between those major markers about which there can be little dispute and those events which are chronologically placed via subtle clues and reason. Further, the biographer must provide the reader with the rationale behind the chronological sequence being employed. However, constantly interrupting the narrative of Abraham's life with reasoned argument as to why "A" preceded "B" is certainly less than satisfactory. As such, most all of the information pertaining to the determination of the chronological sequence of the events in Abraham's life is confined to Appendix IV (Sequential Events in Abraham's Life).

Chapter 2
The Birth and Family of Abraham

Birth and Name of Abraham

Abraham appears to have been born around the year 2,166 BCE.[12] It is interesting to note that *Genesis* rather consistently indicates that Abraham's original name was Abram.[13] (Etymological considerations suggest the name would have actually been Abi-ram, i.e., "the (my) father is exalted".[14]) According to *Genesis*, Abram was not given the name of Abraham, until sometime after the birth of his first son, Ismael.

> No longer shall your name be Abram, but your name shall be Abraham; for I have made you the ancestor of a multitude of nations.[15]

Three factors should be considered in evaluating the name change as reported in *Genesis*. First, the name change is obviously in response to the birth of Ismael, as Isaac, peace be upon him, reportedly was not yet born by then. Second, the etymology utilized in the above quotation from *Genesis* is wrong. "Ancestor of a multitude of nations" or "ancestor of a multitude" would be "Abhamon", not "Abraham".[16] Third, some Biblical commentators have suggested that the name change reported in the *P* strand of *Genesis* was simply an attempt to cover up the fact that traditions about two different individuals, i.e., Abram and Abraham, had been merged in the *Genesis* narrative. Whatever the historical truth regarding whether or not Abraham had the prior name of Abram, the name Abraham is used throughout this book in referring to the friend of Allah.

The Lineage of Abraham: The Account of the *Qur'an*

Regarding the personal lineage of Abraham, the only genealogical information provided by the *Qur'an* is that Abraham was the son of Azar[17], a relationship reiterated in one *Sahih Hadith*.[18]

The Account of the *Torah*

In contrast, the *P* strand of *Genesis* lists a genealogical tree stretching from Abraham back to Adam, peace be upon him: Abraham, the son of Terah, the son of Nahor I, the son of Serug, the son of Reu, the son of Peleg, the son of Eber, the son of Shelah, the son of Arpachshad, the son of Shem, the son of Noah, peace be upon him, the son of Lamech, the son of Methuselah, the son of Enoch, the son of Jared, the son of Mahalalel, the son of Kenan, the son of Enosh, the son of Seth, the son of Adam.[19] In addition, *Genesis* lists two brothers of Abraham, i.e., Nahor II and Haran II, and one nephew, i.e., Lot, peace be upon him, the son of Haran II.[20]

Additions to the account of the *Torah*

In one unreferenced section, *Al-Tabari* inserts the name of Qaynan between that of Arpachshad and that of Shelah, specifically noting that the name of Qaynan was not listed in the *Torah*. In explaining the absence of this name from the *Torah*, *Al-Tabari* states that Qaynan's name was deliberately excluded from the *Torah*, because Qaynan was a magician and sorcerer, who had had the temerity to claim that he himself was a god. As such, the compilers of the *Torah* believed that Qaynan was not worthy of being mentioned in a holy book.[21]

This same assertion is also found in the non-canonical, Jewish writings known as *Jubilees*, where Qaynan is referred to as Kainam.

> In the twenty-ninth jubilee, in the first week, in the beginning thereof Arpachshad took to himself a wife and her name was Rasu'eja, the daughter of Susan, the daughter of Elam, and she bare him a son in the third year in this week, and he called his name Kainam. And the son grew, and his father taught him writing, and he went to seek for himself a place where he might seize for himself a city. And he found a writing which former (generations) had carved on the rock, and he read what was thereon, and he transcribed it and sinned owing to it; for it contained the teaching of the Watchers in accordance with which they used to observe the omens of the sun and moon and stars in all the signs of heaven. And he wrote it down and said nothing regarding it; for he was afraid to speak to Noah about it lest he should be angry with him on account of it. And in the thirtieth jubilee, in the second week, in the first year thereof, he took to himself a wife, and her name was Melka, the daughter of

Madai, the son of Japheth, and in the fourth year he begat a son, and called his name Shelah...[22]

The book of *Jubilees* also states that Abraham's mother was 'Edna, the daughter of 'Abram and of Abraham's paternal aunt, and that 'Edna was married to Terah.[23]

Comparing the *Qur'an* and *P*

Two issues immediately emerge in comparing the lineage information found in the *Qur'an* and in the *P* strand of *Genesis*. First, the *Qur'an* and *P* disagree about the name of the father of Abraham. Second, the *P* account gives a much more complete genealogy, than does the *Qur'an*. In what follows, these two issues are dealt with in reverse order.

Problems with the Abrahamic Genealogy of *P*

Normally, a genealogy as complete as that given for Abraham in *P* would establish some measure of confidence in the historical accuracy of the genealogy. Typically, the more detail provided, the more confident one is of the account given. However, there are a number of reasons to question the accuracy of *P*'s reported genealogy for Abraham. These reasons are presented below.

The First Consideration

The *P* strand of *Genesis* cannot be dated earlier than the fifth or sixth centuries BCE, well in excess of 1,500 years after Prophet Abraham. Such a gap in years should give some pause before accepting the *P* strand genealogy as being historically accurate in all of its details.

The Second Consideration

The source material embodied within the *Torah* can be shown to be contradictory with regard to other genealogies and personal identifications. For example, the *Torah* variously lists the father-in-law of Moses, peace be upon him, as being Jethro, Reuel, and Hobab, the son of Reuel.[24] In addition, as we will see later when discussing the tribal lineage of Abraham, the *Torah* and other Jewish scripture occasionally list Abraham and his offspring as being Aramaeans,[25] which, according to the *P* strand of *Genesis*, would make them descendants of Aram, the brother of Arpachshad, not of Arpachshad himself[26], a finding contrary to the *P* strand genealogy of Abraham.[27] Further, the *J* strand of *Genesis*, predating the *P* strand by about five centuries, suggests that the Aramaeans are the descendants of Aram, the son of Kemuel, the son of Nahor, the son of Terah, the father of Abraham, which contradicts the *P* strand genealogy of Aram, and which contradicts the possibility of Abraham being an Aramaean.[28] In short, the genealogical information in *Genesis* can be accepted only with a certain degree of caution.

The Third Consideration

Many of the names reported in the immediate ancestry of Abraham are the names of ancient towns in the vicinity of Harran in Paddan-aram (Haran in southeastern Turkey), the area from which Abraham migrated to Palestine, according to *Genesis*.[29] For example, Haran, the brother of Abraham can be associated with the city of Harran (Turkey). Nahor, the brother of Abraham, can be associated with a city of the same name. Terah can be associated with the city of Til-Turakhi, Serug with Sarugi, and Peleg with Phaliga. This would suggest that many of the names in the *P* strand genealogy between Shem and Abraham should be read as clan names associated with some eponymous ancestor. If the ancestors listed between Shem and Abraham were merely eponymous ancestors of Abraham for whom clans were named, this suggests that numerous generations of ancestors may have been omitted while reporting Abraham's genealogy.

The Fourth Considerarion

There appears to be a remarkable similarity between the descendants of Seth listed in the *P* strand of *Genesis* and the descendants of Cain listed in the *J* strand of *Genesis*.[30] This similarity is illustrated in the following chart, and suggests that the later *P* strand genealogy of the descendants of Seth may be nothing more than a corrupted version of the *J* strand descendants of Cain.

Table 1: Descendants of Cain and Seth

J	*P*
Cain	Seth
Enoch	Enosh
Irad	Kenan
Mehujael	Mahalalel
Methushael	Jared
Lamech	Enoch
	Methuselah
	Lamech

With only a slight rearranging of the names listed in Table 1, one comes up with the following matches, in which the first name listed is from *J* strand and the second name listed is from *P* strand: Enoch = Enoch; Irad = Jared; Mehujael = Mahalalel; Methushael = Methuselah; and Lamech = Lamech. As noted by at least one Biblical scholar, it seems fairly obvious that the two lines of descent are really one and the same, though attributed to two different sons of Adam.[31]

Conclusions

Given the above considerations, the following conclusions can be drawn. (1) The genealogy given between Adam and Noah may be highly unreliable. (2) The genealogy given between Shem and Abraham is likely to be a listing of only the eponymous ancestors between Shem and Abraham, suggesting that numerous generations may have been skipped over in constructing the *P* strand genealogy.

The Father of Abraham

The *Qur'an*[32] lists Azar as the father of Abraham, as does *Al-Bukhari*[33], and this lineage will be accepted as fact. Yet, the question remains how one is to reconcile the statement in the *P* strand of *Genesis* that the father of Abraham was Terah.[34] At least four possibilities exist. (1) One option would be simply to disregard the *P* strand information. However, this course of action fails to result in any harmony between and any synthesis of the Judaeo-Christian and Islamic information. (2) A second course of action is to assume that Terah and Azar are simply different names for the same individual.[35] However, when confronted with discrepant names between the Judaeo-Christian and Islamic traditions, it would appear to be irresponsible to assume automatically that we have two different names for the same person, especially when there does not appear to be any linguistic similarity. (3) A third option is to consider Terah as a grandfather or some more remote ancestor than the actual biological father, as the use of the word "son" in the *Torah* is often used simply to mean a descendant, however many generations removed. This option does no violence to the information conveyed in the *P* strand of *Genesis*, and is consistent with the fourth option. (4) A fourth option is suggested by the work of several Biblical scholars,[36] i.e., to assume that the name Terah refers to the clan of people to which Abraham belonged. This option has the advantage of not rejecting the information in *P*, of being consistent with the third option, and of accommodating the findings of Biblical archaeology.

Although the second option cannot be dismissed, it is the fourth option that will be incorporated within this book. The inherent difficulty with utilizing this fourth option is deciding whether references to Terah in the *Torah* are merely references to Abraham's eponymous clan leader or to Abraham's actual father. In the course of constructing a biographical sketch of Abraham, the deciding factor as to whether a Biblical reference to Terah is to an eponymous clan leader or to Abraham's actual father will be the specificity of the passage in question. Where specific and detailed information is recorded in the *Torah* about Terah as the father of Abraham, it will be assumed that this information applies to Azar.

Abraham's Family Tree

It has already been determined that the *P* strand information of the genealogy between Adam and Noah may be unreliable. As such, it is omitted from any attempt to construct Abraham's family tree. Focusing on Abraham's descent from Shem, and attempting to integrate the available information, the following family tree can be constructed.

Table 2: Abraham's Family Tree[37]

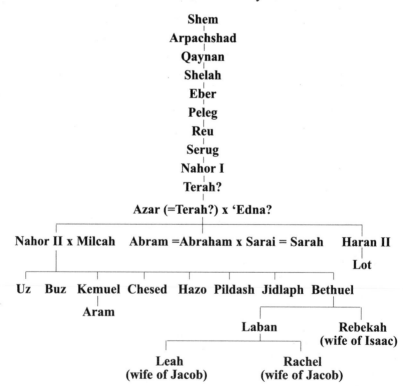

The Family of Sarah

All sources agree that Sarah was the first wife of Abraham. However, there is considerable disagreement as to Sarah's lineage and as to how she was related to Abraham. The following summarizes the different versions that have been presented in the past.

First Version

The received *Torah* states that Sarah was Abraham's paternal half-sister.[38] While this statement occurs only once in the *Torah*, it is reiterated in *Jubilees*[39], and is the version that has traditionally been accepted by the Jewish and Christian communities. Nonetheless, this version raises certain moral and ethical considerations that are repugnant to Muslims and to many Jews and Christians. Granted that the Mosaic Law prohibiting such a marriage had not yet been revealed to Moses[40], as Moses lived many generations after Abraham. Nonetheless, one is still left asking whether a prophet of Allah married his paternal half-sister. In asking this question, one bears in mind that there was no necessity for such a marriage, such as would have existed with the immediate children of Adam and Eve.[41] Given these considerations, it is advisable to search for a more satisfactory version.

Second Version

Al-Tabari suggests several different potential lineages for Sarah, one of which is that Sarah was the daughter of Bethuel, the son of Nahor, the son of Serug, the son of Reu, the son of Peleg, the son of Eber.[42] The problem with this proposed genealogy is immediately apparent when one consults Table 2 above. In short, *Al-Tabari* appears to be confusing: Nahor II, the son of Azar, with Nahor I, the son of Serug; and Sarah, the wife of Abraham, with Rebekah, the wife of Isaac. Given these considerations, this second version needs to be rejected.

Third Version

Al-Tabari also lists Sarah as being the daughter of Hanal, the daughter of Nahor.[43] Consulting Table 2 above, the question immediately arises whether Hanal is the daughter of Nahor II, the son of Azar, or of Nahor I, the son of Serug. In the former case, two generations separate Sarah and Abraham, while in the latter case, if Azar is equated with Terah, there is only one generation separating Sarah and Abraham. In that regard, it is noted that *Genesis* states that there was only a 10 year difference in age between Abraham and Sarah, with Sarah being the younger of the two.[44] If one accepts *Al-Tabari*'s report of Sarah being the daughter of Hanal, the daughter of Nahor, and if one accepts the *P* strand data concerning the relative ages of Abraham and Sarah, it would appear more likely that the Nahor in question was the son of Serug, i.e., Nahor I. However, in the final analysis, it must be acknowledged that this is all speculation, and that no firm conclusions can be drawn regarding the mother of Sarah.

Fourth Version

By far the most intriguing version put forth is that Sarah was the daughter of Abraham's paternal uncle. In a passage in which it is stated that Sarah believed in Abraham's prophetic mission and in the message that Abraham preached, *Al-Tabari* identifies Sarah as being the daughter of "Haran the Elder", the brother of Azar. In presenting this option, *Al-Tabari* introduces a new person to be included in Table 2 above, i.e., Haran I, the brother of Azar, and the paternal uncle of Abraham, Haran II, and Nahor II. In addition, *Al-Tabari* specifically identifies Haran I as being the father of both Sarah and Milcah, the latter being the wife of Abraham's brother, Nahor II.[45]

The *Al-Tabari* information becomes especially relevant when one considers one final piece of information from the *J* strand of *Genesis*.

> Haran died before his father Terah in the land of his birth, in Ur of the Chaldeans. Abram and Nahor took wives; the name of Abram's wife was Sarai, and the name of Nahor's wife was Milcah. She was the daughter of Haran, the father of Milcah and Iscah. Now Sarai was barren; she had no child.[46]

There are two considerations concerning this passage from *Genesis* that tend to support *Al-Tabari*'s position. First, the third person pronoun "she", which begins the third sentence of the above passage, is ambiguous. It could conceivably refer either to Milcah or to Sarah. While Milcah was the last named wife before the use of this pronoun, the fourth sentence is totally specific to Sarah, creating a somewhat jarring change of topics if the "she" in the third sentence refers to Milcah and not to Sarah. Further, if the pronoun refers to Milcah, the third sentence becomes internally redundant, i.e., "Milcah was the daughter of Haran, the father of Milcah and Iscah". This internal redundancy is totally avoided if the pronoun refers to Sarah, i.e., "Sarah was the daughter of Haran, the father of Milcah and Iscah". Of note, Josephus b. Matthias, the first century CE Jewish historian, apparently read the third person pronoun "she" as referring to Sarah, thus making Sarah the daughter of Haran. As Josephus read the passage, Haran was the father of Lot (nephew of Abraham), Sarah (wife of Abraham), and Milcah (wife of Nahor II).[47] However, Josephus failed to distinguish between two potential individuals named Haran, i.e., Haran II, the brother of Abraham, and Haran I, the paternal uncle of Abraham.

Second, the Haran in the above passage from *J* is specifically identified as the father of Milcah and Iscah. These children are nowhere mentioned in the *P* strand information[48] about the offspring of Haran II, the brother of Abraham, used to construct Table 2. Likewise, the *J* passage quoted above nowhere mentions Lot, who was identified in the *P* strand information[49] as being the son of Haran II, the brother of Abraham. It would appear doubtful that the *J* strand information would systematically ignore the child of Haran II, the brother of Abraham, mentioned in the *P* strand information, while the *P* strand information would ignore the children of Haran II, the brother of Abraham, mentioned in the *J* strand information. As such, it becomes probable that there were two individuals named Haran, i.e., Haran II, the son of Azar, and Haran I, the brother of Azar.

Conclusions

While the information presented above is not totally definitive, the considerations raised in the fourth version, coupled with the moral concerns involved in claiming that Sarah was Abraham's paternal half-sister, suggest that Table 2 can now be revised to include the information presented in Table 3 regarding the offspring of Serug, the son of Reu, the son of Peleg, the son of Eber, the son of Shelah, the son of Qaynan, the son of Arpachshad, and the son of Shem.

Table 3: The Family Tree of Abraham and Sarah

Serug
|
Nahor I

Hanal? (mother of Sarah?)   Terah?

Azar (= Terah?) x 'Edna?   Haran I

Nahor II x Milcah Abraham x Sarah Haran II   Sarah Milcah Iscah

Lot

Uz Buz Kemuel Chesed Hazo Pildash Jidlaph Bethuel

Aram

Laban   Rebekah
                         (wife of Isaac)

Leah   Rachel
(wife of Jacob)   (wife of Jacob)

The Akkadian Tribe of Abraham

Based on the above narration, quite a few conclusions can be drawn about Abraham's lineage. For example, to summarize briefly, Abraham's father was Azar[50], a member of the clan of Terah[51], and Abraham traced in his paternal line back to Shem, the son of Noah.[52] As such, Abraham was a Semite, a member of that group of people who claimed to be the descendants of Shem. More specifically, based upon information discussed in some depth in Appendix III, Abraham appears to have been a member of the Akkadian tribe, a Semitic people originating in the Arabian Peninsula and migrating into southern Mesopotamia (southern Iraq) by at least the early years of the third millennium BCE.

The Akkadians were originally a nomadic tribe, being herders of sheep and goats. However, by the late 24th century BCE, the Akkadians, under Sargon I, had established their capital at the newly built city of Akkad (Accad or Agade), north of Ur in the northern portion of southern

Mesopotamia, and had created a large empire including: Iraq, Syria, and Lebanon; parts of Turkey and Iran; and possibly Egypt, Ethiopia, and Cyprus. In short, the Akkadian Empire was essentially an empire of the entire known world at that time. In the process, a large percentage of the Akkadians had become urbanized.

Around the last half of the 23rd century BCE, the Akkadian Empire was ruled by Naram-Sin, the grandson of Sargon I. Naram-Sin was a man of despotic pride and arrogance, who took the royal titles of "king of the four quarters of the earth" and "god of Akkad". It may be noted here that he installed his daughter, Enmenanna, in the office of high priestess of the Akkadian moon god, Sin, at the temple in Ur, which was one of the major cult cities in ancient Mesopotamia where the moon was the center of worship.

It was probably during, or slightly before, the reign of the fourth Akkadian king, Naram-Sin, that Abraham was born.[53] Whether Abraham was born into an urbanized or a nomadic Akkadian family remains unanswered. Judaeo-Christian scripture, the *Qur'an*, and *Sahih Ahadith* provide no concrete evidence regarding whether Abraham's family was urbanized and lived full time in Ur, or whether they were still nomadic and migrated around the rural areas surrounding Ur. Likewise, one simply doesn't know whether Azar and his sons were skilled artisans working in the city, or whether they were agricultural workers or shepherds, who tended their flocks in the countryside. It was only much later, during Abraham's sojourn in Palestine, that he was identified as being a shepherd by the Judaeo-Christian scriptures. However, it is somewhat reluctantly noted that unsubstantiated *aggadic* tales, lacking any known and reliable historical provenance, suggest that Azar, the father of Abraham, was an urbanized Akkadian, who made his living by the manufacture and sale of idols, and that Azar unsuccessfully attempted to enlist Abraham's help in the sale of such idols. Muslim authors later repeated some of these *aggadic* tales about Azar's livelihood.

Chapter 3
Abraham in Ur

Biblical sources indicate that Abraham was born in or near the city of Ur in southern Mesopotamia, and that he migrated from Ur to Harran (Paddan-aram, Aram-naharaim) in southeastern Turkey as an adult.[54] Despite this Biblical identification of Abraham with Ur, the *Torah* is quite silent about the early life of Abraham. As such, almost everything that can be gleaned about Abraham's life in Ur is from the *Qur'an* and from *Sahih Ahadith*. However, archaeological discoveries paint a vivid canvas displaying the secular and religious life of Ur in the latter half of the third millennium BCE, the setting in which Abraham was born and raised.

Life in Ur: Secular life in Ur

Late in the fourth or early in the third millennium BCE, the Sumerians, a non-Semitic people from Anatolia, the geographical region including Turkey, began to build the city of Ur. Located about 200 miles (325 kilometers) southeast of present-day Baghdad, Ur became the capital of the whole of southern Mesopotamia during the 25th century BCE (first dynasty of Ur).

Throughout its history prior to Abraham, Ur had variously been an independent city-state ruled by a king, a city-state in vassalage to some other southern Mesopotamian city, or the seat of power that ruled over the entirety of southern Mesopotamia. In all three phases, a system of city administration and government was established. Labor was highly specialized, and included agriculture, fishing, staff to service the temple, and various skilled craftsmen, such as sculptors, seal engravers, smiths, carpenters, potters, and workers in reeds and textiles. Such specialization in labor was made possible by a system in which part of the population received its daily sustenance from a central distribution supply, in return for its labor in non-agricultural pursuits.

Agricultural enterprises formed the mainstay of the economy of ancient Ur. Utilizing a rotational system, approximately 3,000 acres

(12,372 dunams) of land were cultivated each year, with an additional 3,000 acres left fallow each year, indicating an agricultural work force of approximately 2,500 individuals, i.e., approximately 42% of the entire population of Ur. Irrigation from the Euphrates River was utilized, teams of oxen plowed land, and the harvesting of grain was performed with sickles in the spring. The primary crop was barley, but wheat, flax, dates, apples, plums, and grapes were also grown. Livestock was systematically bred and tended, with sheep and goats outnumbering the cattle. Animal housing and pens were sufficient to keep about 10,000 animals at a time, of which about 3,000 were probably slaughtered annually.

The wealth of ancient Ur is well attested to by the amount of gold, silver, bronze, and semiprecious stones found in the royal tombs of Ur, dating back to the 26th century BCE. Around the same time, the arts had developed and were apparently thriving in Ur, as witnessed by the archaeological discoveries of musical instruments, engraved shell plaques, mosaic pictures, statuary, carved cylinder seals, golden swords, and metal reliefs. With Ur having access by river and canal to the Persian Gulf, shipping and foreign trade were well established by the 24th century BCE, and archaeological evidence suggests that such trade extended to at least Bahrain, Oman, Afghanistan, Turkey, the Mediterranean coast, Crete, Greece, and India, resulting in something of a cosmopolitan flavor to ancient Ur. Cuneiform writing had been developed by the Sumerians, and had been adopted by the Akkadians, thus allowing for detailed written records of business and trade transactions, for governmental and administrative record keeping, and for the development of literature.

A large temple dedicated to Sin, the Akkadian moon god, dominated the city architecture. Massive columns supported the structure, and these columns may have been decorated with colored mosaic and polished copper. In addition, colored mosaics and metal reliefs decorated the walls, and statuary and idols were prevalent. Private architecture during Abraham's life is somewhat more difficult to determine. However, a few hundred years after Abraham, during the early second millennium BCE, individual housing consisted of two-story homes, with sufficient rooms to house family, servants, and guests. Within many of these homes, there was a small chapel in which the family idols were housed and worshipped. When family members died, they were buried under the floor of the chapel.

The typical dress of the men and women of Ur during the time of Abraham consisted of a large piece of tasseled or fringed, woolen material, which was draped in various styles around the body and over a skirt. Men wore the garment with the fullness of the cloth over the back, and with the right arm free to move and to manipulate swords and other tools and objects.

Despite its impressive wealth and civilization, Ur was still a city of the third millennium BCE, and its size was proportionate to its times. Archaeological excavations suggest that Ur covered about 50 acres (206 dunams), and housed a population of about 6,000 individuals. To put the size of Ur into perspective, a millennium after Abraham, i.e., in the second millennium BCE, the population of the entire area comprising Iraq was only about 750,000, failing to reach 2,000,000 until the Assyrian Empire of the seventh century BCE.

Religious Life in Ur

The religious life of ancient Mesopotamia in the fourth and third millennia BCE forms a single strand of tradition that had its beginnings with the Sumerians in the fourth millennium BCE, and this time period may be taken as the first stage of the religious development. The third millennial immigration of the Akkadians did not displace the earlier Sumerian religious strand, but subtly modified and added to it, creating the second stage of religious development. Throughout both millennia, this religious tradition influenced all aspects of life in Mesopotamia, including social, legal, economic, political, military, art, and literature. As such, there can be little chance of understanding ancient Mesopotamian culture without understanding ancient Mesopotamian religious life.

During its first stage of development, Mesopotamian religious life consisted of a vigorous polytheism, focusing on the worship of the forces of nature, often visualized in non-human form. Given the agricultural nature of ancient Mesopotamia, the deification of natural forces frequently focused on agricultural fertility, and encompassed the notion of the "dying god", i.e., a fertility deity who cycled through stages of death and regeneration, just as did the crops tended by the ancient Sumerians and Akkadians. In this ancient stage of religious life, representations of an individual god would have had characteristics specific to the crop or to the agricultural setting most relevant to the worshipper.

However, by the third millennium BCE, Mesopotamian religious life had evolved into a second stage of development. During this period, the gods became arranged into a pantheon, in which each god had its particular sphere of influence, office, and order or place within the cosmos. The popular visualization of the gods became increasingly influenced by anthropomorphism (having human-like shape and physiology) and by arthropopathism (having human-like motivations and emotions). However, the earlier fertility cult aspects of religious life continued as a vigorous substratum.

Religious life was supplemented and enhanced by a combination of written and oral traditions. Through these myths, hymns, and epics, the ancient Sumerians and Akkadians sought to preserve some core of early history, e.g., the flood of Noah, and to explain the origin, nature, and meaning of the cosmos and of the world around them. Cosmogony, the origin of man, agricultural cycles, etc., all found their explanation and place in the religious traditions of ancient Mesopotamia. An examination of creation myths in ancient Mesopotamian religion reveals certain core similarities to the creation as portrayed in *Genesis* and in the *Qur'an*, and also provides evidence of a belief in an afterlife.

The center of organized religious life was the cult temple, which was believed to be the actual, physical home of the god. Within its temple, the primary god of that temple was represented by a wooden idol covered with gold plate. Additional idols represented gods who were associated with the primary god of the temple. In order to serve the god adequately, massive resources had to be dedicated to the temple. As such, each city temple owned abundant agricultural acreage, plentiful orchards, flocks of sheep, herds of cattle, and natural game preserves. A large temple staff prepared and cooked meals for the primary idol, bathed the idol, draped it in costly raiment and finery, and actually placed it in a bed at night. This necessitated that the priestly staff included cooks, bakers, waiters, praise singers, musicians, bathers, and other various and sundry servants. The king was the nominal head of the priests serving the cult temple, and various members of the royal family frequently filled the upper echelons of the temple priesthood.

Typically, each Mesopotamian city had a temple dedicated to the primary cult god of that city, e.g., Anu, the sky god, was the dominant deity worshipped in the city of Erech; Ea, the god of water, in Eridu; Bel, the god of the atmosphere, in Nippur; Shamash, the god of the sun, in both Larsa and Sippar; Ishtar, the goddess of Venus, in Erech; and Sin, the moon god, in both Ur and Harran. These temples dominated the city landscape, and measured anywhere from: (A) 210 feet (65 meters) x 150 feet (46 meters); to (B) 275 feet (85 meters) x 175 feet (54 meters). They could have been multi-storied, and may have reached a height of 40 feet (12 meters).

The pantheon of gods of Mesopotamia in the third millennium BCE reached a theoretical apex with a triad of gods consisting of Anu, Ea, and Bel. Anu was the god of the sky; theoretically, the highest god in the pantheon, although he supposedly had little interaction with humans; father of all the other gods; and the god of kings and of the calendar. Ea was the god of water; and the form-giving god, thus the god of craftsmen and artists. Bel was the god of the atmosphere and of the wind; the embodiment of energy and force; the god of order and destiny; and the god of agriculture. A secondary triad of gods, held in especially great esteem at Ur and at Harran, was an astral triad, consisting of Sin, Shamash, and Ishtar.

Sin, who was also known as Nanna or as Nanna-Sin, was believed to be the son of Bel, and the father of Shamash and possibly of Ishtar. Besides being the god of the moon, Sin was believed to be the god of cattle, and he was intricately associated with fertility in cattle. In addition, Sin was believed to govern the rise of waters, the growth of reeds, and the quantity of dairy products. In the earliest stage of religious development in Mesopotamia, Sin was represented by either a bull or a boat. During the subsequent stage of religious development, Sin was more likely to be represented as a cowherd or boatsman, who was often an old man with a flowing beard and with a four-horned headdress topped by a crescent moon.

Shamash, who was also known as Utu, was the son of Sin, and the god of the sun. He was the god of justice, the judge of both gods and men, and the governor of the universe. He enjoyed the power of light over darkness, and metaphorically of goodness over evil. At night, he was said to rule the underworld. During the second stage of religious development in Mesopotamia, he was frequently depicted as sitting on a throne, holding a staff and a ring.

Ishtar, who was also known as Inanna, was the goddess of Venus, i.e., the morning and evening star. She was also the goddess of war, sex, dates, wool, meat, rain, thunderstorms, the storehouse, brides, the alehouse, and prostitution. Her cult worship probably included temple prostitution, and certainly her cult city of Erich was filled with harlots and prostitutes. In the first stage of religious development, she was frequently represented either as a storehouse gate or as a star with six, eight, or 16 rays within a circle.

As already noted, the primary cult cities of Sin were Ur and Harran. At Ur, the primary temple was dedicated to Sin. Within that temple, the main idol, covered in gold, and draped with fine clothing, was Sin. As Sin was associated in the astral triad with Shamash and with Ishtar, idols of these deities would also have been prominent in Sin's temple at Ur. The importance of Sin, and to a lesser extent of Shamash and Ishtar, to the people of Ur and to the entire Akkadian Empire is well documented by the following additional consideration. During the reign of Naram-Sin, whose very name incorporated the name of the Akkadian moon god, the high priestess of Sin at the temple at Ur was Enmenanna, the daughter of Naram-Sin. In her capacity as high priestess (*Entu*), Enmenanna was believed to be the human wife of Sin, and she would have participated as Sin's bride in the cult rites of the sacred marriage.

The sum total of the above illustrates the religious environment in which Abraham was born, raised, and educated. It is against this backdrop that one finds Abraham struggling to find his way to monotheism.

Sources of Information about Abraham in Ur

As noted earlier, the Biblical tradition is strangely silent about Abraham's early life in Ur, reporting only that he was raised with two brothers, viz., Haran II and Nahor II, and that he married Sarah before immigrating to Harran.[55] In contrast, the *Qur'an* and *Sahih Ahadith* provide information concerning Abraham's initial acceptance of monotheism, Abraham's early preaching, and the resulting persecution of Abraham.

Abraham and Monotheism

The *Qur'an* presents two complementary threads of information regarding Abraham's acceptance of monotheism. The first concerns Abraham's natural reasoning, while the second emphasizes that Abraham was chosen by Allah.

Abraham and Natural Observation: Precursors

Throughout his childhood, Abraham was constantly surrounded by a focus on and the worship of Sin, the Akkadian moon god. Ur's cult temple was dedicated to Sin, and Enmenanna, the daughter of the emperor, Naram-Sin, actually served as the high priestess of Sin in Ur. In this capacity, Enmenanna was seen as the earthly bride of Sin, and she served this function in various cult rituals and rites. A large, gold-plated, wooden idol of Sin, dressed in the finest and most costly of clothing, dominated the interior of Ur's cult temple. Priestly servants cooked for, baked for, bathed, dressed, and sang for the idol of Sin. At night, these priestly servants actually reclined the idol of Sin in a large bed. These factors could only have increased Abraham's acute awareness of the esteem in which Sin was held by Abraham's peers. Surely, Abraham's religious sensibilities were being constantly directed to the contemplation of Sin and to the moon itself.

As Sin formed part of an astral triad with Shamash, the Akkadian sun god, and with Ishtar, the Akkadian goddess of Venus, idols of Shamash and of Ishtar would also have enjoyed prominent display within Ur's cult temple. While the idols of Shamash and of Ishtar would not have been as large as that of Sin, they hardly could have been missed by any observant individual. As such, Abraham's religious attention and contemplation were further directed to the sun and to Venus, also known as the morning and evening star.

However, it was not just within the confines of the cult temple that Abraham's attention was being directed to the moon, to the sun, and to the evening star. One could hardly have walked the streets of Ur without being confronted by the worship of this astral triad. Further, as Azar, Abraham's father, worshipped idols[56], there were probably within Azar's very house idols symbolizing the moon, the sun, and the evening star.[57]

Natural Observation

Given the specific dedications of the cult temple at Ur, the religious climate to be found everywhere around him in the streets of Ur, and the idol worship within his own father's house, Abraham's religious sensibilities were being constantly focused on an astral triad consisting of the moon, the sun, and the evening star. Given this specific context, it was only natural that, as he reached his early teenage years, such a spiritually and religiously attuned individual as Abraham would have begun: to have questioned the religious context that surrounded him; and to have turned his attention to the heavens, and precisely to the three astral bodies primarily associated with worship in Ur, i.e., the moon, the sun, and the evening star. With his focus thus directed, Abraham, although still a youth in his early teens[58], perhaps being only 14 years of age[59], began to contemplate the natural laws within the cosmos that governed and ordered the moon (Sin), the sun (Shamash), and the evening star (Ishtar).

> So also did We show Abraham the power and the laws of the heavens and the earth, that he might (with understanding) have certitude. When the night covered him over, he saw a star: he said: "This is my Lord." But when it set, he said: "I love not those that set." When he saw the moon rising in splendour, he said: "This is my Lord." But when the moon set, he said: "Unless my Lord guide me, I shall surely be among those who go astray." When he saw the sun rising in splendour, he said: "This is my Lord; this is the greatest (of all)." But when the sun set, he said: "O my people! I am indeed free from your (guilt) of giving partners to Allah. For me, I have set my face, firmly and truly, towards Him Who created the heavens and the earth, and never shall I give partners to Allah."[60]

Abraham's own natural reasoning abilities and contemplation, which were focused on the natural laws governing the physical cosmos, and specifically on the natural laws governing the movement of the three primary astral objects most venerated at Ur, led him to reject polytheistic astral worship and idolatry. In so doing, his attention shifted from the created to the Creator. By contemplating the natural laws governing the moon, the sun, and the evening star, Abraham began to appreciate the master plan of a grand architect of the universe. Having made this mental step, the very order and uniformity of the universe demanded the rejection of a multiplicity of architectural plans, which could have only led to chaos and confusion. Having rejected the concept of a multiplicity of architectural plans, Abraham was led to reject the concept of a multiplicity of architects. Within his own mind and within the inner workings of his religious awareness and understanding, Abraham was set free from the polytheism of his environment. Abraham's conclusion was direct and inescapable: Allah is One, and without partners.[61]

This process of natural observation and of contemplation of the cosmos was also attributed to Abraham over 500 years prior to the revelation of the *Qur'an* by Flavius Josephus b. Matthias, the first century CE Jewish historian. Quoting either from still earlier Jewish *Midrashic* sources or from an ancient version of the *Torah* that no longer exists, Josephus reported that Abraham's reasoning was: the movement of the astral bodies betrayed their lack of self-power; therefore, their movements must be ordained by One Who commands them; and therefore, that One Who commands them must be He, Whom alone man ought to worship.[62]

Abraham, The Chosen of Allah

By contemplation of the physical universe that surrounded him, Abraham, although still in his early teenage years, had reasoned to a monotheistic belief in Allah. However, there have been many individuals, often quite older than was Abraham, who have contemplated the heavens, who have watched the orderly movements of the astral bodies, and who have reasoned about lunar and solar movement and action, without coming to the realization of monotheism. What made the youthful Abraham different from these others?

One might be tempted to answer the question by consideration of the special religious sensitivities of Abraham. One might hypothesize some special genius of analytical thought residing within Abraham's cerebral cortex. One might conjecture about some acute nobility within Abraham's character and personality. However, while certainly acknowledging the special religious sensitivities and nobility of Abraham, the fact remains that natural reason is, in and of itself, insufficient to arrive at the truth of the Oneness of Allah, unless Allah selects that reasoning individual to be the recipient of truthful knowledge. As such, without in anyway abrogating the importance of the process of natural reasoning undertaken by the teenage Abraham, it must still be maintained that Abraham, although perhaps only 14 years old, was chosen by Allah to be the recipient of the knowledge of monotheism.

And who turns away from the religion of Abraham but such as debase their souls with folly? Him We chose and rendered pure in this world... [63]

That was the reasoning about Us, which We gave to Abraham
(to use) against his people: We raise whom We will, degree after
degree...We chose them [Abraham and other prophets], and We
guided them to a straight way. This is the guidance of Allah: He
giveth that guidance to whom He pleaseth of His worshippers.[64]

Abraham was indeed a model. Devoutly obedient to Allah, (and)
true in faith, and he joined not gods with Allah. He showed his
gratitude for the favours of Allah, Who chose him, and guided him
to a straight way.[65]

And commemorate Our servants Abraham, Isaac, and Jacob, pos-
sessors of power and vision. Verily We did choose them for a special
(purpose) – proclaiming the message of the hereafter. They were, in
Our sight, truly, of the company of the elect and the good.[66]

Despite his relative youth and inexperience, Abraham had simultaneously reasoned to a monotheistic conclusion and been chosen by Allah
to receive the knowledge of the Oneness of Allah. Abraham was a person
of truth, who had approached Allah with a sound heart, and upon
whom Allah had bestowed righteous conduct.[67] Abraham had accepted
the mantle of prophethood at a most unusually early age, and he had
become a model of obedience to Allah, an excellent example for all to
follow.[68] Although still in his early teenage years, Abraham had been
guided to the straight path of strict monotheism, and he was truly ever
grateful to Allah for that inspiration and for that insight.[69]

And who turns away from the religion of Abraham but such as
debase their souls with folly? Him We chose and rendered pure
in this world: and he will be in the hereafter in the ranks of the righteous. Behold! His Lord said to him: "Bow (thy will to Me):" he said:
"I bow (my will) to the Lord and Cherisher of the universe."[70]

Abraham and *Da'wa* [71]: Abraham's approach to his father

Notwithstanding the straightness of a prophet's path, it is also a path filled
with responsibility, hardship, trial, opposition, tribulation, and heartache.
Such was the case with the teenage Abraham, as he began to witness to
the polytheistic idolaters of Ur. Given his own youthful age of about 14,
given his filial devotion, and given the propensity to discuss profound
truths with those to whom one is closest in love and respect, Abraham

probably began by witnessing to his father, Azar, and to his own immediate family.[72] Either out of an erroneous expectation of rapid success in educating his family to the truth of the Oneness of Allah, or out of the human tendency to ease into profound discussions, it is probable that Abraham's first exhortation to his father was brief and concise.

> Lo! Abraham said to his father Azar: "Takest thou idols for gods? For I see thee and thy people in manifest error."[73]

However, this initial approach to Azar would no doubt have been quickly followed up with other exhortations. In that regard, the pseudepigraphical book of *Jubilees* records the following possible conversation between Abraham and Azar.

> ...Abram said to...his father, saying, "Father!" And he said, "Behold, here am I, my son." And he said, "What help and profit have we from those idols which thou dost worship, and before which thou dost bow thyself? For there is no spirit in them, for they are dumb forms, and a misleading of the heart. Worship them not: worship the God of heaven, Who causes the rain and the dew to descend on the earth and does everything upon the earth, and has created everything by His word, and all life is from before His face. Why do ye worship things that have no spirit in them? For they are the work of (men's) hands, and on your shoulders do ye bear them, and ye have no help from them, but they are a great cause of shame to those who make them, and a misleading of the heart to those who worship them: worship them not."[74]

The Mission to the People of Ur

One can well imagine Abraham's pain and grief when his initial approach to his father and family failed to result in any monotheistic conviction, particularly from his father. Likewise, it is probable that at least one of Abraham's brothers, i.e., Nahor II, consistently rejected Abraham's message of the Oneness of Allah.[75] Further, it has been suggested that Abraham's other brother, i.e., Haran II, also declined to recognize or accept Abraham's message.[76] Nonetheless, despite such momentous setbacks, Abraham persevered in his witnessing to his father, and began to expand his mission among other people of Ur.

...behold, he said to his people: "Serve Allah and fear Him: that will be best for you—if ye understand! For ye do worship idols besides Allah, and ye invent falsehood. The things that ye worship besides Allah have no power to give you sustenance: Then seek ye sustenance from Allah, serve Him, and be grateful to Him: to Him will be your return. And if ye reject (the message), so did generations before you: and the duty of the messenger is only to preach publicly (and clearly)."[77]

Evolution of the Message

Assuming, as is probable, that Abraham continued to receive divine revelation over time, his witness and message would have begun to increase in eloquence, in detail, and in length. Further, in order to reach his listeners more effectively, he began to augment his declaration of faith with attempts at didactic interaction with his audience, with allegory and parable, and with other innovative forms of communication.

Behold, he said to his father and his people: "What worship ye?" They said: "We worship idols, and we remain constantly in attendance on them." He said: "Do they listen to you when ye call (on them), or do you good or harm?" They said: "Nay, but we found our fathers doing thus (what we do)." He said: "Do ye then see whom ye have been worshipping—ye and your fathers before you?—for they are enemies to me; not so the Lord and Cherisher of the worlds; Who created me, and it is He Who guides me; Who gives me food and drink, and when I am ill, it is He Who cures me; Who will cause me to die, and then to live (again); and Who, I hope, will forgive me my faults on the day of judgement...O my Lord! Bestow wisdom on me, and join me with the righteous; grant me honourable mention on the tongue of truth among the latest (generations); make me one of the inheritors of the garden of bliss; forgive my father, for that he is among those astray; and let me not be in disgrace on the day when (men) will be raised up—the day whereon neither wealth nor sons will avail, but only he (will prosper) that brings to Allah a sound heart; to the righteous, the garden will be brought near, and to those straying in evil, the fire will be placed in full view; and it shall be said to them: 'Where are the (gods) ye worshipped—besides Allah? Can they help you or help themselves?' Then they will be thrown headlong into the (fire)—they and those straying in evil, and the whole hosts of Iblis together. They will say there in their mutual bickerings: 'By Allah, we were truly in an error manifest, when we held you as equals with the Lord of the worlds; and our seducers were only those who were steeped in guilt. Now, then, we have none to intercede (for us), nor a single friend to feel (for us). Now if we only had a chance to return, we shall truly be of those who believe!'" [78]

The message of Abraham was evolving. At its core were now at least five fundamental truths: (1) there is no god but Allah; (2) Allah is the sole creator and sustainer of all that is; (3) for mankind, there will be a resurrection after death; (4) upon resurrection, there will be a judgment before Allah for each and every individual; and (5) that judgment will lead either to eternal bliss or to eternal torment. Nonetheless, as had happened to prophets before him, and as would happen to prophets after him, many paid no heed to the message of truth conveyed by Abraham.

His people disputed with him. He said: "(Come) ye to dispute with me, about Allah, when He (Himself) hath guided me? I fear not (the beings) ye associate with Allah: unless my Lord willeth (nothing can happen). My Lord comprehendeth in His knowledge all things. Will ye not (yourselves) be admonished? How should I fear (the beings) ye associate with Allah, when ye fear not to give partners to Allah without any warrant having been given to you? Which of (us) two parties hath more right to security? (Tell me) if ye know. It is those who believe and confuse not their beliefs with wrong—that are (truly) in security, for they are on (right) guidance."[79]

Rejection of the Message

Abraham's message was falling on many deaf ears. His father and probably one of his brothers, i.e., Nahor II, had rejected Abraham's call to true belief in the Oneness of Allah. Perhaps, Haran II had also rejected this message. Abraham had then reached out beyond his family to his fellow citizens of Ur, preaching a message that was expanding beyond the Oneness of Allah to include the concepts of resurrection after death, divine judgment post resurrection, and eternal reward or punishment in an afterlife. Nonetheless, the majority of his people rejected his clarion call, and remained devoted to their idolatry and to the worship of Sin, the Akkadian moon god, and to Sin's cohorts, Shamash, the Akkadian sun god, and Ishtar, the Akkadian goddess of Venus. Further, his peers did not just ignore him, but they actively disputed with him.

The bitter disappointment and rejection must have at times seemed too much to bear for a tender youth in his early teens. Abraham's words and oral message were failing to have their desired effect on the populace of Ur. Although some may have been converted, Abraham's father, Azar, probably Abraham's brother, Nahor II, and perhaps Abraham's brother, Haran II, had not. The worship at the cult temple of Sin continued to flourish. Enmenanna, the emperor's daughter and the high priestess of the temple of Sin at Ur, continued to enact her role as the bride of Sin in the cult rituals. The various temple idols still commanded a legion of priests and servants, who slavishly served them. Food was still cooked for the idols, and bread was still baked for them. The idols were still bathed, and they were still dressed in the best garments that the priests of Ur could acquire. Despite the truth and beauty of the words of Abraham's message, his people were not listening to and comprehending the truth behind the divine message. Perhaps, something more than a strictly oral message was needed.

Abraham destroys the Idols: Context and Setting

There often comes a time in a prophet's life when words of exhortation and preaching must be accompanied by direct physical action. Such was the case with Abraham, who was now planning a bold and decisive stroke against the idolatry of Ur, a stroke that foreshadowed the action of later prophets.[80]

(The exact context in which Abraham carried out his plan is unknown, although it has been suggested that it was at the time of a religious festival, the activities of which demanded that the populace be away from the temple.[81] This hypothesis appears to be as sound as any other, and provides a needed explanation for how it was that Abraham had unrestricted access to the cult temple of Sin, free of interference from the multitude of priests that served that temple. As such, this explanation is used in the following account as a working hypothesis.)

It was the time of a religious festival, probably one dedicated to Sin, but possibly to Shamash or to Ishtar. Abraham's preaching and exhortation about the Oneness of Allah and about the need to reject idolatry had previously drawn significant attention to himself. Further, he had even insinuated that he had some plan involving the idols, a plan that he would carry out when he had an appropriate opportunity free from the watchful eyes of his peers.

> We bestowed aforetime on Abraham his rectitude of conduct, and well were We acquainted with him. Behold! He said to his father and his people, "What are these images, to which ye are (so assiduously) devoted?" They said, "We found our fathers worshipping them." He said, "Indeed ye have been in manifest error—ye and your fathers." They said, "Have you brought us the truth, or are you one of those who jest?" He said, "Nay, your Lord is the Lord of the heavens and the earth. He Who created them (from nothing): and I am a witness to this (truth). And by Allah, I have a plan for your idols—after ye go away and turn your backs"...[82]

Despite Abraham's preaching, or perhaps because of it, Abraham was probably urged to attend this nocturnal festival, and to participate in the idolatrous festivities. Instead, Abraham cast his eyes upward at the astral bodies that would be worshipped during the festivities, and then pronounced the first lie of his life,[83] claiming that he was ill and could not attend. Accepting this explanation, his peers then left him, in order that they might attend the religious event without him.

> Then did he cast a glance at the stars, and he said, "I am indeed sick (at heart)!" So they turned away from him, and departed.[84]

Abraham now had his opportunity. It was night, he was alone, and the cult temple of Sin was deserted. There would be no priests or worshippers present at the temple to interfere with his plans. There would be no one present to report on his actions. There would be no one present to interfere with or to prevent Abraham from taking the major step of transforming his oral preaching into actual physical action.

Destruction of the Idols

The teenage prophet left his home, walked or rode through the streets of Ur to the temple of Sin, and entered the empty or nearly empty temple. He approached the gold-plated, wooden idols dressed in their magnificent finery, in front of which the priests had left the elaborate meal that they had prepared for the idols, and he began to mock them. However, he was not just mocking the specific idols that were in front of him. He was also mocking the very concept of idolatry, i.e., that man could so delude himself as to worship that which man's own hand had created, and he was simultaneously mocking the ideology of polytheism.

> Then did he turn to their gods and said, "Will ye not eat (of the offerings before you)?...What is the matter with you that ye speak not (intelligently)?"[85]

Following his mocking, Abraham then attacked and destroyed the idols, each in its own turn, leaving only the largest of the idols, i.e., the idol of Sin, the Akkadian moon god, untouched.

> Then did he turn upon them, striking (them) with the right hand.[86]

> So he broke them to pieces, (all) but the biggest of them, that they might turn (and address themselves) to it.[87]

Abraham confronts the Masses

It could have been because of the noise caused by Abraham's destruction of the idols or simply because their festival had ended, that the priests and worshippers returned to the temple of Sin, and then witnessed the carnage that had been inflicted on all of the idols except for that of Sin. Whatever the reason for their return, the people apparently found Abraham still within the precincts of the temple. Without initially confirming or denying that he had destroyed the idols, the righteous teenager upbraided his fellow citizens of Ur, and seized on the opportunity to witness to them.

> Then came (the worshippers) with hurried steps, and faced (him). He said: "Worship ye that which ye have (yourselves) carved? But Allah has created you and your handiwork!"[88]

However, Abraham's message merely increased the rage and anger of his listeners, and there were voices crying out for Abraham to be burned to death for his presumed destruction of the idols.

> They said, "Build him a furnace, and throw him into the blazing fire!"[89]

Apparently arriving later, and thus missing the initial confrontation with Abraham, others saw the destruction of their idols, and lamented.

They said, "Who has done this to our gods? He must indeed be some
man of impiety!" They said, "We heard a youth talk of them: he is
called Abraham." They said, "Then bring him before the eyes of the
people, that they may bear witness:" They said, "Art thou the one
that did this with our gods, O Abraham?" He said: "Nay this was
done by—this is their biggest one! Ask him, if they can speak
intelligently!" So they turned to themselves and said, "Surely ye are
the ones in the wrong!" Then were they confounded with shame:
(they said) "Thou knowest full well that these (idols) do not speak!"
(Abraham) said, "Do ye then worship, besides Allah, things that
can neither be of any good to you nor do you harm? Fie upon
you, and upon the things that ye worship besides Allah! Have ye no
sense?"...They said, "Burn him and protect your gods, if ye do
(anything at all)!"[90]

With this second group of people confronting him, Abraham was
even more eloquent than he had been with the first. He answered their
accusations that he had destroyed the idols by pointing to the undamaged
idol of Sin, and claiming that Sin, himself, must have destroyed the other
idols, thus committing the second lie of his young life.[91] In doing so, he
forced his accusers either: to admit to the possibility that the idol of Sin
had destroyed the other idols; or to confront once and for all that the idols,
including that of their chief deity, Sin, were totally incapable of action.
He then taunted his accusers by asking them to inquire of the idols themselves if this weren't the case. The priests and elders of the people were
then mentally and intellectually confounded by the logic of the young
teenager who stood confronting them. The accusers had become the
accused, i.e., accused of illogic and intellectual inconsistency, and they
did not know how to answer. Finally, in their helpless anger, they lashed
back at Abraham by saying that he knew fully well that the idols could
not speak or carry out the act of destruction that had taken place. At that
point, the teenage Abraham had the priests, the elders of the people,
and his other accusers in the tightening grip of his inescapable logic.
Why were they worshipping that which could neither act nor speak?
Had they no sense, no logic, no intellectual consistency? The righteous
teenager of Allah was now lecturing his supposed intellectual and educational superiors.[92] However, rather than learning from their intellectually

inconsistent predicament, they responded with rage and fury, lending their cry to that of the first group that Abraham should be burned for his supposed improprieties.

Abraham versus Naram-Sin: A Trial in the Making

Among those at the temple of Sin, either as an observer of the conflict between Abraham and his fellow citizens of Ur or as one of Abraham's accusers, would likely have been Enmenanna, the high priestess of the temple of Sin and the daughter of the emperor, Naram-Sin. If Abraham's destruction of the temple idols had not been enough of a reason to draw the personal attention of the emperor to him, and if the demands for his death by his peers had still not been enough of a reason, surely a personal appeal from his own daughter, the high priestess of the defiled cult temple at Ur, would have garnered Naram-Sin's imperial concern.

The idols, over which Naram-Sin's own daughter presided, had been destroyed. Further, Naram-Sin, as emperor, was ultimately in charge of the cult temple of Sin at Ur. As such, the destruction of the idols was not just a rejection of idolatry. It was also an act that struck at the very foundations of imperial power and of the religiously sanctioned legitimacy of the Akkadian Empire itself. Given the intimate intertwining of religion and government within the Akkadian Empire, the blow against the idols was also a blow against the very legitimacy of the Akkadian Empire. As such, it was inescapable that Abraham would be called to account before the emperor, Naram-Sin.

The Trial of Abraham

Whether Abraham was taken north to Akkad to stand trial before the emperor, or whether Naram-Sin journeyed south to Ur to preside at Abraham's trial, is not known. However, in either case, Abraham was called forth to stand accused before the pompous and arrogant ruler of the Akkadian Empire. The emperor was the presiding judge, Abraham probably stood alone from all human support in the docket, and the accusers were the multitudes of Ur, probably including Enmenanna, the emperor's own daughter and the high priestess of Sin. How does any accused person respond to such a trial, especially when that accused person is only a youth in his early to mid teens? However, while Abraham probably stood alone from all human support, he was immeasurably strengthened by his faith in Allah.

Hast thou not turned thy vision to one who disputed with Abraham
about his Lord, because Allah had granted him power? Abraham
said: "My Lord is He Who giveth life and death." He said: "I give
life and death." Said Abraham: "But it is Allah that causeth the sun
to rise from the east: do thou then cause him to rise from the west?"
Thus was he confounded who (in arrogance) rejected faith. Nor doth
Allah give guidance to a people unjust.[93]

The weakness and frailty of human nature are such that, if
confronted by truth, a person may generally respond with anger and
fury, rather than with any understanding derived from his having been
confounded and forced to face a truth. This is more likely to happen
especially if the irrefutable nature of that truth has been driven home by
unanswerable reason and logic, and especially if the person concerned
is trapped by his own overbearing pride and arrogance. This had been
exactly the case with both groups of people who had confronted Abraham
in the temple after his destruction of the cult idols. Such was now also
the case with the emperor, Naram-Sin, the self-styled "king of the four
quarters of the earth" and "god of Akkad". Heeding the demands of those
who had previously called for Abraham's death by fire[94], and perhaps also
wishing to show that, as master of life and death within the Akkadian
Empire, he could hand out the same punishment and torment by fire as
Abraham had claimed was the punishment bestowed by Allah for the
unbelievers at the final judgment[95], Naram-Sin condemned Abraham to
death by fire.

Death by Fire

Though only in his early to mid teens, at least once source says that he
was 16 at the time[96], Abraham had been condemned to death by fire. With
the possible exception of the events surrounding his birth and infancy, no
other event in Abraham's life resulted in more *aggadic* tales than his
having being thrust into the fire. There are detailed stories about how
much wood was collected for the fire, how big the fire was, how many
days the fire burned, the actions of various angels, etc. However, despite
the rapid succession of miraculous events reported in these *aggadic* tales,
the final effect of such stories on the reader is actually to detract from the
miraculous nature of Abraham's escape from the fire. Quite simply, one
miracle in the midst of too many miracles can lose its aura of divine

intervention. The miraculous becomes commonplace, and the divine becomes mundane. In the process, Abraham emerges more as an exaggerated and mythological figure, than as a historically-based prophet of Allah.

In marked contrast to these *aggadic* tales, the *Qur'an* and *Sahih Ahadith* report Abraham's miraculous escape from the fire of his intended death with remarkable brevity and conciseness. In an *Hadith* narrated by 'Abdullah b. 'Abbas, the reader is informed that:

> The last statement of Abraham when he was thrown into the fire was "Allah is sufficient for us and He is the best disposer (of affairs for us)".[97]

There are at least two points that need to be emphasized with regard to Abraham's statement as he was thrown into the fire. Firstly, one is struck by the remarkable faith of this teenage prophet. Secondly, one notes that this faith is not merely an intellectually-based monotheistic belief. One can theoretically hold to a concept of monotheism without being prepared to submit to the will and pleasure of Allah. How many self-proclaimed monotheists, whether Jew, Christian, or Muslim, conceptually adhere to monotheistic principles, yet rail against and protest their own lot in life? In marked contrast, consider Abraham's total acceptance that Allah is the "best disposer" of Abraham's own affairs, even if that should result in a fiery death at a very young age.

However, Abraham did not die in the fire, as Allah miraculously saved His young prophet.

> They said, "Burn him and protect your gods if ye do (anything at all)!" We said, "O fire! Be thou cool, and (a means of) safety for Abraham!"[98]

> So naught was the answer of (Abraham's) people except that they said: "Slay him or burn him." But Allah did save him from the fire. Verily in this are signs for people who believe.[99]

Continued Persecution

Allah had miraculously delivered Abraham from the fire of Naram-Sin. Yet, despite the witnessing of this miracle, by and large, Abraham's people still refused to accept the message preached by him. Rather than being persuaded to accept Abraham's message of monotheism by the divine miracle that they had witnessed, the people continued to plot against Abraham, and continued to persecute him. However, such plots and persecutions came to naught.

> Then they sought a stratagem against him: but We made them the ones that lost most![100]

> (This failing) they then sought a stratagem against him but We made them the ones most humiliated![101]

The Conversion of Lot

Despite the refusal of the majority of the populace of Ur to learn from the monotheistic message of their teenage prophet, there was at least one who did listen and who did understand. Lot (Lut) was the son of Abraham's brother, Haran II.[102] Lot knew Abraham quite well, and may have even been raised with him. As such, he was in an excellent position to assess the honesty, character, and moral fiber of his youthful uncle. That assessment, coupled with Abraham's miraculous escape from the fire and with Abraham's continued preaching and exhortation following his escape from the fire, was sufficient to lead to the conversion of Lot.

> So naught was the answer of (Abraham's) people except that they said: "Slay Him or burn him." But Allah did save him from the fire. Verily in this are signs for people who believe. And he said: "For you, ye have taken (for worship) idols besides Allah, out of mutual love and regard between yourselves in this life; but on the day of judgement ye shall disown each other and curse each other: and your abode will be the fire, and ye shall have none to help." But Lut had faith in him: he said: "I will leave home for the sake of my Lord: for He is exalted in might, and wise."[103]

Thus began an association between Abraham and Lot that was to last for many years, through their subsequent migration to Harran, through their time spent in Harran, and through their continued relationship in Egypt and Palestine. It has even been suggested that Abraham, at some point in time after he reached adulthood, took the orphaned Lot as an adopted son.[104]

Marriage to Sarah: Sarah's Conversion

One may safely assume that Abraham persevered in delivering his message throughout his teenage years and into his adulthood. Quite likely, there continued to be a majority rejection of his message, accompanied by a minority of additional converts to monotheism. One of those converts was probably Abraham's bride-to-be, Sarah, who was said to have believed in the message of Abraham.[105]

Discrepancies regarding Sarah

There are at least two areas of discrepancy regarding Sarah. The first discrepancy is easily summarized, and involves the issue of whether Sarah's name was changed later in life to Sarah from Sarai. The *Torah* rather consistently states that Sarah's original name was Sarai[106], and that Sarai's name was changed to Sarah at the time Abraham's name was changed from Abram to Abraham.[107] In reality, Sarai is merely an older form of the name Sarah[108], and the more common and familiar name of Sarah will be used throughout this book.

The second area of discrepancy has to do with the ancestry of Sarah, and was previously discussed in some depth in Chapter 2. It would suffice here to say that Sarah was probably the daughter of Haran I, who was: the paternal uncle of Abraham, Nahor II, and Haran II; and the son of either Terah (if Terah were not identical with Azar) or the son of Nahor I (if Terah were identical with Azar). It is possible that Sarah's mother was Hanal, probably a daughter of Nahor I, but possibly a daughter of Nahor II.

Age at Marrying

Neither the *Torah* nor the *Qur'an* and *Sahih Ahadith* give any indication of the age of Abraham at the time of his marriage to Sarah. However, *Genesis* does state that Abraham was 10 years older than Sarah[109], and assuming that Sarah would have been at least 14 years old when she married, this places Abraham's age when marrying Sarah as being at least 24 years. However, the pseudepigraphical book of *Jubilees* indicates that Abraham was 49 years old when he married Sarah.[110] If this figure is accepted, then it would appear that Sarah was 39 years old at the time of the marriage.

Postscript to Abraham in Ur

The book of *Jubilees* suggests that Abraham continued to reside in Ur until he was 60 or 61 years old.[111] Assuming that Abraham began his preaching and exhortation at Ur during his early teenage years, at around age 14, this would suggest that the total length of Abraham's mission in Ur covered 46 to 47 years. Despite these 46 or 47 years of Abraham's preaching and exhortation at Ur, Azar, probably Nahor II[112], perhaps Haran II[113], and certainly the majority of the populace of Ur continued to reject Abraham's message of the hereafter and of the Oneness of Allah.

One does well to stop and contemplate the amazing perseverance and steadfastness of Abraham, who continued to preach his message of monotheism to the antagonistic population of Ur for what appears to have been 46 to 47 years. How much rejection and persecution did he have to withstand for the sake of Allah during that tremendously long tenure at Ur? During that same lengthy time span, he must have made countless approaches to his father, Azar, and to his brothers, Nahor II and Haran II, urging them to submit to Allah, only to be rebuffed at the end of the discussion.

Granted, there had been some conversions, with the submissions of Sarah and Lot being the most prominent. Nonetheless, the frustration and apparent futility of the endeavor would have surely overwhelmed anyone whose faith in Allah was any less strong than that of Abraham.

Chapter 4
Abraham in Harran

(Information on Abraham's stay in Harran is quite limited. Basically, source material is confined to that found in the *Qur'an*, in *Genesis*, and in *Jubilees*.)

I t was after his marriage to Sarah that the adult Abraham, perhaps 60 or 61 years old at the time[114], migrated to Harran in southeastern Turkey. However, he did not go alone. Going with him were Sarah, Abraham's father, and Lot.[115] Further, based upon information in *Genesis* placing them at Harran some years later[116], it is likely that Nahor II and his wife, Milcah, Sarah's sister, also accompanied them[117]. One suspects that the members of this extended family group had vastly different reasons for making the pilgrimage from Ur to Harran.

Motivations to migrate to Harran: The Motivations of Azar

Archaeological discoveries have identified Harran as a cult center for the Akkadian moon god, Sin, the very same astral deity that was the primary deity worshipped at Ur. In line with these archaeological discoveries, it appears that Harran was a favorite pilgrimage site for the worshippers of Sin, with people coming from across the Akkadian Empire to worship at the cult center and to make homage to the idols within it. This may well have been the primary reason that prompted Azar and Nahor II to make this trip, as certainly Azar[118], and probably Nahor II[119], continued in the idolatrous worship of Sin. Azar and Nahor II were probably making a religious pilgrimage to worship at the sanctuary of Sin in Harran.

However, there may have been a secondary reason for Azar and Nahor II to have made this major relocation. As previously noted, Haran II, the son of Azar and the brother of Nahor II and of Abraham, had died in Ur.[120] Perhaps, on a psychological level, Azar and Nahor II needed to escape from any traumatic memories associated with Haran II's premature death and subsequent burial in Ur. This is the explanation proposed by Josephus in his *Jewish Antiquities*.[121]

The Motivation of Lot

For Lot, the motive for the pilgrimage to Harran would have been quite different to that of the primary reason of Azar and of Nahor II. Lot had already accepted the message of monotheism preached by Abraham and was a convert to the belief in the Oneness of Allah. He was a follower of Abraham, and he had previously proclaimed his faith and devotion.

> But Lut had faith in him: he said: "I will leave home for the sake of my Lord: for He is exalted in might and wise."[122]

No doubt the people of Ur had persecuted Lot for his monotheistic beliefs, just as they had persecuted Abraham. If, as hypothesized in Chapter 3, Lot had submitted to Allah shortly after Abraham's encounter with the fire, and if Abraham were about 16 years old at the time of the fire and around 61 years of age when he left Ur, then based on this assumption, Lot may have experienced almost 45 years of religious persecution for the sake of Allah. As such, for Lot, the pilgrimage to Harran may have represented hope for religious freedom and for an escape from persecution. Further, the pilgrimage to Harran provided Lot the opportunity to continue his association with Prophet Abraham. However, in the final analysis, Lot now had his chance to "leave home for the sake of my Lord."

The Motivation of Abraham

One cannot be completely sure of the reasons behind Abraham's departure from Ur to Harran. Perhaps he wanted to continue his attempted monotheistic conversion of Azar and Nahor II. As they were probably making a cult pilgrimage to the temple of Sin in Harran, he probably felt compelled to go along with them, in order to attempt continuously to convert them to the path of Allah. It could also have been very likely that he was escaping from the ongoing persecution he had been experiencing at Ur for perhaps as long as 46 to 47 years, thus foreshadowing a similar pilgrimage from Makkah to Madinah made about 2,800 years later by Prophet Muhammad.[123] It is also possible that Abraham had to leave Ur, because once again he may have made a strong, physical statement against the idol worship at Ur and once more Abraham may have directly attacked the temple of Sin at Ur.

This last consideration must be regarded only as a hypothetical possibility, because the source supporting this hypothesis may only be reporting a corrupted version of Abraham's destruction of the idols during his teenage years, coupled with a corrupted version of the attempt to kill Abraham by fire, also during Abraham's teenage years. Nonetheless, it cannot be totally ignored that a non-canonical, pseudepigraphical book within the Judaeo-Christian tradition, viz., *Jubilees*, states that Abraham had to flee Ur. *Jubilees* maintains that, at 60 years of age, Abraham had surreptitiously and stealthily crept to the temple at Ur while hidden by the darkness of night, had set a raging fire, and had burned the temple of Sin to the ground, destroying the entire building, the idols within it, and all it housed.[124] This same source suggests that Haran II, Abraham's brother, was actually killed attempting to help put out this fire.[125] If accepted at face value, the *Jubilees* narrative suggests that Abraham's father and both of Abraham's brothers had continued their idolatrous worship in the face of Abraham's message of monotheism. The account in *Jubilees* would then also provide a specific reason for Haran II's premature death and as to why Lot had been left an orphan.[126]

Pilgrimage to Harran

Whatever the respective motives of the individual members of Abraham's family for making the trip to Harran, the actual itinerary of the caravan comprising Abraham's family can probably be deduced from geographical considerations. The caravan probably traveled from Ur to Harran along the classic migration route of the Fertile Crescent. This would have necessitated a journey of about 500 miles (812 kilometers) on a straight line, but considerably longer when one considers the meandering of the rivers being followed and the need to find suitable grazing for any animals they were herding. As such, the journey was no weekend outing, but a long and time consuming march through almost the entirety of Iraq and into southeastern Turkey.

Abraham's family would have began their journey on the banks of the Euphrates River by Ur, traveled northwest up the Euphrates through Iraq until reaching the Balikh River, and then veered almost straight north as they went up the Balikh River to Harran in southeastern Turkey. By taking this route, Abraham's family would have assured their animals suitable water and grazing throughout the journey.

Life in Harran: Secular Life

Less is known about the ancient Harran of Abraham's time, than is known about the city of ancient Ur. However, it can be stated that Harran was situated along the Balikh River, about 24 miles (38 kilometers) southeast of Urfa. Situated as it was, Harran would have been a city of some strategic importance for the Akkadian Empire, which was based in southern Mesopotamia, as Harran would have provided a natural outpost, by which to guard the northern flank of any such empire. It can also be stated that about one and a half millennia after Abraham, during the time of the Assyrian Empire, Harran was located on the road that ran from Nineveh to Carchemish, thus being ideally placed to capitalize on the trade, travel, and transportation industries of that day. A little over two millennia after Abraham, during the period of the Roman Empire, the city of Harran would be known as Carrhae.

Religious Life

As previously noted, Harran's religious life, like that of Ur, centered on the worship of the Akkadian moon god, Sin. As a pilgrimage site for the worship of Sin, Harran would have boasted an impressive cult temple, although probably not as large as that of its sister city of Ur. Although likely on a lesser scale than at Ur, one would have found the same display of idols, viz., Sin, Shamash, Ishtar, and others, the same type of temple staff, and the same basic rituals and religious festivals. In short, the daily religious life of Harran would likely have been a scaled down version of that previously found at Ur.

Abraham at Harran

There is probably less concrete information about Abraham's life during his time in Harran than there is about any other period in his life. As was the case regarding Abraham's life in Ur, there is again no indication as to whether Abraham lived in the city, or whether he lived in a surrounding village or in the countryside. Likewise, there is no indication as to whether he worked in the city, or whether he performed some sort of agricultural work in the countryside. To a great extent, one is reduced to informed speculation regarding Abraham's life in Harran.

Relationship with Lot

One might posit that Abraham and Sarah continued to form some special attachment to Lot, Abraham's orphaned nephew, while living in or near Harran. In part, that attachment would have been based on the normal feelings of compassion any caring individual would have had for an orphaned nephew. In addition, if one accepts the account of *Jubilees* that Haran II, Lot's father, was killed fighting the fiery destruction of Sin's temple in Ur, and that Abraham had set that very fire, then the responsibility felt by Abraham for Lot might have been all the greater. However, it must be remembered that the attachment to Lot was also grounded in a shared belief in the Oneness of Allah and in a shared submission to Allah. One cannot easily overestimate the importance of that bond of shared submission. Considering all of the above factors, perhaps, as suggested by Josephus[127], Abraham actually went so far as to adopt Lot. If so, it is possible that such an adoption took place during the time they spent together in the vicinity of Harran.

Married Life

One can also imagine that the married life of Abraham and Sarah was an island of tranquillity and calm in an otherwise stormy sea. Surrounded by polytheistic idolatry, the shared monotheistic beliefs of Abraham and Sarah would have naturally pulled them closer together as a husband and wife. However, the marriage would also have had its disappointments, chief of which was that Sarah continued to be barren. No child had yet been born to Abraham and Sarah, despite what may have been 11 to 12 years of married life in Ur, and despite what may have been an additional 14 years of marriage in Harran.[128] No doubt, this was an ongoing source of personal frustration to both of them. Had it not been for their faith in Allah and for their acceptance of Allah's divine plan, this could well have festered into a source of significant marital friction between the two of them.

Abraham and *Da'wa*

Given Abraham's prior preaching and exhortation to the citizens of Ur, it is difficult to conceive of Abraham not having continued to deliver his monotheistic message of submission to Allah while he was in Harran. One suspects that attempts to convert others to a belief in the *Tawheed*

(Oneness of Allah) formed an ongoing and crucial part of Abraham's daily life. His exhortations and preaching would have continued to be developed and refined, and his actual message would have become more elaborate and detailed as his revelations from Allah continued.

Of special importance to Abraham would have been his continued and persistent attempts to convert his father, Azar, and his brother, Nahor II, to the worship of Allah. Certainly Azar, and probably Nahor II, had resisted Abraham's message of monotheism while in Ur. Despite such resistance, Abraham would have persevered.

> (Also) mention in the Book (the story of) Abraham: he was a man of truth, a prophet. Behold, he said to his father: "O my father! why worship that which heareth not and seeth not, and can profit thee nothing? O my father! to me hath come knowledge which hath not reached thee: so follow me: I will guide thee to a way that is even and straight. O my father! serve not Satan: for Satan is a rebel against (Allah) Most Gracious. O my father! I fear lest a penalty afflict thee from (Allah) Most Gracious, so that thou becomes to Satan a friend.[129]

Nonetheless, Azar continued to reject the monotheistic message of his son. Despite Abraham's persistence in approaching his father with the message of the *Tawheed* and of the hereafter, and despite the eloquence of Abraham's spoken message, Azar remained trapped in his own polytheistic and idolatrous belief system. He continued to worship the idol of Sin, and probably those of Shamash, Ishtar, and others. In fact, as Abraham's preaching to his father became more persistent and ongoing, Azar's rejection of that message became all the more adamant.

> (The father) replied: "Dost thou hate my gods, O Abraham? If thou forbear not, I will indeed stone thee: now get away from me for a good long while!"[130]

Not only was Azar continuing to reject the message of Allah delivered by his son, he was now also prepared to reject that very son. Furthermore, Azar had even prepared himself to kill his own son by stoning him to death, and Azar directly threatened Abraham with that fate if Abraham did not cease his monotheistic message and belief. Perhaps, something more than the rejection of Abraham's monotheistic message was fueling Azar's rejection of Abraham. If one accepts the account of *Jubilees* that one of Azar's sons, i.e., Haran II, was killed in Ur in the temple fire, which Abraham had supposedly set, then it may well be that Azar's rejection of Abraham was also partially grounded in his blaming Abraham for the death of his other son. Whether this hypothetical possibility has any historical merit or not, it is obvious that the rage, hurt, and hatred burning within Azar must have been virtually uncontrollable, while the sorrow and rejection experienced by Abraham must have been practically unbearable.

Abraham separates from Azar

Azar banished Abraham from his sight, and Abraham could do nothing in response, but leave his father with a kind word.

> Abraham said: "Peace be on thee: I will pray to my Lord for thy forgiveness: for He is to me Most Gracious. And I will turn away from you (all) and from those whom ye invoke besides Allah: I will call on my Lord: perhaps by my prayer to my Lord, I shall be not unblest!" [131]

Perhaps, Abraham was more tenderhearted and forbearing than should have been the case after his many years of trying unsuccessfully to convince Azar to submit to Allah. Nonetheless, Abraham's anguish at his father's idolatry, at his father's probable fate in the hereafter, and at his father's rejection of him are only too understandable to any child, who has seen his parent blunder down the path of life. As such, perhaps against his better judgment, Abraham kept his promise to pray for his father, the one who had rejected Allah.[132]

> It is not fitting, for the prophet and those who believe, that they should pray for forgiveness for pagans, even though they be of kin, after it is clear to them that they are companions of the fire. And Abraham prayed for his father's forgiveness only because of a promise he had made to him. But when it became clear to him that he was an enemy of Allah, he dissociated himself from him: for Abraham was most tender-hearted, forbearing.[133]

Abraham leaves Harran: The Narration of the *Qur'an*

Abraham was now finally forced to separate himself totally from Azar and Nahor II, as was Sarah from her sister, Milcah. Abraham and presumably Sarah had come to accept the inevitability of their family's polytheistic idolatry, and Abraham knew that he must bring together himself, his wife, Sarah, his nephew, Lot, and the rest of his converts, and leave behind the idolatry and the unbelievers of Harran once and for all.

> There is for you an excellent example (to follow) in Abraham and those with him, when they said to their people: "We are clear of you and of whatever ye worship besides Allah: we have rejected you, and there has arisen, between us and you, enmity and hatred forever—unless ye believe in Allah and Him alone": but not when Abraham said to his father: "I will pray for forgiveness for thee, though I have no power (to get) aught on thy behalf from Allah."[134]

Having made the final break from the idolatrous and polytheistic members of their families, these early monotheists then turned to Allah in prayer.

> (They prayed): "Our Lord! in Thee do we trust, and to Thee do we turn in repentance: to Thee is (our) final goal. Our Lord! make us not a (test and) trial for the unbelievers, but forgive us, our Lord! for Thou are the exalted in might, the wise." There was indeed in them an excellent example for you to follow—for those whose hope is in Allah and in the last day. But if any turn away, truly Allah is free of all wants, worthy of all praise.[135]

The Narration of *Genesis* and the First Promise to Abraham

There is also an account given in *Genesis* of Abraham leaving Harran. This narrative, which is not inconsistent with that given in the *Qur'an*, emphasizes that the migration out of Harran by Abraham and the believers was in direct response to a command from Allah, and includes a blessing upon Abraham and his house. This blessing directly implies that Abraham would not remain childless forever, and constitutes Allah's first recorded promise that Abraham would have offspring.

Now the Lord said to Abram, "Go from your country and your kindred and your father's house to the land that I will show you. I will make of you a great nation, and I will bless you, and make your name great, so that you will be a blessing. I will bless those who bless you, and the one who curses you I will curse; and in you all the families of the earth shall be blessed." So Abram went, as the Lord had told him; and Lot went with him.[136]

Postscript # 1 to Abraham in Harran

It has been suggested that Abraham, Sarah, and Lot resided in or near Harran for a total of 14 years.[137] If so, these 14 years, coupled with the earlier estimate that Abraham may have spent 46 to 47 years preaching in Ur[138], would indicate that by the time he left Harran, Abraham had been preaching the Oneness of and submission to Allah for approximately 60 to 61 years. This would have given more than ample opportunity for Azar and Nahor II to convert to the worship of Allah.

Given the previously reported estimate that Abraham was possibly 60 or 61 years of age when he left Ur[139], these 14 years at Harran, if accepted as historically accurate, would indicate that Abraham was approximately 75 years old when he left Harran. This is consistent with *Genesis*, which indicates that Abraham was 75 years old when he left Harran.[140] By extension, given that Sarah was Abraham's junior by 10 years[141], this would indicate that Sarah was about 65 years of age when she left Harran.

Postscript # 2 to Abraham in Harran

The fifth or fourth century BCE compiler of the book of *Genesis* has so arranged the *P* strand of *Genesis* 11:32 with the *J* strand of *Genesis* 12: 1 as to suggest that Abraham's father died in Harran before Abraham left Harran.

The days of Terah were two hundred five years; and Terah died in Haran. Now the Lord said to Abram, "Go from your country and your kindred and your father's house to the land that I will show you."[142]

This suggestion is contradicted by the Qur'anic accounts, wherein Abraham specifically disassociates himself from his father, Azar, and leaves only after his father has threatened him with death by stoning.[143] It also creates an internal inconsistency within the *P* strand of *Genesis*, which simultaneously states that: (1) Abraham was born by the time his father was 70 years old; (2) Abraham left Harran when he was 75 years old, making Abraham's father 145 years old at the very oldest; and (3) Abraham's father did not die until 205 years of age, resulting in Abraham's father living for 60 years after Abraham left Harran.[144] Through all this, one can safely assume that Abraham's father died many years after Abraham left Harran.

Chapter 5
Abraham in Palestine – I

From Harran to Palestine: The Pilgrims

Those making the journey from Harran to Palestine included: Abraham (presumably 75 years old at the time[145]); Abraham's wife, Sarah (presumably 65 years old at the time[146]); Abraham's nephew, Lot; fellow monotheists who had accepted Abraham's message; and whatever servants Abraham and Sarah had acquired.

> Abram took his wife Sarai and his brother's son Lot, and all the possessions that they had gathered, and the persons whom they had acquired in Haran; and they set forth to go to the land of Canaan.[147]

The Journey

Geographical factors, such as terrain and proximity to pasture and water, would have probably dictated the route of Abraham's migration from Harran to Palestine. Thus, one can assume that Abraham and his band of followers left Harran, traveling southwest, to where the Euphrates River would have eventually blocked their path. As the Euphrates can be forded at times of low water at Carchemish, which is close to the present Turkish-Syrian border, one assumes that this was the place, at which this dedicated group of monotheists made their crossing. Having forded the Euphrates, they would then have picked up once again the classic migratory route of the Fertile Crescent, journeying southwesterly until reaching the vicinity of Aleppo (Haleb), Syria.

A pleasant legend about Abraham relates to a hypothesized stop by Abraham's migratory group at Aleppo. According to this legend, Aleppo was one of the places along the migratory path of Abraham, at which he stopped to milk his grey cow, Al-Shahba. As the Arabic word for "milked" is "*Haleb*", it has been posited that this hypothesized event in Abraham's life provides the origin of the name of the city of Aleppo (Haleb Al-Shahba in Arabic). In reporting the above legend, it must be noted that the author is uncertain about the historical provenance of the above hypothesized event, and that the author can find no mention of this story in any early and authoritative reference work on the subject. Nonetheless, with the above disclaimer firmly in mind, the author has included the above legend, because it is such a charming story.

Leaving Aleppo, Abraham and his followers would have journeyed south towards Palestine. However, before reaching Palestine, Abraham's group apparently stopped for a stay of unknown length in Damascus, where, according to Josephus, Abraham may actually have ruled for a while.[148] After their halt at Damascus, the caravan would have then crossed the plain of Bashan (Hawran or Hauran), a large area east and north of the Sea of Galilee (Lake Tiberias), which includes the Golan Heights. Perhaps, the caravan slowed its journey as it moved through the rich agricultural plain of Bashan. Although devoid of trees, Bashan, spreading southeast from Mt. Hermon to the Jordanian frontier, consisted of fertile soil and had sufficient rainfall to enable large fields of wheat, barley, beans, and beats to be grown. Continuing south, they probably crossed the Jabboq (Jabbok) River, and then turned west to cross the Jordan River at the ford of Damiya. From there, they would have arrived in that northern portion of Palestine, which was known to later genera-tions as Samaria, where they went to the plain of Shechem (Balatah), at the foot of the Gerizim and Ebal mountains.[149]

The distance covered in the move from Harran to Shechem would have totaled to about 410 miles (667 kilometers), which included about 60 miles (98 kilometers) between Harran and Aleppo, about 210 miles (341 kilometers) between Aleppo and Damascus, about 120 miles (195 kilometers) between Damascus and the crossing of the Jordan River into Palestine, and about 20 miles (33 kilometers) between the Jordan River and Shechem.

Life in Palestine

Before presenting Abraham's life during his first sojourn in Palestine, it is helpful to examine the secular and religious setting in which Abraham would live.

Secular Life

The Palestine of the late third millennia BCE served as a land bridge between the two great civilizations of Mesopotamia and the River Nile, and thus had an extensive flow of trade and commerce thriving there. However, such travel and commerce were basically confined to the western or coastal lowlands of Palestine, while Abraham was consistently located in the hill country of Palestine, some miles east of these lowlands. As such, one imagines that secular life in ancient Palestine would have been far removed from that which Abraham had known in the cosmopolitan centers of the Akkadian Empire.

Life within the interior of Palestine was chiefly nomadic, with the countryside being dotted with a succession of small city-states, most, if not all, of which had been in some sort of vassalage to the Akkadian Empire. Individual architecture was far more primitive than that which Abraham had experienced in Ur and in Harran. Even a millennia after the time of Abraham, houses in the hill country of Palestine were still just simple four-room affairs, a far cry from the two-story homes of Ur, with their capacity to house family, servants, guests, and a chapel. However, even these simple four-room homes would have been a luxury for Abraham, who remained a tent dweller during the early days of his first sojourn in Palestine.[150]

Likewise, the architecture of the various temples and holy sites was far more primitive than the massive temple of Sin at Ur. The various cult temples in the area were simple rectangular buildings, with a door on the long wall, and a small altar or niche containing a cult idol. However, outdoor shrines were probably even more common than actual temples. A typical outdoor shrine might have consisted of nothing more than an altar for sacrifice, a "sacred" tree, and standing stones, which had been placed on some local high ground.

The population of Abraham's Palestine was chiefly composed of Canaanites and Amorites, not the Sumerian and Akkadian people, who had dominated life in and near Ur. The dominant languages were Canaanite and Amoritic, both languages of the Northern Central Group of Semitic languages, unlike Akkadian, which was a language from the Northern Peripheral Group of Semitic languages. Judging from these findings, it is very probable that Abraham would have had some trouble communicating with the native population of Palestine.

Religious Life
Religious life in Palestine varied considerably across different millennia,

and there is limited information available on the religious life in Palestine during the time of Abraham, which was in the latter part of the third millennium BCE. However, it is more or less certain that there was no single, official religion, and that religious beliefs and practices varied from one region of Palestine to another. Despite this difference in regional beliefs and practices, it is possible to note some similarities in religious life, which existed across many different regions within the Palestine of Abraham's time.

Cosmology and Cosmogeny

In most Palestinian regions, the official religious life centered on the polytheistic worship of an assembly or extended family of deities, who were symbolized in anthropomorphic form. El, the chief deity, was the father of all the other gods besides Baal, was typically represented as an old man with a long beard, and was frequently portrayed with two wings. El's female consort was Asherah, who reportedly was the mother of 70 gods.

Throughout Palestine, cosmogony was understood in terms of an epic battle between Baal (the son of Dagan) and Yam (Yamm), also known as Leviathan (Lotan). Yam was the god of the primordial sea, i.e., chaos, and when known as Leviathan, he was portrayed as the dragon or serpent of chaos. Yam was appointed king of the gods by El, and then demanded that Baal, the god of the thunderstorm, become his servant. Baal refused, and waged a civil war, resulting in the death of Yam, and the creation of an orderly universe. Thereafter, Baal ruled, presumably at El's pleasure, as king of the gods.

The Fertility Cult

Not having access to the potential for river irrigation, as was enjoyed at both Harran and Ur, agricultural fertility issues were far more prominent in Palestine, which was totally dependent on natural rainfall to insure successful crops and harvests. As such, fertility cults and fertility cult practice assumed an even greater prominence in Palestine than they did in Ur and in Harran. In that regard, the typical fertility cult of ancient Palestine centered on: belief in a dying and regenerating deity; and the cult practices of sacrifice, ritual sex, and sacred prostitution.

The dying god motif within ancient Palestinian religion served two functions: to explain the seasonal variations between the winter rains, i.e., the time of life, and the summer of no precipitation, i.e., the time of death; and to explain periodic famines and times of plenty, which were believed to follow seven-year cycles. As typically portrayed, Baal, whose name can be translated as "lord", was the god of the thunderstorm, the rain, and the dew, thus being intricately tied to agricultural production. According to the dying god myth of Palestine, Baal was annually killed each spring by Mot, the god of death, resulting in the cessation of rain. In turn, Mot was killed each fall by Anath (Anat), Baal's sister or wife, who would then regenerate Baal from the underworld, resulting in the coming of the winter rains.

Fertility cult practice was primarily devoted to insuring bountiful crops and the production of livestock and children. With this goal in mind, the people of ancient Palestine attempted to insure the fertility of land, livestock, and people through two primary cult practices. The first cult practice consisted of ritual sacrifices to the gods, and especially to Baal. Typically, the sacrificial victims were animal livestock, but occasionally consisted of children. The second cult practice to insure fertility can be understood within the framework of sympathetic magic, i.e., attempting to create fertility in the natural world by engaging in individual and ritual acts of "fertility" in one's personal world. In this regard, the ancient Palestinians practiced ritual sex and cult prostitution, both during agricultural festivals and at sacred sites and temples. It would suffice to say that the ancient Palestinian religion had an extreme emphasis on sex and reproduction.

El

As pointed out earlier on, within the ancient and polytheistic Palestinian cosmology, El was conceived of as the father god figure. However, it is likely that there is a second possible explanation regarding the worship of El. El is a word from the ancient Canaanite language, one of the Northern Central Group of Semitic languages, and can be translated as "god". As such, it is linguistically similar to the Hebrew name "Elohim" and to the Arabic words "*Al-Ilahi*" ("the god", or by implication "the one god"), from which the contraction "Allah" is derived.

Given the above, it appears that there may have been two types of El worship in ancient Palestine. The first, and most prevalent, type consisted of viewing El as the father of a pantheon of gods, and placed the worship of El within a polytheistic setting. This type of worship is not wholly dissimilar from the way in which most residents of Makkah worshipped Allah, before the revelations given to Prophet Muhammad, i.e., seeing Allah as only one of many gods, as having daughters, etc. In contrast, the second, and less frequent, type would have consisted of belief in the *Tawheed*. Throughout the rest of this book, the above distinction will be employed where possible, and the word "El" will be used within the polytheistic setting and where the setting is unclear, and the word "Allah" will be used within the monotheistic setting.

Sources of Information on Abraham in Palestine -I

While the *Qur'an* was the primary source of information about Abraham's life in Ur, and while informed speculation was the primary source of information about Abraham's life in Harran, information pertaining to Abraham's first sojourn in Palestine is basically limited to *Genesis* and to *Jubilees*.

Abraham in Palestine -I

Having provided the secular and religious setting of Abraham's life in Palestine, one now turns to an examination of what little is known of Abraham's life during his first brief stay in Palestine.

If he had not lived a nomadic lifestyle before, Abraham was certainly living a nomadic lifestyle during the early days of his first sojourn in Palestine. What limited information exists from *Genesis* and from *Jubilees* indicates that Abraham moved through Palestine on a north to south axis. He began his first Palestinian sojourn in the vicinity of Shechem, then moved to the vicinity of Bethel, then moved to the vicinity of Hebron, where he briefly settled, and finally moved to the vicinity of Bealoth in the Negeb.

Shechem and the Second Promise to Abraham

Upon entering Palestine by crossing the Jordan River at the ford of Damiya, Abraham and his followers moved northwest into the hill country of Palestine to the plain of Shechem.[151] At or near the Canaanite city of Shechem, Abraham and his family and followers stopped for an undetermined, but probably fairly brief, length of time. The city of Shechem was located about 32 miles (52 kilometers) north of Jerusalem, and about one mile (1.6 kilometers) east of the pass between Mt. Gerizim and Mt. Ebal. Shechem was strategically located at the junction of the main north-south and east-west routes of travel in ancient Palestine, and it boasted a good supply of water.

Genesis specifically states that Abraham went to "the oak of Moreh"[152] at Shechem, suggesting that he went to a Canaanite religious site, i.e., one of the outdoor shrines with a sacred tree. At this site, Abraham reportedly received a revelation from Allah, in which the childless Abraham was first promised that he would have future offspring and descendants, and in which Abraham was then promised that his descendants would inherit the land that he now beheld.[153]

Genesis goes on to indicate that Abraham, presumably as an act of thanksgiving, then built an altar to Allah in the midst of this Canaanite outdoor shrine.[154] Without minimizing the intention of thanksgiving in Abraham's construction of an altar to Allah at Shechem, there is also another possible explanation. In that regard, it is noted that *Da'wa* is not merely verbal exhortation. In fact, the most effective *Da'wa* is often *Da'wa* by behavioral example, i.e., so living one's life that it is an example for others to emulate. Abraham may well have taken some personal risk in constructing an altar to Allah at the oak of Moreh at Shechem. The native Canaanites may well have seen Abraham's behavior as an act of defilement of their holy place. Nonetheless, despite the personal risk involved, Abraham practiced *Da'wa* by example, perhaps because he was having some difficulty communicating with the indigenous population, who spoke a different dialect of Semitic language, than did Abraham. In any case, he constructed an altar to Allah, and he demonstrated the worship of Allah to anyone who was present to witness it.

Bethel

Having probably stayed at Shechem only for a brief time, Abraham and his followers now moved almost straight south towards Bethel, presumably driving their flocks with them. In doing so, they kept to the Palestinian hill country, which was far less densely populated than the coastal lowlands. Thus, intentionally or otherwise, Abraham was minimizing his contact with the native Palestinian population of Canaanites and Amorites, although he may well have met fellow travelers of this north-south axis on the way. In traveling through the sparsely populated hill country between Shechem and Bethel, Abraham and his company journeyed about 22 miles (36 kilometers), which would have required a two to three day journey, if one allows time for flocks to graze and water, for the setting up of camps at night, and for the elevated terrain of the land. Arriving at a mountain to the east of Bethel and to the west of Ai[155], Abraham was now only about 10 miles (16 kilometers) north of Jerusalem.

The name "Bethel" can be translated as "house of El". From this fact, one can conclude that Abraham had journeyed to an important cult center devoted to the Canaanite worship of El. The importance of Bethel as a cult site may have been due to its abundant water supply, which was so sufficient that no cisterns had to be dug at Bethel until the population growth experienced under the Roman Empire, about two millennia after Abraham. As such, Bethel would have supplied an easy source of water for Abraham, Sarah, Lot, Abraham's servants, fellow monotheists from Harran, and their flocks.

Having arrived in the hill country between Bethel and Ai, Abraham pitched his tent on a mountain or high place.[156] Given the association of Bethel, i.e., "house of El", and mountain or high place, one can again conclude that Abraham had briefly settled at a Canaanite place of worship, a sacred site which was devoted to the worship of El. As had previously been the case at the oak of Moreh at Shechem, Abraham once again practiced Da'wa by example. Despite whatever personal risk Abraham might have been taking in having the observing Canaanites conclude that he was defiling their sacred place, Abraham proceeded to build an altar to Allah, upon which he performed a sacrifice and he invoked the name of Allah.[157]

Hebron

According to *Genesis*, upon leaving Bethel, Abraham "journeyed on by stages toward the Negeb."[158] (The Negeb is a roughly triangular-shaped, dry highland in the far south of Palestine, with corners defined by the northern most part of the Gulf of 'Aqaba, the southern most point of the Dead Sea, and Gaza on the Mediterranean Sea.) In contrast, *Jubilees* provides a more detailed itinerary for Abraham's movements between Bethel and the Negeb, stating that Abraham initially moved south from Bethel to Hebron[159], a distance of about 31 miles (50 kilometers). Again, given the need to pasture and water his flock, one assumes that this journey from Bethel to Hebron would have taken a few days. Based upon multiple accounts of later occasions when Abraham stayed in the vicinity of Hebron[160], one assumes that he came to the oaks of Mamre the Amorite, which were apparently located about 1.5 miles northwest of Hebron at Ramat Al-Khalil. Presumably, the oaks of Mamre were the sacred trees of another outdoor shrine to some Canaanite deity. Here, Abraham apparently stayed for approximately two years[161], although one assumes that Abraham's life as a shepherd required episodic travel, in order to find suitable pasture for his flocks.

There is no source of information regarding Abraham's life during these two years at Hebron. One can assume that he continued to preach and instruct his followers, that he maintained his close association with Lot, and that his marital life with Sarah continued to be good, if childless. Further, based upon Abraham's consistent movement to outdoor shrines to Canaanite deities (the oak of Moreh at Shechem, the high place at Bethel, and the oaks of Mamre at Hebron), and based upon his *Da'wa* of action at both Shechem and Bethel, one assumes that Abraham continued a vigorous *Da'wa* to the Canaanites and Amorites in the neighborhood of Hebron.

Bealoth

Jubilees offers no clue as to why Abraham left Hebron. One is simply informed that after their two-year stay in and around the vicinity of Hebron, Abraham, Sarah, and Lot moved south to Bealoth[162], an unidentified, although elsewhere mentioned[163], city in the Negeb.

Abraham leaves Palestine I

Upon reaching Bealoth in the Negeb, Abraham and his family were surrounded by a severe famine. In the face of this famine, and with the need for pasture for their flock, Abraham, Sarah, and Lot migrated west across the arid steppes and desert into Egypt.[164]

Postscript to Abraham in Palestine I

Assuming that Abraham was 75 years old when he left Harran for Palestine[165], and assuming an initial sojourn in Palestine of only two to three years[166], makes Abraham about 77 or 78 years old when he left Palestine. Being 10 years his junior[167], Sarah would have been at that time about 67 or 68 years old.

Chapter 6
Abraham in Egypt

From Palestine to Egypt: The Pilgrims

As noted previously, the migration from Palestine to Egypt was caused by a great famine in the Negeb.[168] From the main story concerning Abraham in Egypt, which is presented later, it is clear that Sarah accompanied him to Egypt. From scattered references to Lot and Abraham growing rich in Egypt, to Lot marrying while in Egypt, and to Lot leaving Egypt with Abraham and Sarah, one deduces that Lot also accompanied Abraham and Sarah to Egypt. However, during a time of widespread famine in the Negeb, it is likely that there were many others, who also migrated into Egypt, and who were attempting to find sustenance there. Unfortunately, there is no reliable way of knowing how many of Abraham's converts to the *Tawheed* accompanied him, Sarah, and Lot into the land of the pharaohs.

The Journey

Lacking a specific location for Bealoth, aside from the fact that it was in the Negeb, the exact itinerary of Abraham's migration from Palestine to Egypt remains a bit shrouded in ambiguity. However, it appears safe to assume that he would have followed one of the two main routes between Palestine and Egypt.

The first alternative would have been the road on the way to Shur. If he had taken this route, he would have in all probabilities moved as far as 20 miles (32 kilometers) in a southerly direction from the Negeb, where he would have been skirting the northwest edge of the Wilderness of Zin. He would then have most likely moved southwesterly about 100 miles (162 kilometers), traveling along the Wilderness of Shur in the northern area of the Sinai. Next, he would have probably swung in a more north-westerly direction for about 60 miles (97 kilometers), arriving at Lake Timah, about seven miles (11 kilometers) north of the Great Bitter Lake and about 40 miles (65 kilometers) north of the Gulf of Suez. From thereon, he could have easily moved west about 40 miles (65 kilometers) into the land of Goshen in northeastern Egypt.

The second alternative would have had Abraham traveling due west from the Negeb until reaching the Mediterranean coast, and then following the coast in a westerly direction until entering the land of Goshen in northeastern Egypt. This would have resulted in a journey of about 185 miles (301 kilometers).

Whichever of the two routes Abraham, Sarah, and Lot took from the Negeb into Egypt, their trip would have been long and arduous, especially in a time of famine. The total distance traveled to reach Goshen would appear to have been somewhere between 185 and 220 miles (301 to 357 kilometers). Having arrived in Goshen, Abraham and his family would still have needed to travel to the capital of Egypt, in order to have had their subsequent contact with the pharaoh, which is described below. In that regard, the capital of Egypt may have been located at Memphis (during first through eighth dynasties of Egypt), but may have been moved to Heracleopolis (during ninth through 10th dynasties of Egypt).

Life in Egypt

There are two special difficulties attendant to attempting to review life in Egypt during the time of Abraham, both of which have to do with chronology. The first such difficulty has been confronted repeatedly in formulating this biography of Abraham, i.e., what was the time of Abraham. By a combination of means, it was determined that Abraham was probably born around 2,166 BCE, perhaps during the reign of Naram-Sin of the Akkadian Empire, although common sense suggests that one should allow for a significant margin of error of up to a century, with such margin of error secondary to vagaries in Biblical dating and to the unreliability in dating kings in ancient Mesopotamia.[169] This is a margin of error that has been previously taken into account by the author in presenting life in Ur, Harran, and Palestine during the time of Abraham.

Assuming that Abraham was about 77 or 78 years old when he entered Egypt[170], Abraham would have entered Egypt around 2,089 or 2,088 BCE. However, when attempting to date events in ancient Egypt, one is confronted with the second chronological difficulty. Simply stated, the academic discipline of Egyptology is currently in the midst of a fierce internal debate regarding chronological dating systems in ancient Egypt. The traditionally held chronological system for dating dynasties, kings, and events in ancient Egypt is under attack by a new coterie of scholars, which holds that major mistakes were made in constructing the traditional chronological system. While the specifics of this debate are beyond the scope of this book, it must be acknowledged that the implications of this debate may affect traditional dating of events in Egypt at the time of Abraham by as much as 377 years.[171]

This second chronological difficulty, especially in combination with the margin of error previously noted for placing Abraham chronologically, makes it virtually impossible to be specific about people and events in Egypt during the time of Abraham. It would suffice to say that Abraham probably could have entered Egypt anywhere between the fourth and ninth dynasties of Egypt, with the former estimate derived from the new chronological system[172], and with the latter derived from the traditional chronological system.[173] As such, the following discussion of life in Abraham's Egypt is more or less of a general nature.

Secular Life: A Brief History

Upper and Lower Egypt were first unified into a single kingdom by the semi-mythical Menes, who was originally the king of only Upper Egypt, and who probably may be identified with Aha, the first king of the first dynasty of unified Egypt. During the first dynasty of Egypt, three significant events took place. First, the capital of Egypt was firmly established at Memphis. Second, the kings of Egypt began to take a Horus name, i.e., a name connecting them with Horus, one of the Egyptian sky gods, as the first of their five names. Third, papyrus was invented as an artificial writing material.

During the third dynasty, the city of Memphis became the royal burial site, and *nomes* were created as governmental, administrative units or provinces in Egypt. The fourth dynasty found the kings or pharaohs beginning to take the titles of "perfect god" and "son of Re", with Re being the Egyptian god of the sun. It was also during this fourth dynasty that the pharaohs of Egypt began a massive building program, which inevitably resulted in their subjects being overly worked and overly taxed. During the fifth dynasty, sea expeditions were launched to

Lebanon, in order to import timber, and trade was well established with such areas as Turkey, Syria, and Eritrea. In addition, meticulous record keeping and accounting systems were established during this fifth dynasty.

During the sixth dynasty, the governors and local officials of the various *nomes* began to establish greater independence from the pharaohs. Egypt lost control of Lower Nubia, and more and more high-level officials began to build their homes in the provinces, and not at the capital of Memphis. Of note, one pharaoh of the sixth dynasty, Pepi II, ruled for an astonishing 94 years. Throughout both the seventh and eighth dynasties, the pharaohs were relatively weaker in power than they had been previously, and the end of the eighth dynasty saw widespread famine and violence erupting throughout the land of Egypt.

During the ninth dynasty, the capital of Egypt was moved from Memphis to Heracleopolis. Droughts and famine continued, there were a series of major earthquakes throughout the Middle East, and Egypt was flooded with starving refugees from Asia. Inscriptions pertaining to the pharaohs of the ninth dynasty often recorded praise to the pharaohs for their irrigation works projects and for their supplying of food to the populace during the trying times of famine.

Architecture

Mastabas began to be constructed during the first dynasty of Egypt. A *mastaba* was a tomb, which was constructed as a large, flat-topped, rectangular structure of mud brick, with a shaft descending to a burial chamber far underground.

The pyramids of Egypt, which were massive funerary edifices, have their beginnings in the third dynastic period, with the most celebrated of such construction being the step pyramid at Saqqarah, which was the first known monumental stone building in the history of the world, and which was constructed under the supervision of Pharaoh Djoser's royal architect, Imhotep. This step pyramid began as a *mastaba*, which was about 26 feet (eight meters) high, and which had a square base with each side being about 205 feet (63 meters) in length. Imhotep later expanded the base of this *mastaba*, and added rectangular additions of diminishing size, which were superimposed upon this base, resulting in a terraced edifice of six steps rising to a height of 195 feet (60 meters), and with a base of 390 feet (120 meters) by 351 feet (108 meters). However, it was not until the fourth dynasty that the first true pyramids were built, and this was only then achieved through the intermediate step of the Bent Pyramid, which was built by Pharaoh Snefru, and which changed slope about halfway up, being steeper in the lower half than in the upper half.

Of the pyramid tombs built during the fourth dynasty, the most notable were the three pyramids at Giza (Ahramat Al-Jizah). The oldest of the three was built by Khufu, the second pharaoh of the fourth dynasty, and is known as the Great Pyramid. The four sides of the Great Pyramid's base averaged just over 755 feet (231 meters) in length, and its original height was just over 481 feet (148 meters). Its four sides are accurately oriented to the four points of the compass, and rise at an angle of 51 degrees, 52 minutes. It was built from an estimated 2,300,000 blocks of yellowish limestone, each of which weighed about 2.5 tons. It has been estimated that it took 20 years and 100,000 laborers to build this funerary monument to Pharaoh Khufu. The second of the three Giza pyramids to be built was the pyramid of Khafre, the fourth pharaoh of the fourth dynasty. At its base, this pyramid averaged just over 707 feet (217 meters) in length for its four sides, and was originally 471 feet (145 meters) in height. The third and last of these three pyramids was built by Menkaure, the sixth pharaoh of the fourth dynasty. Averaging just over 356 feet (109 meters) in length at the base of its four sides, it rose to a height of 218 feet (67 meters).

The Sphinx (Abu Al-Hawl) was built during the reign of Khafre, the fourth pharaoh of the fourth dynasty, and it is Pharaoh Khafre's face that is represented in the head of the Sphinx. Despite having the face of Khafre, the body of the Sphinx was that of a recumbent lion. The Sphinx was carved out of a knoll of rock, and measured 240 feet (73 meters) in length and 66 feet (20 meters) in height.

During the fifth dynasty, seven pyramids were built, although all were smaller than those of the fourth dynasty, and the great period of pyramid building was to end in the sixth dynasty. However, the fifth dynasty marked the beginning of the period of great temple building, with six massive temples being built and dedicated to Re, the Egyptian sun god. Of these six temples, the ruins of the temple of Pharaoh Neuserre at Abu Jirab give some indication of the architectural and engineering skills involved in temple construction.

The temple of Neuserre consisted of: (1) a reception pavilion situated at the edge of the desert; (2) a long, covered corridor, which connected the reception pavilion to the open court of the temple; (3) the open court of the temple; and (4) corridors on two sides of the open court. The cult object (*Benben*), which was a squat obelisk of limestone, and an alabaster altar were situated within the open court of the temple, with the cult object being placed in direct sunlight. Elaborate reliefs decorated the covered corridor, as well as the two corridors on the sides of the open court.

In contrast to the pyramids and temples, common domestic housing was typically built from mud bricks and from wood, although stone was occasionally used for doorjambs, lintels, column bases, and window placements. These were relatively modest affairs, commonly consisting of a master bedroom, a reception room, and a kitchen. The kitchen typically lacked a ceiling, and was open to the sky, probably to aid in ventilation. A cellar for storage and a flat roof, which was reached via stairs, completed the structure. In contrast, houses for important officials may have consisted of up to 30 rooms, and may have contained bathrooms and lavatories, wooden columns to support the ceiling, high windows to reduce the sunlight, and hooded roof vents to allow for ventilation. In still greater contrast, palaces were probably vast and monumental buildings with broad halls, harem suites, kitchen areas, wide courts, murals, and floor decorations.

Art

Statuary was already well developed by the first dynasty, with the typical statues being wooden representations of standing male figures, which portrayed the left leg being slightly advanced beyond the right. By the second dynasty, statuary included seated figures. By the fourth dynasty, royal statues were made of stone, had become truly magnificent, and demonstrated subtle carving techniques. Thereafter, individual expression and individual facial characteristics were admirably displayed in Egyptian statuary.

Mural decorations were developed by the third dynasty. Such decorations consisted of paintings, where the materials used were mud bricks or stone of poor quality, and of relief work, where the walls were of good stone suitable for intricate carving. A high level of art was achieved in the paintings of the fourth dynasty, and low-relief work reached its artistic zenith during the fifth dynasty.

By the third dynasty, faience was much in use for artistic expression. Faience was typically blue or green in color, and consisted of a glazed composition of ground quartz. It was used for making decorative tiles, wall decorations, beads, amulets, and small figures representing animals and humans. Gold was used extensively by the fourth dynasty, and the gold-plated, gold-inlaid furniture of Queen Hetepheres of the fourth dynasty has survived to date. Gold was also molded into statues, probably by being beaten, as opposed to by casting, as exemplified by the falcon head of a cult statue from the sixth dynasty. By at least the fourth dynasty, gold was commonly used in making settings, beads, and chains for fine jewelry. Semi-precious stones, such as carnelian, amethyst, garnet, jasper, lapis lazuli, feldspar, turquoise, and agate, were also utilized in jewelry making. Silver was also used in jewelry, being occasionally inlaid with carnelian, turquoise, and lapis lazuli. However, because silver was much less accessible in ancient Egypt than was gold, silver was actually a much more valuable and expensive commodity than gold.

Copper metalwork was prevalent in ancient Egypt by the start of the first dynasty, and by at least the end of the third millennium BCE, copper was alloyed with tin to form bronze. Copper and bronze were used to make fine bowls, jugs, etc., with the artistic process of creation apparently being to beat a metal ingot over a wooden anvil. Copper plate was also used to cover wooden statues.

Summary

In many ways, the secular civilization that Abraham entered into in Egypt was much more reminiscent of his homeland of Ur, than it was of either Harran or especially Palestine. Southern Mesopotamia and the Nile Valley represented the two great centers of civilization of the day, and Abraham was journeying from one to the other, after having spent an interlude in Harran and Palestine. Of special note to the later discussion of Abraham's sojourn in Egypt is the fact that silver was much more valuable than gold in the ancient Egypt of Abraham's day.

Religious Life: Cosmology

Ancient Egyptian religion was both polytheistic and idolatrous, with the gods often being depicted as having a human body and an animal's head. The gods in the Egyptian pantheon were neither omnipotent nor omniscient. They were generally benevolent to humans, but their favor had to be curried by propitiation and sacrifice. The number of gods in the pantheon was large, and constantly changing, with new gods emerging, and with old gods ceasing to be worshipped. From the third dynasty on, the gods tended to be grouped into enneads, or groups of nine.

The most common ennead of ancient Egypt was that consisting of the following nine deities. (1) Re or Re-Atum was the sun god, and was the creator god. (2) Shu was the god of the air, who was created without a mother by Re-Atum, was often portrayed in statues in human form, and was the father of Geb and Nut. (3) Tefnut was the goddess of moisture, the sister of Shu, and the mother of Geb and Nut. (4) Geb was the god of the earth, the brother of Nut, and the son of Shu and Tefnut. (5) Nut was the goddess of the sky, was often portrayed as a female human or as a cow, was the sister of Geb, and was the daughter of Shu and Tefnut. (6) Osiris, also known as Usiri, was a fertility god and the god of the dead, was the son of Nut, the husband of Isis, and the father of Horus, and was believed to be the god that each deceased pharaoh became. (7) Isis, also known as Aset or Eset, was the goddess most associated with magic, was often portrayed as a human female or as a human female with a cow's head, and was the sister of Seth and of Osiris, the wife of Osiris, and the mother of Horus. (8) Seth, also called Setekh, Setesh, or Set, was the god of chaos, disorder, the desert, violence, and storms, was frequently represented with a canine body and a composite animal head, was the slayer of Osiris, and was the perpetual antagonist of Horus. (9) Nephthys was the daughter of Nut, and was the wife of Seth.

The Cult of the Dead

Ancient Egyptian religion was heavily focused on death and the concept of a life in the next world. For those wealthy enough to afford it, vast sums were spent to insure a safe and successful passage to the next life. In that regard, two aspects of the burials of the wealthy can be noted. First, elaborate burial tombs were constructed, and were stocked with objects that might be needed in the next life. These tombs also contained religious texts, i.e., *The Book of the Dead*[174], that were believed to help guide the deceased in attaining the next world and in prospering in it. Second, the deceased's body was specifically prepared through elaborate mortuary techniques, including mummification, in order to ensure a safe and successful passage into the next life.

Such elaborate preparation and the expenditure of such vast resources on burial suggest that there was a common belief that the journey to the next world was fraught with many dangers and obstacles. Among other such dangers and obstacles was a judgment after death. Those failing this judgment were denied entry into the next world, and were cast out of the ordered cosmos into absolute chaos.

Order versus Chaos

A central aspect of ancient Egyptian religious thought was the concept of an ongoing struggle between order (*Ma'at*) and chaos or disorder (*Izfet*). This struggle had its manifestation both in the world of the gods and in the world of man. In the pantheon of the gods, the struggle between order and disorder was best exemplified in the Osiris story, which also has implications for the aforementioned cult of the dead. In the world of man, the struggle between order and chaos was exemplified by the role of the pharaoh, which needs to be understood within the context of the Osiris story.

According to the ancient Egyptian traditions, Osiris was a fertility god, who was the son of Nut, the brother of Seth and Nephthys, and the brother and husband of Isis. At some point, Seth, the god of chaos, violence, storms, the desert, and disorder, tricked Osiris into entering a chest, which Seth then closed, locked, and dropped into the ocean, thereby drowning and killing Osiris. Afterwards, Seth recovered the corpse of Osiris, cut the body into 14 different pieces, and scattered them throughout Egypt. Isis (Osiris' grieving wife) and Nephthys (Osiris' sister and Seth's wife) then dutifully recovered all the pieces of Osiris, except the phallus, and buried the recovered parts. Post burial, Isis, through her unsurpassed skill in and use of magic, brought Osiris back to life. Thereafter, Osiris became the god of the dead, and, out of Isis, fathered a son, Horus, who was typically represented by a man's body with a falcon's head, one eye of which was the sun and one eye of which was the moon. Isis carefully hid Horus from Seth, until Horus had gained his maturity. Horus then waged a war of revenge against Seth, and finally defeated Seth, but only after Seth had damaged the eye of Horus that was the moon, which eye was later healed by the god Thoth, thereby providing ancient Egyptians with an explanation for the phases of the moon.

The struggle between order and chaos was also seen as being a crucial element of man's existence. Here, Egypt itself was perceived as order, while the surrounding desert was seen as the embodiment of chaos, violence, and storms. Just as the surrounding desert (*Deshret*) was constantly threatening to engulf and overwhelm the fertile black land (*Kemet*) of the Nile River valley, so was chaos threatening to engulf ordered life. As such, the impressive pyramids of the third through sixth dynasties can be seen, not only as tombs emphasizing the importance of the cult of the dead, but also as: (1) attempts to pierce the heavens and commune with Re, the Egyptian sun god; and (2) mighty machines within which the departed pharaoh attempted to manipulate the universe and to keep a stable equilibrium between the order of the Nile Valley and the chaos of the desert. Seen from this latter vantage point, the departed pharaoh had become Osiris, attempting to help his son, Horus, i.e., the new pharaoh, fulfill his supreme task of suppressing Seth's ambitions, i.e., of holding back the chaos and danger of the desert from engulfing the order and structure of the Nile Valley. In short, the most recently deceased pharaoh had become Osiris, the reigning pharaoh was Horus, the queen mother was Isis, and the desert was Seth.

The Divinity of Pharaoh

As noted previously, as early as the pharaohs of the first dynasty, each pharaoh, upon accession to the throne, took as the first of his five names, a Horus name. This Horus name identified the pharaoh, as the personification and embodiment of Egypt, as the living Horus. By the fourth dynasty, two important additions had been made to the pharaoh's list of regal titles: "son of Re", i.e., son of the Egyptian sun god; and "perfect god". As one can see, both from these titles and from the above discussion of order versus chaos, the pharaoh had a unique status between humanity and the gods, and was in something of an intermediary position between the profane and the divine. On the one hand, he was already the living embodiment of Horus; on the other hand, only with his death could he seek full divinity as the embodiment of Osiris.

Conclusions

The ancient Egyptian religion confronting Abraham upon his arrival in Egypt was a strange and confusing morass of beliefs. The pantheon of the gods was not stable, and gods came and went from the pantheon, providing some sense of impermanence in the worship of the people of Egypt. The elaborate cult of the dead would have been something new for Abraham to confront, as there had been no parallels to this cult in Ur, Harran, and Palestine.

However, certain aspects of religious belief and practice in ancient Egypt would have been familiar to Abraham. As had been the case in Ur, Harran, and Palestine, idolatry was prevalent. As had been the case in Ur, Harran, and Palestine, polytheism was the order of the day. As had been the case with Naram-Sin in Ur, the pharaoh had pretensions of divinity. The struggle between Horus, as order, and Seth, as chaos, had certain parallels to the story of the battle between Baal and Yam, to which Abraham had probably been exposed while in Palestine. Likewise, the belief in a regeneration of Osiris, and in the deceased pharaoh becoming Osiris, had their parallels in Palestine in the belief of the annual regeneration of Baal from the death inflicted upon him by Mot. Further, the ancient Egyptian belief in an afterlife, and in a judgment that had to be passed, in order to enter the next world, may have sounded to Abraham like a thoroughly corrupted and contaminated version of his own preaching of a resurrection, afterlife, and final judgment.

Abraham and Lot prosper in Egypt

The book of *Jubilees* claims that Abraham and Sarah lived in Egypt for five years.[175] During this time, Abraham would have had ample opportunity to witness the architectural and artistic triumphs of ancient Egypt. The pyramids and the Sphinx were already present for Abraham to see. Yet, Abraham's time in Egypt was not that of a sightseeing tourist. Abraham and his family were attempting to escape a devastating famine, and there was much to do. Apparently, Abraham was quite successful in escaping the economic hardships of the famine, because he reportedly began to experience significant economic advances, riches, and prosperity. In particular, while in Egypt, Abraham was said to have acquired vast amounts of sheep, cattle, donkeys, horses, servants or slaves, gold, and silver.[176]

In addition, it is said that Lot also became wealthy during these years in Egypt.[177] Further, it has been reported that Lot married an Egyptian wife while in Egypt.[178]

Abraham and *Da'wa*

However, one hypothesizes that Abraham's five years in Egypt were not totally devoted to the acquisition of material wealth. For about 46 to 47 years in Ur, for the next 14 years in Harran, and for two to three years in Palestine, Abraham had been continuously engaged in preaching the message of *Tawheed*, of the need to submit to Allah, of a resurrection after death, and of an eventual day of judgment. Such preaching was carried out in the face of continuous opposition from the idolatrous polytheists of his day, and despite extreme personal risk. Given this history, and given the polytheism that surrounded him in ancient Egypt, it is hard to imagine that Abraham did not also carry out an active program of *Da'wa* during his five years in Egypt.

Specific support for this hypothesis is found in the works of the Jewish historian, Josephus b. Matthias, who wrote in the first century CE. Josephus, who probably had access to a variety of ancient Jewish books that no longer exist, and to a more ancient version of the *Torah* than is available today[179], maintained that Abraham carried out an active program of *Da'wa* while in Egypt. According to Josephus, Abraham talked with and preached to the Egyptian priests and laity, attempted to show them the errors of polytheism, and taught them the scientific knowledge that he had previously learned in Mesopotamia.[180]

Pharaoh and Sarah –The Setting

If one accepts the account in *Jubilees* regarding Abraham and Sarah having spent five years in Egypt, then based upon the previous estimates of the ages of Abraham and of Sarah when they left Palestine[181], it appears that Abraham was about 82 to 83 years old and that Sarah was about 72 to 73 years old at the time of their encounters with the pharaoh. However, despite her age (see Postscript to Abraham in Egypt below), Sarah was a very charming and beautiful woman[182], and her loveliness and allure had begun to draw inappropriate attention from many of the male Egyptians, with whom they came into contact. Eventually, these men began to report to the pharaoh about this attractive foreigner in their midst[183]. With his curiosity and libido being piqued by these reports that were reaching him, the pharaoh sent for Abraham.[184]

Upon meeting Abraham, the pharaoh probably wasted little time on social amenities and pleasantries. After all, he was the pharaoh of Egypt, the living embodiment of Horus, the "son of Re", and the "perfect god", and Abraham was a mere foreigner, who was being allowed to live in Egypt only by the pharaoh's indulgence. As such, the pharaoh quickly turned to Abraham, and inquired as to the relationship, if any, that existed between Abraham and Sarah.[185] At that point, Abraham told the third, and presumably, last lie of his life, and responded by saying that Sarah was his sister.[186]

Abraham's Motivation

The motivation behind Abraham's statement that Sarah was his sister has troubled Biblical commentators throughout the ages. The *J* strand of *Genesis* clearly states that Abraham's motivation was to save his own life[187], thus portraying Abraham as a prophet with feet of clay, who was willing to save his own life by "selling" his wife into sexual servitude to another man. This shabby portrayal of Abraham in the *J* strand is only worsened by the *J* statement that Abraham's economic prosperity in Egypt was directly tied to the pharaoh having dealt kindly and favorably with Abraham on account of Sarah.[188] *Jubilees* does not even mention Abraham's lie, and thus provides no statement concerning Abraham's motivation in lying. *Sahih Ahadith*[189], while clearly stating that Abraham lied in saying that Sarah was his sister, fail to address directly the issue of Abraham's motivation in lying.

One explanation that has been offered by Biblical commentators is that technically Abraham did not lie, because Sarah was his paternal half-sister. This is the explanation proposed by the *E* strand of *Genesis*[190], whose author apparently experienced some need to justify Abraham's actions. However, there are two arguments against this technical justification of Abraham's action by the author of *E*. First, as already documented in Chapter 2 (The Birth and Family of Abraham: The Family of Sarah), it is probable that Sarah was not Abraham's half-sister, but was the daughter of Abraham's paternal uncle. Second, despite the parsing and semantics to which *E* reduces Abraham, *E* still maintains that Abraham feared for his life.[191]

Another explanation that has been offered is again based upon the notion that technically Abraham did not lie. Abraham had been living among the Horites in Harran, and Hurrian (Horite) legal tradition held that sisterhood was a transferable relationship, in which a woman given in marriage by her brother became legally her husband's sister. Be that as it may, while offering a technical defense that Abraham did not lie, this explanation fails to address the much larger issue of Abraham turning over his wife to the pharaoh of Egypt.

One final explanation remains, and that is one drawn from a close inspection of *Sahih Ahadith*. Two points need to be noted in the *Sahih Ahadith* stating that Abraham told his third lie when he told the pharaoh that Sarah was his sister. First, the two previous times that Abraham had lied, he had done so for the sake of Allah.[192] Second, Abraham reportedly told his third lie in the face of there not being any other believers in Egypt, besides Abraham and Sarah, and presumably Lot.[193] Given the juxtaposition of these two points in the *Sahih Ahadith*, it appears to this author that: if Abraham's first two lies were for the sake of Allah, it seems reasonable to conclude that Abraham's third lie was also for "the sake of Allah"; and that "the sake of Allah" can be understood within the context of there being no believers in Allah among the native Egyptian population. In other words, Abraham lied in saying that Sarah was his sister, precisely because he knew that the following event (see below) would take place, and that this event would be a powerful statement to the people of Egypt about the need to submit to Allah. Seen from this perspective, Abraham's lie was no craven act of moral cowardice, but a bold act of faith in the omnipotent nature of Allah.

Pharaoh takes Sarah

The pharaoh now believed that Sarah was simply Abraham's sister. Accordingly, the pharaoh wasted no time in summoning Sarah to his palace.[194] Sarah, having been previously instructed by Abraham not to disavow Abraham's lie[195], said nothing to the pharaoh about her real relationship to Abraham.

One can but assume that if verbal reports of Sarah's beauty had initially stirred the pharaoh's libidinous desires, the actual presence of

Sarah in his palace had reduced him to a state of overwhelming lust. Anticipating that such would be the case with the pharaoh, Sarah turned to Allah in prayer. But not even Sarah's state of prayer could distract the pharaoh from the desire to satisfy his basest cravings. As such, even though Sarah remained praying, the pharaoh advanced upon her, and reached out to her. However, as soon as he reached for Sarah, he was afflicted with what sounds similar to an epileptic fit or to a conversion reaction, i.e., a stiffening and rigidity of his upper extremity and an agitated twitching of his legs.[196]

Crying out from his distressed state, the pharaoh promised that he would release Sarah unharmed, if she would pray for his cure. Sarah complied, and Allah answered her prayer. However, as soon as the pharaoh had regained his equilibrium and physical prowess, he again advanced upon Sarah. Again, Sarah pleaded to Allah for aid, and again Allah answered her prayer. For the second time, the pharaoh was reduced to his afflicted state of stiffening upper extremity and of agitated trembling of lower extremities. For the second time, the pharaoh promised Sarah her safety and release, if she would pray for his cure. For the second time, Sarah complied with the pharaoh's request. For the second time, Allah answered Sarah's prayer to cure the pharaoh. But once again, cured from his affliction, the pharaoh attempted to attack sexually the seemingly helpless Sarah. For the third time, Sarah prayed for deliverance from the pharaoh, and Allah answered her prayer yet again. For the third and final time, the pharaoh was reduced to a state of stiffening and trembling, and had once again to beg Sarah to pray for his cure. For the third time, Sarah did so, and Allah answered her prayer. This time, the pharaoh kept his word to Sarah, and ordered Sarah released.[197]

Of note, *Jubilees* and the *J* strand of *Genesis* reduce the above narrative to a simple statement that the pharaoh and his house were afflicted with great plagues[198]. The *E* strand of *Genesis* reports only that Sarah's antagonist received a dream that he would die if he molested Sarah, and that he and his wife and his concubines needed healing.[199] In contrast, the *Sahih Ahadith* offer a rich narrative, in which Sarah's prayers are answered on six separate occasions, i.e., three times for protection from the pharaoh, and three times for the cure of the pharaoh.

The Return of Sarah

Sarah was returned to Abraham while he was praying [200], no doubt for Sarah's safety and protection. One can well imagine the rejoicing of Abraham and Sarah, upon their reunion with each other. Abraham's faith had been justified, and Abraham's and Sarah's prayers had been answered. The pharaoh of Egypt had been humiliated [201], and a powerful message had been delivered to the polytheists of Egypt.

However, it was not just Sarah that the pharaoh sent to Abraham. Sarah came accompanied by gifts of reparation from the pharaoh. The confabulated *E* account in *Genesis* of Sarah's return lists a thousand pieces of silver being among those gifts. [202] In evaluating this gift, one needs to remember that silver was much more valuable than gold in the ancient Egypt of Abraham's day. However, of more relevance to Abraham's and Sarah's later life, there was at least one additional gift sent by the pharaoh, i.e., a female slave, who was named Hagar. [203]

Abraham leaves Egypt

It would be nice to think that the pharaoh learned from his experience, and that he came to accept the *Tawheed* and came to submit to Allah. However, that apparently was not the case, as the pharaoh ordered Abraham and his family to leave Egypt, taking with them all that they had. [204]

Postscript # 1 to Abraham in Egypt

The modern reader of the story of the pharaoh's sexual infatuation with Sarah must come to grips with the fact that Sarah was probably about 72 or 73 years old at the time, with Abraham being 82 or 83 years old. [205] How is it that this septuagenarian wife of Abraham could have been so beautiful, and so sexually alluring, as to have completely turned the head of the pharaoh of Egypt? Hypotheses about the pharaoh having some particular fetish for or sexual deviation about elderly women must be quickly rejected, as soon as one remembers that various Egyptian men had previously praised Sarah's beauty and charm to the pharaoh, and when one considers that it would have been most unlikely that such a fetish would have been commonplace. Thus, at first glance, the situation seems most perplexing.

However, this apparent perplexity is based upon two assumptions that may not be viable. The first assumption is that the normal life span in Abraham's day was similar to that of today. The second assumption is that the rate or process of aging in Abraham's day was similar to that of today. With regard to the first assumption, it has been reported that Abraham lived to be 175 years old, Sarah lived to be 127, Abraham's father lived to be 205, Abraham's paternal grandfather lived to be 148, and Abraham's paternal great-grandfather lived to be 230.[206] Further, the archaeological record clearly verifies that Pepi II of the sixth dynasty of Egypt ruled for an incredible 94 years.[207] With regard to the second assumption, it has been stated that Abraham was the first person to begin to show such signs of aging as graying of hair.[208] In short, neither assumption appears to be valid.

Judging from the above discussion, there is no reason to doubt that, upon leaving Egypt, Abraham was about 82 or 83 years old, and that Sarah was about 72 or 73 years old.

Postscript # 2 to Abraham in Egypt

The impression conveyed by most sources is that Sarah was at the palace of pharaoh only very briefly. However, it is noted that the *Genesis Apocryphon* claimed that Sarah was held prisoner by the pharaoh for two years.[209] This length of time appears to be quite doubtful, given the afflictions suffered by the pharaoh while Sarah was at his palace.

Chapter 8
Abraham in Palestine – II

Information regarding Abraham's second sojourn in Palestine is basically dependent on the *J* strand of *Genesis*. Only minimal information is provided by other sources, primarily a few scattered details from the *E* and *P* strands of *Genesis, Jubilees,* and *Sahih Ahadith.*

Abraham's Return to Palestine

Abraham, presumably now 82 or 83 years old[210], and his family had been ordered by the pharaoh to leave Egypt, secondary to the pharaoh's disastrous and humiliating encounter with Sarah. However, Abraham, Sarah, and Lot did not leave Egypt empty-handed. Indeed, they were a far cry from being penniless refugees. While in Egypt, Abraham had acquired at least a thousand pieces of silver[211], as well as gold, multiple servants or slaves, flocks of sheep, and herds of oxen or cattle, donkeys, and horses.[212] Sarah had acquired a personal female slave, Hagar.[213] Reportedly, Lot had also grown rich[214], and had married an Egyptian woman.[215] As such, it was probably quite a large caravan, which began the journey to return to Palestine from Egypt.

In returning to Palestine, Abraham probably took one of two possible routes: (1) following the coastal plain bordering the Mediterranean, until reaching a suitable place in the Gaza Strip, at which to have turned due east into the Negeb; or (2) following the way to Shur, and moving past the Wilderness of Shur and the Wilderness of Zin, before reaching the Negeb. Regardless of which route was traversed, Abraham and his company reached the Negeb, and then apparently traveled north in stages to Bethel.[216] One assumes that these stages in travel between the Negeb and Bethel were to accommodate the need for his and Lot's livestock to find suitable grazing and watering.

Abraham at Bethel: Abraham's *Da'wa* at Bethel

When Abraham had initially entered Palestine after leaving Harran, he and his family first stopped at the oak of Moreh near Shechem where Abraham built an altar to Allah – an event which signified Abraham's undaunted devotion to the One and Only Allah. Abraham supposedly then moved to a mountain east of Bethel and west of Ai, where he had again built an altar to Allah, thereby witnessing for Allah. On his return to Palestine from Egypt, Abraham went to Bethel, the site at which he had previously built an altar to Allah some seven or eight years earlier.[217]

There is, of course, no way of knowing for sure why Abraham returned to Bethel. However, it can be reasonably speculated that one of his reasons for returning to Bethel was to monitor and reinforce the result of his having built an altar and witnessing in that area some seven or eight years before. Perhaps, there were converts to the belief in the *Tawheed*, who had been left in the area. If so, it appears reasonable to assume that these converts needed Prophet Abraham's spiritual guidance on a continuing, if only periodic, basis. Perhaps, Abraham merely wanted to witness once again to the polytheists of Bethel, and thereby give them yet another chance to submit to Allah. Whatever must have been the case, it seems probable that Abraham would have again carried out a vigorous program of *Da'wa* while in the area. Likewise, it seems probable that Abraham's *Da'wa* would have consisted of both a verbal message, i.e., preaching and exhortation, and a behavioral message, i.e., the example of Abraham's worship and life.

Abraham and Lot separate

Prelude: At times, abundant prosperity can be as much of a curse as it is of a blessing. The owner of large flocks and herds of livestock assumes a heavy responsibility to find appropriate pasture and water for his animals. The greater the size of his flocks and herds, the greater his responsibility, and the greater the demands that are placed on him by the basic needs of his animals. Such was now the case with Abraham and Lot, both of whom had acquired vast flocks and herds during their sojourn in Egypt. Certainly, the semi-arid and arid Negeb was not a region that could sustain such large flocks and herds in close proximity to each other. There was neither enough pasture nor enough water in the Negeb to maintain such a vast number of livestock. Perhaps this was one of the reasons that had prompted Abraham's move north from the Negeb to Bethel. However, even in the vicinity of Bethel, the natural agricultural resources were insufficient to sustain herds as vast as those owned by Abraham and Lot.[218] As such, rather inevitably, the shepherds and herders of Abraham and the shepherds and herders of Lot began to quarrel with one another over the available pasture and water.[219] Given that the natural water supplies of Bethel were so abundant that there was no need to dig cisterns at Bethel until the time of the Roman Empire, which was some 2,000 years after Abraham, one must stop and marvel for a moment about the size of the flocks and herds owned by Lot and by Abraham. They were obviously so great, that they were causing a shortage of available water and pasture in the vicinity of Bethel, a location which was known for its abundant water supplies.

The animosity and strife that had begun to develop between the servants of Abraham and those of Lot must have been a source of great personal distress for the two prophets of Allah. They were not only biological uncle and nephew, but also spiritual brothers in their submission to Allah. Abraham may have even adopted the orphaned Lot[220], thus additionally cementing their relationship. Further, they had lived and shared together for many years: for as much as 40 or more years during their initial lives in Ur; through their 14-year immigration in Harran; through the two or three years they spent together during their first stay in Palestine; through their five-year sojourn in Egypt; and through the vicissitudes of their return to Palestine.[221] One may assume that Lot had been a vigorous assistant to Abraham during the difficult periods of Abraham's life, when Abraham's preaching and exhortation about the *Tawheed*, and about the need to submit to Allah, had fallen on deaf ears. Perhaps, Lot had already begun to share Abraham's load in actively witnessing and preaching. One may also assume that Lot had raised his own prayers for Sarah's safety when Sarah had been abducted by the pharaoh of Egypt. In short, one may assume that Lot had been an active assistant, if not an actual partner, in sharing Abraham's trials and tribulations.

Parting Ways: Ironically, Abraham's and Lot's current prosperity and wealth accomplished what none of their shared travails and difficulties had done, i.e., force them apart, if not emotionally and spiritually, at least locationally. So it was that Abraham and Lot came to stand together on a mountain or high ground, and to survey the land around them. As they stood there meditating on what was transpiring between them,

Abraham turned to Lot, his voice probably tinged with both sadness and love, and reportedly said:

> Let there be no strife between you and me, and between your herders and my herders; for we are kindred. Is not the whole land before you? Separate yourself from me. If you take the left hand, then I will go to the right; or if you take the right hand, then I will go to the left.[222]

Then, Lot looked around him, and surveyed the land across the vast distances that he could see. To the east, along the plains surrounding the Jordan River, Lot saw an area of great beauty and abundance, with sufficient water to turn the land into a veritable garden of agricultural delight.[223] Here was an agricultural potential to rival the richness of the Egyptian delta that they had so recently left. Here was a land, which had sufficient water from the Jordan River, and which had sufficient flat lands for grazing, so that the need to be constantly migrating would be minimized. There was the potential to settle down, and to enter the life of the city and town. Here was also a new population of people, to whom one could take the message of the *Tawheed*. Here was an opportunity for Lot to establish his own mission of preaching, of exhortation, and of witnessing by example.

To the west, Lot gazed out upon the hill country of Palestine, with its innumerable slopes and varied terrain. Here, there was no river to supplement the winter rainfall. Here, the rich flat land was less abundant and less centrally located. Here, life would always remain at least semi-nomadic, at least for someone with as much livestock as possessed by Lot and by Abraham. Perhaps, an additional consideration was that this was a country already known to Lot and to Abraham. In Palestine, Abraham had already begun preaching the message of the *Tawheed*, at least at Shechem, Bethel, and Hebron. Palestine had already been established as part of Abraham's mission, and Abraham had already built altars to Allah, both at Shechem and at Bethel.

Whether Lot's choice was based upon economic and agricultural considerations and potential, or whether Lot's choice was based upon the opportunity to begin his own mission for Allah to a new people, is something that cannot be determined so many years after the event. Whatever must have been his motivation at that time, Lot chose the plains of the Jordan River region as his abode, leaving to Abraham the whole of the remainder of Palestine.[224]

Having made his choice, Lot then prepared to move his tent[225] and his possessions to his selected habitat on the plains of the Jordan River. No reliable source known to this author documents the events during the interval between Lot's choice and his eventual move. However, one can speculate that the interval was filled with great sadness at the looming separation. Perhaps, there was also an element of anticipatory joy, in that Lot would now be taking the message of the *Tawheed* to a new population of people living in the plains of the Jordan River, just as Abraham had previously carried that message to the people of Ur, Harran, Palestine, and Egypt. In any case, Lot moved his people and his possessions eastward, to and beyond the Jordan River, eventually exchanging his nomadic, tent-dwelling life for the settled life of Sodom[226], a town that was probably located on what was then a fertile plain on the southeastern edge of the Dead Sea.

Comment: At the time of the separation of Abraham and Lot, there were five so-called "cities of the plain" on the southeastern side of the Dead Sea. These were Sodom, Gomorrah, Admah, Zeboiim, and Zoar. These five cities were located on what was then a rich and fertile plain, which was sustained by an abundance of fresh water flowing into the Dead Sea. However, around the beginning of the second millennia BCE, a violent earthquake along the Great Rift Valley, which extends from the Jordan River to the Zambesi River in eastern Africa, forever changed the geographical terrain and climatic conditions prevailing along the southeastern side of the Dead Sea. Prior to the earthquake, the Dead Sea had probably been a large fresh water lake, which drained southward through a southern extension of the Jordan River that culminated in the Gulf of 'Aqaba. At the time of the earthquake, Sodom and Gomorrah were dropped down in elevation, and were buried by the waters of the Dead Sea, which then expanded to include the area south of the Al-Lisan Peninsula. This giant earthquake released sufficient petroleum and gases into the air to turn what had been a verdant agricultural paradise into a land of desolation and despair.

The Third Promise to Abraham

Shortly after Lot's departure from Abraham at Bethel, Abraham reportedly received his third promise from Allah that he would have offspring and descendants. Further, he was reportedly promised that his descendants would be so multitudinous that they would be almost impossible to count. Still further, Abraham was reportedly promised that his descendants would inherit and possess all of the land that Abraham now saw from the high ground by Bethel.[227]

Such is the mercy and love of Allah. The childless Abraham had not only been promised that he would have offspring and descendants, but that very promise had now been repeated on two occasions. The initial promise had been delivered to Abraham just before he had left Harran.[228] That initial promise had then been reiterated at Shechem[229], during Abraham's first stay in Palestine. Now, at Bethel, that promise had been made to Abraham for the third time. No doubt, the childless Abraham found much comfort and reassurance in the continuing promises of Allah. While there is certainly no reason to suspect that Abraham ever doubted even the first promise from Allah, Allah's continuing reassurances to Abraham could only have bolstered Abraham's spirits, providing him with a constantly renewed belief in the love and mercy of Allah.

Abraham at Hebron

There is no way of reliably determining how long Abraham stayed in the vicinity of Bethel during his second sojourn in Palestine. However, *Genesis* states that Abraham left Bethel, remained a tent-dweller, and moved to the oaks of Mamre by Hebron.[230] One assumes that Abraham's large flocks and herds necessitated that he then keep constantly moving around the vicinity of Hebron, in order to sustain his livestock with sufficient pasture and water. Nonetheless, the oaks of Mamre by Hebron appear to have been the hub, around which Abraham's movements in the vicinity of Hebron centered.

Da'wa **at Hebron**

During his first sojourn in Palestine, Abraham had built an altar to Allah at the oak of Moreh by Shechem.[231] Later, he had built a second altar to Allah at the mountain between Bethel and Ai.[232] As noted previously in Chapter 5, both these sites were presumably associated with outdoor shrines to various gods in the Canaanite pantheon, with the outdoor shrine near Bethel being supposedly dedicated to the Canaanite god, El.[233] No doubt, Abraham was taking a great personal risk in building these two altars to Allah. In that regard, it should be noted that it was quite likely that the local population of Canaanites and Amorites might have viewed Abraham's behavior as an act of defilement of their holy places. However, Abraham, armed and girded with the faith and zeal of a prophet of Allah, had not been deterred by considerations involving the safety of his life and limbs. In erecting these altars, Abraham had boldly practiced *Da'wa* by example. His very behavior had been a statement of the *Tawheed*, and of the need to submit to Allah. Having now returned to the oaks of Mamre by Hebron, which must also be considered as having been an outdoor shrine to some local deity in the Canaanite pantheon, Abraham continued his pattern of *Da'wa* by example. Once again, he built an altar to Allah.[234] Once again, he risked life and limb, in order to illustrate the proper worship of Allah. *Da'wa,* once again took precedence over everything and everyone in Abraham's life.

The Fourth Promise to Abraham

While residing in the vicinity of Hebron, Abraham then received a vision from Allah, wherein Abraham was reportedly told that Allah would protect and reward him.

> After these things the word of the Lord came to Abram in a vision,
> Do not be afraid, Abram, I am your shield; your reward shall be very
> great."[235]

Perhaps, this reassurance from Allah came as the result of some unrecorded and specific threats that were being made against Abraham, secondary to Abraham having erected an altar to Allah at the oaks of Mamre. Probably, this reassurance was only a general statement of support, and was unrelated to any residual resentment amongst the local population to Abraham having erected the altar to Allah at the oaks of Mamre.

Whatever the case, Abraham then reportedly supplicated for a rapid end to his childless state, noting that at present his only heir was Eliezer, a slave whom Abraham had acquired from Damascus. Allah reportedly answered Abraham's supplication by telling him that Eliezer would not be his heir; and that Abraham would have offspring and descendants, who would be as numerous and uncountable as the stars in the sky. Abraham, whom one can safely assume had never doubted Allah's initial promise to him, continued to have faith in and to believe the promise of Allah, and Allah reportedly weighed it as a sign of Abraham's righteousness that Abraham remained so steadfast in his faith in Allah's promise.[236]

Abraham's Sacrifice

The *Genesis* narrative: According to *Genesis*, after having received Allah's promise for the fourth time that he would have descendants, Abraham was directed by Allah to prepare a sacrifice. This sacrifice was to consist of a three-year-old heifer, a three-year-old female goat, a three-year-old ram, a turtledove, and a pigeon. Reportedly, Abraham was directed to split each of the carcasses in two, except for the birds, and was to protect the sacrifice from carrion birds of prey.[237]

A Qur'anic interlude: The above account from *Genesis* of Abraham's sacrifice has certain, minimal similarities with a story of Abraham from the *Qur'an*. These similarities are as follows. First, the *Genesis* account of the sacrifice takes place within a context of Abraham talking about death, albeit his own, in that Abraham raised the issue of dying with only Eliezer as his heir. Second, Abraham's actions are specifically carried out under the direct command of Allah. Third, the *Genesis* account specifically mentions birds as part of the sacrifice, and specifically mentions birds (of prey) gathering together where Abraham stood at the place of sacrifice. Given these three considerations, it is possible, although very far from certain, that the *Genesis* account of Abraham's sacrifice is a much contaminated and confabulated version of the following story from the *Qur'an*, which story the author has no way of definitively placing in the sequence of events comprising the life of Abraham.

> Behold! Abraham said: "My Lord! Show me how Thou givest life to the dead." He said: "Dost thou not then believe?" He said: "Yea! but to satisfy my own understanding." He said: "Take four birds, tame them to turn to thee; put a portion of them on every hill, and call to them; they will come to thee, (flying) with speed. Then know that Allah is exalted in power, wise."[238]

The First Covenant with and the Fifth Promise to Abraham

According to *Genesis*, shortly or immediately after the above events, Allah made a covenant with His prophet, Abraham, in which Allah promised Abraham for the fifth time that Abraham would have descendants. Specific to the covenant between Allah and Abraham, Abraham was reportedly told that Allah would give to Abraham's descendants all of the land from the Nile River in Egypt to the Euphrates River in Iraq and Syria.[239]

Again, one marvels at the love and mercy of Allah, Who not only promised Abraham descendants, but also promised that Abraham's descendants would be a multitude beyond counting. Further, having made this promise to Abraham, Allah was gracious enough to reiterate this promise on a second, a third, a fourth, and a fifth occasion. Still further, Allah promised Abraham that his descendants would inherit the land all the way from the Nile to the Euphrates, a promise that has already been fulfilled, as one can readily see by examining the distribution of the Arab population in the Middle East.

Abraham and Hagar

Establishing the Setting: As reported previously in Chapter 6, as a result of the pharaoh's humiliating and debilitating encounter with Sarah, the pharaoh of Egypt had given to Sarah a female slave, who was named Hagar.[240] The pharaoh had then demanded that Abraham and his family leave Egypt[241], with Abraham being about 82 or 83 years old and Sarah being about 72 or 73 years old at that time.[242] Abraham, Sarah, and Hagar then entered Palestine, where they lived together for two to three years.[243] During this interval, Sarah and Abraham continued to be childless, despite the repeated promises of Allah that Abraham would have descendants. Given this continued state of being childless, Sarah apparently decided to attempt to alter the equation.

Sarah's Gift to Abraham: According to *Genesis*[244], Sarah suggested to Abraham that he take Sarah's Egyptian slave, Hagar, as his second wife, in order that he might have children by Hagar. In regard to this gift from Sarah, three points should be considered. First, *Genesis* states that Sarah's motivation in giving this gift was that she wanted to claim and raise the resulting children from Hagar as being her own. This would imply a rather selfish motivation on Sarah's part. Certainly, a more charitable interpretation would be to hypothesize that Sarah was motivated by an altruistic desire that her husband might soon have children. Second, *Genesis* suggests that Abraham took Hagar as a second wife, not as a mere concubine, nor as the slave of Abraham's right hand. This point will become crucial much later in the life of Abraham, when one considers the issue of Abraham's legitimate heirs. Third, despite becoming Abraham's second wife, Hagar remained the slave of Sarah. This latter point is critical in understanding what happened within months of Abraham accepting Sarah's gift, and of Abraham marrying Hagar as his second wife.

Conflict between Sarah and Hagar: Human nature being such as it is, it would appear almost inevitable that conflict would quickly arise between the two wives of a man, if the wives could not relate to each other as total equals, because the second wife was the slave of the first; and if the second wife quickly conceived, whereas the first wife had been barren throughout 36 years of prior marriage.[245] Given the frailties of the human psyche, one would posit that such conflict would arise even where both of the wives and the husband had the best of motives and intentions. Such was the case in Abraham's household, as Sarah and the pregnant Hagar began to experience a most difficult, strained and conflicted relationship.[246]

Perhaps, as suggested by *Genesis*, the pregnant Hagar began to look with contempt upon the barren Sarah.[247] Perhaps, as suggested by what happened at a later time[248], Sarah simply became jealous of Hagar. Such jealousy, if it existed, may have had to do with Hagar's relationship with Abraham, or it may have been based on the fact that Hagar was pregnant by Abraham and Sarah was not. Perhaps, some or all of the above scenarios occurred simultaneously. Whatever the historical reality of the conflicted situation between Sarah and Hagar, Sarah reportedly complained to Abraham that Hagar was acting contemptuously to her mistress, Sarah.[249] One suspects that this complaint by Sarah was not an isolated occurrence, but was repeated on more than one occasion. Nonetheless, Hagar was Sarah's slave, and Abraham's options for intervening between his two wives were sorely limited by this consideration. In short, in the final analysis, Hagar was still Sarah's slave, and was thus subject to Sarah's power, direction, and command.

According to *Genesis*, with the conflict growing between Sarah and Hagar, Sarah began to abuse her power and authority over her slave, who also happened to be her co-wife. No specifics of this abuse are given, but *Genesis* clearly states that Sarah "dealt harshly with" Hagar.[250] Finally, after an unknown length of time of accepting Sarah's abuse, and with no hope of immediate reconciliation with Sarah in sight, the pregnant Hagar could simply take the abusive situation no longer. Hagar desperately wanted to be out of her untenable and burdensome situation. In fact, she had reached the point where she was willing to take considerable personal risk to resolve the situation with Sarah once and for all. Despite the fact that it meant leaving her husband, Abraham, Hagar could see no alternative but that of escaping from Sarah, whatever the personal cost and risk.

The Flight of Hagar: Hagar fled south from Hebron, south from her harsh mistress, Sarah, and south into the arid and semi-arid Negeb.[251] She apparently fled on foot, dragging her girdle behind her, in order to cover her tracks from Sarah.[252] Her flight took the pregnant Hagar some 75 to 80 miles (122 to 130 kilometers) south of Hebron, past Beersheba, and into the Wilderness of Zin, where she finally stopped at a spring or well between Kadesh and Bered.[253] From the route of her path, Hagar appears to have been heading toward the road on the way to Shur[254], thus suggesting that Hagar was attempting to return to her native Egypt, a country which Abraham and Sarah were barred from entering, by order of the pharaoh.[255]

The desperate and untenable plight of Hagar at Hebron is only emphasized by considering the extent to which she was willing to go, and the personal risk that she was willing to undertake, in order to escape from Sarah. Alone, pregnant, and on foot, Hagar had traveled some 75 to 80 miles (122 to 130 kilometers) through a sometimes harsh and forbidding wilderness. Food and water would have been scarce along the way. Finally, exhausted, she rested at a spring or well between Kadesh and Bered.

According to *Genesis*, it was at the well between Kadesh and Bered that an angel of Allah approached the troubled Hagar, and inquired of her to where she was going, and from where she was coming. One assumes that Hagar unburdened herself in talking to the angel, and that she obtained some measure of cathartic release, as she explained that she was fleeing from Sarah, and from Sarah's treatment of her. In response, the angel of Allah noted that Hagar was pregnant, that she was carrying Abraham's son, and that she should call her to-be-born son Ismael, meaning "Allah (El) hears", because Allah had indeed heard the cries of Hagar in the midst of her affliction.[256]

Apparently, Hagar's encounter with the angel of Allah enabled Hagar to find new resolve and fortitude, in regard to her conflicted relationship with Sarah. Perhaps, the angel's words, as recorded in *Genesis*, were sufficiently reassuring to Hagar, in and of themselves. Perhaps, there was more to the message of the angel, than the sparse information recorded in *Genesis*. In that regard, it is noted that a later editorial gloss of or editorial insertion into the narrative in *Genesis* includes a statement that the angel of Allah informed Hagar that from her son, an uncountable multitude of descendants would arise.[257] As such, one might speculate that there was more said by the angel of Allah about Hagar's future descendants through Ismael. Although it is nothing more than sheer speculation, one might even wonder if there was something said about a specific descendant of Hagar, one who would not yet be born for over two millennia. Could this passage in *Genesis* have originally contained an angelic promise about the future birth and life of Prophet Muhammad?

Given the extent of currently available information, the above speculation must remain firmly in the realm of the unknown. Nonetheless, following her encounter with the angel of Allah, Hagar apparently began the difficult and painful trek back to Hebron. Whatever the specific reassurance Hagar had received, she was now reconciled to her life, and to Allah's plan for her life.

The Birth of Ismael: There is no surviving account of Hagar's return to Hebron, to her husband, Abraham, and to her mistress, Sarah. One can but assume that the reunion between husband and wife was one of great joy and happiness. One might also speculate that, during the time that Hagar was away from her, Sarah had experienced some guilt about her prior treatment of Hagar, and that Sarah's behavior toward her returning slave and co-wife was thereby altered, at least for a while. In any event, Hagar remained with Abraham and Sarah at Hebron, where she later gave birth to Ismael when Abraham was 86 years old.[258] Five times Allah had previously promised Abraham that he would have offspring and descendants. That promise was now fulfilled.

Abraham leaves Palestine

Unfortunately, it appears that the hypothesized cessation of, or easing of, the conflict between Hagar and Sarah was short-lived. Apparently, while Ismael was still nursing at his mother's side, this conflict began or escalated once again, secondary to Sarah's jealousy of Hagar. Finally, with no apparent alternative in sight, and reportedly in response to a directive from Allah, Abraham took Ismael and Hagar and left Palestine, presumably leaving Sarah behind at Hebron.[259]

Postscript to Abraham in Palestine–II

It is fitting to pause for a few moments to reflect a little about the second wife of Abraham. Hagar had been acquired in Egypt as a slave, having been a gift of reparation from the pharaoh of Egypt to Sarah. At the time, Hagar was apparently an unbeliever in the *Tawheed*, as noted by Abraham's statement to Sarah that there were no believers among the native Egyptian populace. One therefore assumes that Hagar had been a polytheist and an idolater, who had practiced the indigenous religion of her native Egypt.[260]

Upon being given to Sarah as a slave, Hagar had then immediately been forced to leave Egypt, along with Abraham, Sarah, and Lot. She had been uprooted from whatever family and friends she might have had in Egypt, she had been ripped apart from her native culture and dialect, and she had been forced to wander throughout Palestine with Abraham and Sarah. Finally, after two to three years in Palestine, she had been given by Sarah to be Abraham's second wife, although remaining Sarah's personal slave. She had quickly conceived, and had then been subjected to abuse and harsh treatment from Sarah.[261]

Despite the obvious probability that Hagar had quickly come to respect and to love her husband, Abraham, her situation with Sarah is reported by Biblical sources to have been totally untenable and totally unbearable. As such, Hagar made a desperate attempt to flee from Sarah. In that regard, it is worth noting that linguists occasionally associate the name of Hagar with an Arabic word meaning "flee".[262] However, it is unknown whether Hagar derived the name by which she was known by later generations from her action of fleeing, or whether a derivative of her name later entered the Arabic vocabulary as a synonym for "flee". In either case, Hagar's flight was long and desperate, and was made while Hagar was alone, pregnant, and on foot.

Finally, an exhausted Hagar stopped at a spring or well by Kadesh. Here, her cries of affliction were answered, and an angel of Allah appeared to Hagar, informing her that her to-be-born son should be named Ismael, meaning "Allah (El) hears". In addition, *Genesis* notes that the well, by which Hagar stopped, was later known as Beerlahairoi, meaning "Well of the Living One Who sees me". Hagar then returned to Hebron, and to Abraham and Sarah, where she gave birth to Ismael, when Abraham was 86 years old.[263]

Either at some point in the above story after Abraham's return to Palestine, or during the next two years following Ismael's birth[264], Hagar submitted to Allah, as would be shown by the story, which is recounted in Chapter 8, of her remarkable faith in Allah.[265] If one attempts to become more specific as to the time of Hagar's submission to Allah, it is tempting to point to her encounter with the angel of Allah near Kadesh. There is even some support for this speculation to be found in *Genesis*, where it implies that, during her encounter with the angel of Allah, Hagar referred to Allah as the "God Who sees"[266], i.e., sees Hagar's own affliction, needs, and troubled state.

At whatever point during her first five to six years with Abraham that Hagar accepted the *Tawheed*, her submission to and faith in Allah were certainly an example for all to see by the time of the events narrated in Chapter 8. Quite obviously, Hagar was a most remarkable woman, whose personal story has received far less attention than it deserves, and one wishes that a great deal more were known about her. The story of Hagar's childhood and early life as a polytheist in Egypt is unknown, as is any account of how it was that she entered into slavery. These details, if known, would probably add much to one's understanding of her. Likewise, one wishes that more were known about Hagar's five to six years with Abraham and Sarah in Palestine, and about her conversion to a firm belief in the *Tawheed*. Finally, a thorough account of Hagar's life in Makkah, after her eventual separation from Abraham, would surely contain much material to captivate one's attention. Taken together, her early life in Egypt, her life with Abraham and Sarah in Palestine, and her subsequent life in Makkah, would certainly make a most fascinating biography in its own right.

Chapter 8
Abraham in Makkah – I

Information on Abraham's first journey to and stay in Makkah are basically confined to three *Sahih Ahadith*, as recorded in *Al-Bukhari* 4: 582-584. In addition, some fragments of information are gleaned from the account of the *E* strand of *Genesis* 21: 8-21, which appears to be a confabulated merging of: the *J* strand of *Genesis* 16: 5-8, 11-14 account of Hagar's attempt to escape from Sarah; and the *Al-Bukhari* accounts noted above.[267]

From Palestine to Makkah

Apparently within the first two years of Ismael's young life, and certainly while Ismael was still nursing at his mother's breast[268], conflict again broke out between Sarah and Hagar. Sarah had become increasingly jealous of Hagar[269], who had successfully provided to Abraham what Sarah had not, i.e., a son. No doubt the sight of Abraham joyfully playing with his only child, the infant Ismael, fueled Sarah's jealousy.[270] As Abraham watched Ismael play and frolic and cavort around him, Abraham's heart rejoiced in this blessing, which Allah had granted to him, while Sarah's heart grew increasingly jealous of Hagar, and now became jealous of Ismael, as well.[271]

Although Hagar was the wife of Abraham and the mother of Ismael, Hagar was also the slave of Sarah. Hagar was still Sarah's possession and property, and Sarah still held power and authority over her. By extension, since Ismael was Hagar's son, Ismael was also Sarah's slave and Sarah's possession. In the past (see Chapter 7), Sarah's jealousy had apparently caused her to lash out at Hagar, to treat Hagar harshly, and to abuse her power and authority over Hagar in various and unspecified ways.[272] This time, however, Sarah's jealousy drove her in a new direction. Sarah lashed out in a different way, and she followed a radically different, although still highly abusive, set of tactics.

Sarah now went to Abraham, and told him of her fateful decision. She emphasized that Hagar was her "slave woman", and that Hagar was her property. Sarah had the right to do with Hagar, as Sarah wished. Having set out and specified her claim upon Hagar, Sarah demanded that Hagar and Ismael were to leave, that they were to be finally and irrevocably banished from the lives of Sarah and Abraham, once and for all. Upon hearing these words of Sarah, Abraham was sorely distressed. Hagar and Ismael had brought him much joy and happiness, and one must assume that his love for them was very great. Hagar was his wife, and Ismael was his only child. How could he bear to part with them?[273]

Apparently, later that night, in the midst of his despair, Abraham turned to Allah in prayer. As had happened so many times before, Allah reportedly answered Abraham's supplications, and He informed Abraham that Abraham should adhere to the dictates of Sarah's decision. However, Allah also reportedly informed Abraham that He would insure Ismael's safety and health, so that a great nation would yet arise out of Ismael's descendants.[274]

The Pilgrims

Early the next morning[275], after having reportedly received Allah's assurances regarding Hagar and Ismael, Abraham came out of his tent, which was probably pitched in the vicinity of Hebron. He gathered together Hagar, Ismael, and what supplies and animals would be needed on the long and difficult journey, which was facing them. Preparations having been completed, the three of them left the camp, heading south into the wilderness areas.

Given the context of the departure of Abraham, Hagar, and Ismael from Abraham's campsite near Hebron, it appears probable that Sarah was left behind. As supporting evidence, there is no mention of Sarah having made this trip in the accounts reported in *Al-Bukhari*.[276] Certainly, there were more than enough servants and slaves at the Hebron campsite to attend to and to take care of Sarah, during Abraham's coming absence. Further, Sarah's presence on this trip would have been most awkward and stressful, and would have created the context for constant interpersonal difficulties. Thus, one may assume that the only people making this trip were Abraham, Hagar, Ismael, and perhaps a few servants.

The Journey

Leaving the area of Hebron, Abraham, Hagar, and Ismael traveled southeast into the arid and semi-arid wilderness. Whether Abraham already knew his eventual destination, or whether he was simply having faith in and being guided along the way by the providence of Allah, is unknown. In either case, their direction of travel was southeast, probably along an ancient caravan route known as the Incense Route, which was so named because it was a caravan route carrying perfumes and incense from the southern edge of the Arabian Peninsula to the Mediterranean world. This southeasterly route would eventually lead them to a narrow, barren valley, located over 700 miles (about 1,200 kilometers) southeast of Hebron.

This valley was surrounded on all sides by the Sirat Mountains, whose primary peaks included: Jabal Ajyad, which rose to a height of 1,332 feet (410 meters); Jabal Abu Qubays, with an elevation of 1,220 feet (375 meters); Jabal Qu'ayq'an, at 1,401 feet (431 meters); Jabal Hira', at 2,080 feet (640 meters); and Jabal Thawr, at 2,490 feet (766 meters). Through these Sirat Mountains, four passes led to the valley: one from the northeast, which in later years would connect with the towns of Mina, Al-'Arafat, and Al-Taif; one from the northwest, which shows the way to Madinah; one from the south, which leads onward to Yemen; and one from the east, which leads to the Red Sea, about 50 miles (80 kilometers) to the west of the valley. Vegetation within the valley was sparse, primarily consisting of tamarisks and acacia, due to an annual rainfall of only about five inches. Animal life consisted of wild cats, wolves, hyenas, fox, mongoose, and kangaroo rats. Throughout the year, temperatures were high in the valley, and could easily reach 113 degrees Fahrenheit (45 degrees Celsius) during the summer months.

When Abraham, Hagar, and Ismael entered the valley, it was still devoid of any permanent settlement. However, it apparently was a frequented campsite, and probably was a periodic marketing center and exchange point on the Incense Route. The valley was called Bakka (Baca), and linguists have posited two different origins for its name: one derived from the concept of a narrow valley[277]; and the other derived from the concept of a valley that was fit for nothing other than growing balsam trees.[278] It was here that Abraham, Hagar, and Ismael finally stopped.

As already noted, a straight-line estimate of the distance between Hebron and Bakka would be one of over 700 miles (about 1,200 kilometers). However, the Incense Route, being subject to the dictates of terrain and of available watering holes, did not conform to anything resembling a straight line. As such, the distance actually traveled by Abraham, Hagar, and Ismael would have been considerably longer than the straight-line estimate. In that regard, it has been hypothesized that the actual route between Hebron and Bakka would have entailed a journey of some 40 days by camel.[279] However, camels were not yet domesticated at the time of Abraham, and would not be domesticated for almost a millennia after Abraham.[280] As such, the actual time spent on the journey, assuming travel by donkey or similar conveyance, would have been considerably longer than the estimate of 40 some days. A fair assumption about the length of the journey could be as long as two months or more.

One can but speculate about the nature of events during those two months or more. Probably, given his knowledge of upcoming events, Abraham would have had a welcome opportunity to do some anticipatory grieving, thus making his later separation from Hagar and Ismael somewhat easier to bear. One imagines that Abraham was especially attentive to and tender with both Hagar and Ismael, knowing that an eventual separation was looming. In their nightly camps, and when stopping for meals and for prayer, Abraham's joy in watching the infant Ismael frolic and play must have been especially bittersweet. For her part, Hagar may have been inwardly questioning the whole purpose of their journey.[281] However, given that sixth sense that a devoted wife has about her husband's attitudes, feelings, and plans, she probably already had some unconscious realization of what was happening. For his part, Ismael probably would have been enjoying all the new stimulation that was everywhere confronting his senses, but was probably also having his fussy moments, as all young children do during periods of prolonged travel.

Speculation aside, Abraham, Hagar, and Ismael eventually reached the semi-isolated valley of Bakka, which, in later centuries, would come to be known as Makkah.

Abraham leaves Hagar and Ismael at Makkah:
Hagar and Ismael entrusted to Allah's Care

It is unclear how much time Abraham, Hagar, and Ismael spent together after they reached Makkah. However long or short it was, Abraham eventually sat Hagar and Ismael down under a tree, and handed Hagar a skin of water and a leather bag containing dates. Then, Abraham apparently turned aside silently, and began walking away. As Abraham continued walking farther and farther away, Hagar apparently became anxious about what was happening. Temporarily leaving Ismael under the shade of the tree, Hagar jumped to her feet, ran after Abraham, and called out to him.[282]

Abraham neither stopped his walking, nor looked back, nor even said a word. Perhaps, his grief and pain were too much to permit him to speak at the moment. However, Hagar continued chasing after him, calling out: "O Abraham, where are you going, leaving us in this valley where there is no person whose company we may enjoy, nor is there anything (here)?". Still, Abraham continued his steadfast and deliberate walking out of Makkah, neither looking back nor speaking. Receiving no response, Hagar raised her voice to call out again to her husband, but again Abraham did not respond. Finally, after numerous repetitions of her initial question, Hagar raised her voice to ask Abraham, "Has Allah ordered you to do so?". Having received this question, Abraham stopped, turned, and answered in the affirmative. Allah had ordered Abraham to leave Hagar and Ismael in this desolate valley.[283]

Receiving this answer, Hagar had only one additional question, "O Abraham, to whom are you leaving us?". Abraham's response was concise, and it was directly to the point, "I am leaving you to Allah's care." At that moment, despite what must have been a multitude of unanswered questions erupting in her mind, and despite what must have been an almost overwhelming churning of conflicting emotions within her heart, Hagar's resolute faith in and submission to Allah took over. Her goodbye to her husband was brief, although it spoke volumes about her character and about her spiritual commitment to Allah: "I am satisfied to be with Allah."[284]

Hagar then turned, and retraced her steps to the infant Ismael, whom she had left under the shade of a tree.[285] She was still a mother, and she still had a mother's responsibilities and obligations. More than ever before, Ismael would need her devoted care.

Abraham's Prayer

As for Abraham, he continued walking out of the valley of Makkah. Despite his faith in and total submission to Allah, one can assume that this walk must have been very difficult for him. Each step probably took enormous effort on his part. One assumes that his feet were weighed down, that his heart was grieving, and that his eyes were watering. So many times before, Allah had tried Abraham, and had always found Abraham deserving and righteous. Abraham had been tried in Ur, during his confrontation with Naram-Sin and with the fiery furnace. He had been tried in Harran, when having to leave his father. He had been tried in Egypt, when the pharaoh took Sarah. He had been tried in Palestine, when Abraham had built altars to Allah at outdoor shrines to Canaanite deities, and when Sarah had demanded the expulsion of Hagar and Ismael. Always, Abraham had acted righteously, and in full accordance with the wishes of Allah. Abraham's behavior and conduct during this Makkan trial were no exception, although this trial, of leaving Hagar and Ismael behind in a lonely and desolate valley, was probably Abraham's most difficult trial to date.

When Abraham had finally walked far enough so that he could no longer be seen by Hagar and Ismael, he turned around to face Makkah. Standing there, he raised both hands, and invoked the name of Allah. He committed and entrusted both Hagar and Ismael into the care of Allah, and he supplicated to Allah for the continued safety and well being of Hagar and Ismael.[286]

Hagar's Moments of Desperation

Having returned to her infant son, Hagar opened the leather bag of dates, which had been left by Abraham, and she ate. Likewise, she opened the skin of water, and she drank deeply, for she was still nursing Ismael, and needed to keep her milk flowing abundantly. The dates and water sustained Hagar and her milk supply for a while, and Ismael nursed accordingly. However, the temperature in Makkah was very hot[287], and in that environment, Hagar's skin of water did not last long. Eventually, the water was exhausted, and shortly thereafter was Hagar's ability to nurse the infant Ismael. One doesn't know exactly how long Hagar went without water, nor does one know exactly how long her milk supply had been dried up. However, she had been dry long enough that the infant Ismael was now tossing and thrashing about in the agony of his dehydration and hunger. Being unable to watch Ismael's agony, being unable to do anything constructive to mitigate Ismael's distress, and knowing that she must quickly do something to alleviate Ismael's condition, Hagar tore herself away from her child, in order to search for help. Perhaps, there might be some caravan, which was happening to pass by Makkah. Perhaps, even in her own precarious physical condition, Hagar could find some way to hail it, and could somehow secure the water, which she and Ismael so desperately needed.[288]

Hagar rose unsteadily to her feet, and wearily spotted the nearest hill. Slowly, through the squelching heat of Makkah, she began forcing her dehydrated body to stagger the short distance to the hill, leaving Ismael in the shade of the tree, at a spot on the valley floor, which would become known as Zam-zam. Arriving at the base of the hill known as Safa, she clawed her way along the sometimes treacherous footing of the rocky incline to the top, hoping that from that vantage point she could see some passing caravan. However, straining her vision to her utmost in all directions, there was no person to be seen. The increasingly desperate Hagar then dragged her exhausted body down the slippery and uneven rock surface to the valley below.[289]

Perhaps, Hagar had intended to go and to sit with Ismael once she reached the valley floor. However, once off of Safa, her desperate concern for Ismael drove her body onward, in order to look for any new sign of others. She tucked up her robe, and began to run frantically through the valley. However, even with the burst of energy she had experienced, she was just not physically able to run far, and her run quickly turned into a staggering walk. Nonetheless, she somehow managed to proceed to the base of another hill, which was Marwa, and which was almost 490 yards (about 450 meters) from Safa.[290]

As she had before with Safa, Hagar, reaching deep inside herself, found some hidden reserve of strength, which allowed her to make the painful climb up the inclined surface of Marwa. Reaching its peak, she again scanned the valley and the horizon for any sign of life. Finding none, she dejectedly climbed down Marwa. Heading back towards Ismael, she again experienced the sudden rush of desperate energy, and again she began to run. As before, her run did not last long. However, she was now relatively close to Safa, and so she forced herself up its rocky incline one more time. Standing on its peak, there was nothing to be seen except for the desolation and emptiness of the valley itself. Once more, Hagar descended down the sometimes slippery, rocky surface of Safa.

Reaching the valley floor, Hagar again experienced the strange, driven energy, which had propelled her forward twice before. As such, she returned to the peak of Marwa, but to no avail. Descending Marwa, the pattern was continually repeated, until Hagar had completed traveling between the two hills a total of seven times.[291]

In her weakened, and physically and emotionally desperate, state, it is probable that Hagar had fallen one or more times against the rocks of Safa. One may thus assume that Hagar was not only critically dehydrated, and in a state bordering on heat exhaustion and sunstroke, but that she was also physically battered and bruised. One may also assume that, at some point in her wanderings between Safa and Marwa, Hagar had stopped to check on Ismael, and had found her infant exhibiting all the signs of being in the midst of his death throes.[292]

The Miracle of Zam-zam

The Story: Thus, standing for the last time on the peak of Marwa, Hagar must have wondered if she were hallucinating, when she thought that she had heard a voice. She forced herself to be quiet, and she listened harder than she probably ever had before. It was a voice! Fighting down the flood of relief that threatened to engulf her completely, Hagar cried out: "O, (whoever you may be)! You have made me hear your voice; have you got something to help me?". Then looking down into the valley below her, Hagar saw an angel of Allah standing beside the dying Ismael.[293]

The angel, who was Gabriel (Jibril), then used the heel of his foot to strike the ground near Ismael. At the very spot that Gabriel struck, water came miraculously gushing out of the ground, spreading in all directions. Despite her precarious and weakened state, Hagar struggled down off Marwa, and hurried as best she could to Ismael, and to the newly formed Well of Zam-zam. Dropping to her knees at the edge of the water, Hagar formed an earthen basin around the spreading water, thus preventing Zam-zam from becoming the spring-fed headwaters of a river. She then began to scoop the water into her water skin.[294]

Hagar quickly drank her fill from the healing waters of *Zam-zam*. Immediately thereafter her milk miraculously returned, and Hagar was able to suckle Ismael, who was unexpectedly revived by Hagar's milk. Once both mother and infant were refreshed and invigorated, Gabriel spoke to Hagar. "Don't be afraid of being neglected, for this is the House of Allah which will be built by this boy and his father, and Allah never neglects His people."[295]

How great must have been Hagar's gratitude and thanksgiving to Allah! Her initial faith in having had herself and Ismael entrusted into the care of Allah had been totally vindicated.

A Comment: It is often maintained that the miracle of Zam-zam was Gabriel's digging of the well with his heel. However, in reality, there was a succession of miracles, each following quickly on the heels of the preceding one: (1) Gabriel's arrival and his digging of the well of Zam-zam; (2) Hagar's surprisingly quick revival; (3) the immediate return of Hagar's milk supply; and (4) the escape of the infant Ismael from a state precariously close to death.

The Arrival of the Jorhamites

Thanks only to the divine intervention of Allah, Hagar and Ismael had survived the rigors of the desolate and barren valley of Makkah. They now had a constant water supply from the Well of Zam-zam, and Hagar was able to scrounge enough dates and other edibles to keep the two of them nourished and alive. Either Abraham had left some tent material with them, or Hagar had been able to find enough natural material, e.g., palm leaves, to construct some sort of makeshift shelter. In either case, having been entrusted into the care of Allah, mother and son were able to sustain their isolated existence in Makkah for an undetermined length of time.

Eventually, however, the isolation of Hagar and Ismael came to an end. A band of Jorhamites, who were apparently moving northward from their original home in the southern reaches of the Arabian Peninsula, entered the southern end of the valley of Makkah.[296] The Jorhamites were a tribe of people, who reportedly descended from Jorham (Hadhram), the son of Eber, the son of Siba, the son of Qahtan, the son of Eber, the son of Shelah, the son of Qaynan, the son of Arpachshad, the son of Shem, the son of Prophet Noah.[297] Thus, they were distant cousins of Abraham and of Ismael.

As the Jorhamites crossed through the southern pass into the valley of Makkah, they saw a bird flying in the distance. Wondering what this bird was doing so far from fresh water, they hurried forward to find the bird circling over the Well of Zam-zam, and to find Hagar sitting next to the well. Seeing that there now was an abundant supply of fresh water in Makkah, the Jorhamites respectfully approached Hagar, and sought her permission for them to settle down in Makkah. Hagar agreed, but stipulated that the Jorhamites must acknowledge her and Ismael's ownership of the well and of its water supply. The Jorhamites adhered to Hagar's stipulation, sent back south for their families and relatives, and began to build the first permanent settlement at Makkah. Thus, Ismael grew up in the midst of the Jorhamites, and learned their particular dialect of speech.[298]

Postscript # 1 to Abraham at Makkah – I

The two-month or more journey back to Palestine from Makkah must have been a difficult one for Abraham. The route was long, and the terrain was often desolate, and sometimes dangerous. Watering holes were few and far between. Yet, one surmises that the real difficulty for Abraham was in having left Hagar and Ismael back behind him in Makkah.

Abraham had passed another one of Allah's trials, this one probably more difficult than any he had previously faced. Now, however, as Abraham entered Palestine, he was most likely anticipating another trial. Not one necessarily ordained by Allah, but one arising out of the human psyche. Abraham would soon meet Sarah, the wife from whom he had been separated for more than four months. It was Sarah, who had initially ordered the expulsion of Hagar and Ismael. Nonetheless, Sarah remained Abraham's wife, and Abraham had to find it within himself to continue the loving relationship, which they had previously enjoyed throughout the length of their nearly 40 years of marriage.

In the course of normal human events, one would predict on the basis of interpersonal psychology, that a person in Abraham's position would be unable to reconcile fully with his first wife. One would also predict that such a person would, consciously or unconsciously, blame his first wife for the expulsion of his second wife and of his only son. Finally, one would predict that marital friction would be inevitable, and that a future divorce was only a matter of time. However, as a prophet of Allah, Abraham's character and psyche, while still having its roots in the normal human condition, were elevated above that of normal men. As such, despite Sarah's role in the banishment of Hagar and of Ismael, Abraham was successful in re-establishing a loving marriage with Ṣarah, and that marriage was to last until Sarah's death, approximately 49 years later.[299]

Postscript # 2 to Abraham in Makkah – I

The journey of Abraham, Hagar, and Ismael to Makkah (Bakka or Baca), as well as the miracle of the Well of Zam-zam, is vaguely recalled in one passage, attributed to an earlier hymnbook of the sons of Korah, which appears in the Biblical book known as *Psalms*.

> Happy are those whose strength is in you, in whose heart are the highways to Zion. As they go through the valley of Baca they make it a place of springs; the early rain also covers it with pools. They go from strength to strength; the God of gods will be seen in Zion.[300]

Chapter 9
Abraham in Palestine – III

Information pertaining to the events described during Abraham's third sojourn in Palestine is basically limited to the 14th chapter of *Genesis*. This chapter stands outside of and independently of the four main literary strands (*J, E, P,* and *D*) comprising the various books of the *Torah*. The events recounted in the 14th chapter of *Genesis* appear to have occurred between Abraham's 83rd and 98th year of life, and, more specifically, probably happened when he was 88 years old. Unfortunately, there is no way to identify definitively any of the individuals named in these events, with the obvious exceptions of Abraham and of Lot.

Abraham's Rescue of Lot

At the time this story begins, the kings of the five cities of the plain, which were located on a plain south and southeast of the Dead Sea, had been in a state of vassalage to King Chedorlaomer of Elam for 12 years. These five city-states of the plain were: Sodom, ruled by King Bera; Gomorrah, ruled by King Birsha; Admah, ruled by King Shinab; Zeboiim, ruled by King Shemeber; and Zoar, aka Bela. During their 13th year of servitude, the five kings of the plain joined forces, entered into open rebellion, and threw off their yoke of vassalage.[301]

It took some extended period of time for news of this rebellion to reach King Chedorlaomer back in Elam, as Elam was located on the slopes of the Iranian plateau, some 750 to 800 miles (1,218 to 1,300 kilometers) straight east of the cities of the plain in Jordan. However, news would not have traveled back to Elam on a straight-line basis, because of intervening deserts, etc. Rather, the news of this rebellion would have been carried from Jordan up north through Syria, then down the Euphrates River into Iraq, and then east to Elam in Iran, a distance of about 1,200 miles (1,950 kilometers). Having received the news that his vassals were rebelling, it would have taken Chedorlaomer some time to raise and equip his army. Further, Chedorlaomer took some time to arrange for allied armies to march with him, including those of King

Amraphel of Shinar (Sumeria), King Arioch of Ellasar, and King Tidal of Goiim.[302] Thus, it was not until the 14th year that the four kings began their military campaign to reclaim the suzerainty of Chedorlaomer over the five cities of the plain.[303]

One assumes that the route of the advancing armies was westerly until reaching the Euphrates River. They would have then marched north-westerly up the Euphrates, through Iraq, and into Syria. Assuming they passed by Aleppo, they would have then marched south through Syria and into Jordan. However, they apparently skirted well to the east of the Sea of Galilee (Lake Tiberias), and remained well to the east of the Jordan River, as they continued their southern advance into Jordan. At this point, their advance of military conquest becomes documented in *Genesis* 14.

Advancing southward from Syria, but staying quite a ways east of the Sea of Galilee, the invading armies conquered the Rephaim at Ashterothkarnaim, which was located about 23 miles (37 kilometers) east of the northern part of the Sea of Galilee. Next, they moved about 27 miles (44 kilometers) southwest, where they conquered the Zuzim at Ham, a city which was located about 20 miles (32 or 33 kilometers) southeast of the southern tip of the Sea of Galilee. Following that conquest, they again marched south, until stopping to conquer the Emim at Shavehkiriathaim, a city which was apparently located about nine miles (14 or 15 kilometers) due east of the north-central portion of the Dead Sea, and about 15 (24 kilometers) miles southwest of contemporary Madabah, Jordan. Skirting well to the east of the five city-states on the plain, they then moved southwesterly to Seir in Edom, which was located south of the Dead Sea in the vicinity of what would later become Petra, Jordan. There, they conquered a Horite community. Next, they moved south about 90 miles (146 kilometers), continuing their advance to El-paran (probably the Gulf of 'Aqaba). Following a presumed encampment at 'Aqaba, they moved northwesterly about 80 miles (130 kilometers) into the Negeb, where they conquered the Amalekites [304], who were in the vicinity of Kadesh. They then marched about 55 miles (89 kilometers) to the northeast, and conquered the Amorites near Hazazontamar, a city which was located only about eight miles (13 kilometers) west of Zoar. Zoar, it will be remembered, was one of the rebelling city-states of the plain, and was located only about three miles (5 kilometers) south of the Dead Sea.[305]

The Capture of Lot

Having made this circuitous route of conquest noted above, King Chedorlaomer and his allied kings were poised to begin their campaign against the five rebelling city-states of the plains. The city of Zoar was only eight miles (13 kilometers) to their east. The remaining four city-states, i.e., Zeboiim, Admah, Gomorrah, and Sodom, were all within a 10 mile distance north of Zoar, being located in the Valley of Siddim, a geographical area which currently lies under the southeastern portion of the Dead Sea.

Rather than remaining in their walled city-states and being easily vanquished, one by one in rapid and isolated succession, by the invading armies of King Chedorlaomer, the five kings of the cities of the plain led their armies out of their walled fortresses. They united their armies in the Valley of Siddim, made their stand, and met the armies of Chedorlaomer in head-to-head combat. The author of *Genesis* 14 portrays this battle as being four kings against five kings. However, that portrayal is quite misleading. The combined armies of the four kings from Iraq and Iran must have had a huge numerical advantage over the armies of the five small city-states. The battle quickly turned into a complete military rout. The king of Gomorrah was killed, the king of Sodom fled for his life, and the five small armies of the cities of the plain fled to the surrounding hill country. Sodom, Gomorrah, Zeboiim, and Admah were sacked, the cities of the plains were stripped of all their possessions and valuables, and their men and women were led off into slavery. Among the men of Sodom, who were summarily captured and enslaved, was Lot, the nephew of Abraham.[306]

Having won the war, the five kings of Iraq and Iran began to travel north, moving through Jordan, on their way back home. They had already gained enormous booty in possessions and slaves, had thoroughly punished the rebellious cities of the plain, and had apparently extended the suzerainty of King Chedorlaomer to include southern Jordan as far south as 'Aqaba, as well as parts of the Negeb. No doubt, their trek north through Jordan was one of nightly celebrations. These were relaxed and victorious armies, who believed that all their enemies had been vanquished, and who believed that they had nothing left to fear.

The Rescue of Lot

Not all of the men of Sodom had been taken into slavery by the forces of King Chedorlaomer. At least one man escaped the sacking of Sodom. However, instead of running into the surrounding hill country of Jordan, as had some members of the vanquished armies of the cities of the plain, he had escaped to the west. As fast as whatever his means of conveyance, if any, could take him, he traveled to the northwest, rushing the approximately 35 miles (57 kilometers) to Hebron. At Hebron, he apparently wasted no time in searching out Abraham, and in informing Abraham of the sacking of cities of the plain and of the capture of Lot.[307]

Upon hearing this report, Abraham acted immediately. First, he sought out his allies among the Amorites, namely the brothers Mamre, Eshcol, and Aner. Abraham apparently persuaded them to assemble their own male relatives, servants, and slaves, in order to aid Abraham, in what certainly appeared to be a Quixotic pursuit.[308] Abraham then went and armed his male servants and slaves, 318 men who had been specifically trained for armed combat.[309] Together, the retainers of Abraham, Mamre, Eshcol, and Aner must have made a sizable force for the times. However, they had to have been a far cry from the size of the four armies of the kings of Iraq and Iran. Nonetheless, Abraham led his force north out of Hebron, presumably double-timing through the hill country of Palestine.

Even with a rapid march by Abraham's forces, traveling northward through the hill country of Palestine, it would have taken several days for them to have caught up to the four armies under the command of King Chedorlaomer. Finally, after having marched about 130 miles (211 kilometers) to the north, Abraham's forces saw the camp of the enemy near the city of Dan (Laish)[310], which was located about 25 miles (40 to 41 kilometers) north of the Sea of Galilee. Awaiting the dead of night, when the enemy would be groggy with sleep, and presumably intoxicated with drink from their evening's celebration[311], Abraham divided his much smaller force, and attacked the camp from several angles at once.[312] Having achieved the element of total surprise over his numerically superior, but intoxicated and sleepy, foes, Abraham and his force killed many, and routed the rest.[313]

The armies under the command of King Chedorlaomer were routed and panic-stricken. Running blindly through the night, they dashed northeastward, leaving their booty and their possessions behind them. No doubt, as panic built upon panic, the soldiers of the numerically superior army did not even bother to stand and fight. They simply ran for their lives from the far inferior number of Abraham's men, who pursued them, and who presumably captured or slew the stragglers along the way. That pursuit reportedly lasted from the city of Dan to Hobah, a city somewhere to the north of Damascus[314], implying that the pursuit covered a distance of over 45 miles (73 kilometers).

Allah had delivered a resounding, a totally unexpected, and a miraculous military victory to a small band of probably well under 1,000 men, who had attacked a vastly superior force. The five armies of Iraq and Iran had to have been many times the size of Abraham's force. Further, these five armies were comprised of seasoned soldiers who had previously conquered Ashterothkarnain, Ham, Shavehkiriathaim, Seir (Edom), El-paran ('Aqaba), Kadesh, and Hazazontamar.[315] Yet, despite their tremendous numerical advantage and superiority, and despite their advantage in military and combat experience, they had been completely routed in one panic-filled night. Allah, Most High, had delivered Abraham's enemies into his hand.[316]

Lot had been rescued, and Lot and Abraham had been reunited. That reunion between uncle and nephew must have been quite emotional. One doesn't know for sure how long it had been since the two of them had last seen each other. However, one does know that Lot had already been held captive for many days, perhaps for a week or more. One can assume that Lot had been subjected to various forms of rough treatment, and to a multitude of physical and emotional abuse. As he had been marched northward in bonds, he had probably wondered if he would ever see his uncle again. For his part, Abraham had been pursuing the armies of Chedorlaomer at break-neck speed for several days. During that pursuit, it would have been only human for Abraham to worry about, and to have questions about, the safety and health of his nephew. No doubt, Lot's name had been frequently mentioned in Abraham's many prayers along the way. Now, after this amazing military victory, each of their questions had been answered positively, and they were together once again.

The Return

However, it was not just Lot, who had been rescued. There were many other members of the populace of the cities of the plain that had also been rescued by Abraham and his band, including both men and women.[317] (One can only wonder if Lot's wife and two daughters were also in the group that had been led out of Sodom as slaves.) Some of those people were probably ill or injured, having endured the hardships of their temporary slavery, and having been made to march from the Valley of Siddim to the city of Dan, a distance of about 160 miles (260 kilometers). Those, who were ill or were injured, would have greatly slowed the trip back home, which apparently took place through the hill country of Palestine.[318] Also slowing the return trip would have been the logistics of transporting all the booty and riches, which Abraham and his force had captured. As such, one assumes that the return trip may have taken a couple of weeks. However, Abraham apparently sent out runners ahead of the returning group, in order to announce the success of his military mission. As such, on their way south through the hill country of Palestine, the group was met in the Valley of Shaveh (the King's Valley)[319], which was near to Jerusalem.

Abraham and Melchizedek

When Abraham's victorious band reached the vicinity of Jerusalem, there was apparently quite a crowd to greet them, including King Bera of Sodom and King Melchizedek of Salem (Jerusalem).

Melchizedek

King Melchizedek is mentioned in the *Bible* in very few places[320], and nothing is known about him other than from the *Bible* or from sources dependent upon the *Bible*. *Genesis* 14:18 identifies Melchizedek as the king of Salem, and as a priest of "El Elyon". Several points need to be made in terms of this brief identification. First, Melchizedek can be translated as "my king is Zedek" or, perhaps, as "my king is righteousness". Second, Salem was most probably the city of Jerusalem. Third, as noted previously in Chapter 5, El was one of the gods in the pantheon of gods worshipped in Palestine, but El could also refer to Allah. In the current context, as will be seen below, El clearly refers to Allah, and "El Elyon" can thus be translated as "Allah, Most High". In short, Melchizedek, like Abraham, appears to have been a believer in the *Tawheed*, and appears to have been one who had submitted to Allah.

Melchizedek had journeyed out from Jerusalem to meet Abraham at the Valley of Shaveh. He reportedly brought with him food and drink, and prepared a feast to refresh Abraham and his men.[321] Presumably after Abraham had then eaten and rested, Melchizedek blessed Abraham, and in so doing, invoked the name of Allah.

> Blessed be Abram by God Most High, maker of heaven and earth; and blessed be God Most High, who has delivered your enemies into your hand![322]

Following this blessing, Abraham gave King Melchizedek ten percent of all the booty that had been captured in the preceding military expedition.[323] Thereafter, there is no more mention of King Melchizedek in the recorded life of Abraham.

The King of Sodom

Bera, the king of Sodom, had somehow survived his wild flight from the Valley of Siddim. His army had been routed, his city had been sacked, and his subjects had been led away in slavery. His despair and depression must have been palpable. One can well imagine him having been sitting and bemoaning his fate in the remains of his sacked city, when word first reached him of the miraculous, military triumph of Abraham. How quickly the deepest despair can turn to heights of joy! His city had been saved after all! Wasting no time, Bera had prepared a small caravan from what he could scrounge together from his sacked city, and he journeyed to the Valley of Shaveh to greet the victorious Abraham.

Approaching Abraham at the Valley of Shaveh, Bera would have no doubt begun his conversation with felicitations and congratulations. However, Bera eventually got to the point. Abraham's victory had given him ownership of the booty that had been taken from the cities of the plain, as well as ownership of the rest of the booty that had been taken from the routed armies of Iraq and of Iran. Further, given the prevailing rules of warfare at that time, the captives from the cities of the plain, who were being led away into slavery, were now the captives and slaves of Abraham. If Bera could not retrieve something from this situation, he would only be the king of a sacked and fairly depopulated city.

Given this situation, Bera attempted a compromise, which was no compromise at all. He started out by asking for the return of his people. In exchange for them, Bera offered that, which he did not even possess, i.e., the material goods and booty that had been taken from his sacked city. In response to Bera's proposal, Abraham reportedly stated:

> I have sworn to the Lord, God Most High, maker of heaven and earth, that I would not take a thread or a sandal-thong or anything that is yours, so that you might not say, "I have made Abram rich." I will take nothing but what the young men have eaten, and the share of the men who went with me—Aner, Eshcol, and Mamre. Let them take their share." [324]

Aside from what his forces had eaten to sustain themselves during their campaign, aside from the ten percent of the spoils and booty that he had previously set aside for King Melchizedek, and aside from the share of the spoils that belonged to Aner, Eshcol and Mamre, Abraham insisted on the full return of all property and peoples to the cities of the plain. In short, Abraham was foregoing any share of the spoils, because he had previously sworn an oath to "El Elyon (Allah, Most High), maker of heaven and earth" that he would take nothing from the campaign for his own personal aggrandizement. In making this statement, Abraham's words of "El Elyon, maker of heaven and earth" were identical to the phrase used by King Melchizedek in blessing Abraham, thus appearing to confirm that King Melchizedek was in fact a monotheistic worshipper of Allah.

Postscript to Abraham in Palestine–III

Assuming that Abraham was 88 years old at the time of the events described in this chapter[325], and assuming that Abraham was 14 years old when he began preaching his message of the *Tawheed*[326], Abraham had been proclaiming the message of Allah for 74 years. Yet, for all the *Da'wa* that Abraham had done during those 74 years, the historical record allows one to identify only three converts to Abraham's message, prior to the events described in this chapter: Lot; Sarah; and Hagar. Now, the historical record suddenly introduces four more people, who can probably be identified as converts to Abraham's monotheistic message: King Melchizedek of Jerusalem; and the three Amorite brothers of Hebron, Mamre, Eshcol, and Aner, who were Abraham's allies. While one assumes that there had been many other converts to Abraham's message prior to this time, the historical record does not allow for specific identification of these individuals.

Chapter 10
Abraham in Makkah – II

At first glance, the author's presentation of the events recorded in this chapter may appear to be controversial, highly subjective, and arbitrary. However, the author's presentation is based upon a critical analysis and synthesis of the available information that is preserved in the historical record. This analysis and synthesis is discussed in some depth in Appendix IV (Sequential Events in Abraham's Life: Events in Makkah – II), and the reader is urged to consult that material for an understanding of the process and methodology, whereby the author has arrived at his current presentation of the events covered in this chapter.

~

There are three main events that transpired during Abraham's second sojourn in Makkah: (1) the sacrifice of Abraham's son; (2) Allah's covenant with Abraham; and (3) the introduction of the rite of circumcision. The primary sources for the first event are the *Qur'an* and a reconstruction of a narration from the *E* strand of *Genesis*.[327] The primary source for the second event is *Genesis*, while the primary sources for the third event are *Genesis* and *Sahih Ahadith*.

The Setting

It had been 11 or 12 years since Abraham had entrusted Hagar and Ismael to the care of Allah, left them in the desolate valley of Makkah, and returned to Palestine to live with Sarah. Abraham was now approaching, or had just entered, his 99th year of life[328], and his thoughts had often lingered on the fate of Hagar and of Ismael. His faith in Allah's care of them had never wavered, but there were so many questions, which he had about them, for which he wanted answers. What were they doing? What kind of youngster had Ismael become? What did Ismael look like? Did his wife and son miss him, as much as he missed them? Yes, there was still the constant ache of missing them. Finally, whether by his own authority, or whether by the explicit direction of Allah, Abraham decided to return to Makkah, and to visit his second wife and only son.

It would have taken some considerable time for preparations to be completed for the arduous trip ahead. There were supplies to gather, e.g., food to last Abraham and his two accompanying servants[329] along the over 700 mile (1,200 kilometer) trek through the wilderness ahead, and forage and grain to be collected for the riding and pack animals, presumably donkeys, which they would be taking with them. Allowing time for a round trip and for a month's visit in Makkah, Abraham and the two servants, who would go with him, would be gone for five months or more. There was also physical preparations that had to be made for Sarah's well being and care during the time that Abraham would be absent from her. Fortunately, Abraham had hundreds of servants by this time[330], many of whom could be directed to see to Sarah's comfort and needs. However, instructions would still have had to be given, and plans would still have to be made.

However, physical preparation was not the only issue. Perhaps, a much larger concern was that of emotional preparation. Sarah, who was still childless, and who had initially demanded the banishment of Hagar and of Ismael, would have to be emotionally prepared to accept Abraham's absence, and to accept the amount of time Abraham would be spending with Hagar and with Ismael. One would suspect that Sarah was deeply troubled by Abraham's proposed visit to Makkah. From a psychological perspective, massive self-doubt and fears of abandonment must have been front and center in her psyche. Wasn't she good enough for Abraham? Didn't Abraham love her any more? Would Abraham stay in Makkah, and not return to her? Quite likely, a substantial portion of Abraham's time prior to his journey was spent in listening to Sarah's concerns, and in providing her with the reassurance, which she so desperately needed.

The Reunion

Physical and emotional preparations having been completed in Palestine, Abraham, his two servants, and their riding and pack animals set off southeast from Hebron, in order to begin their journey to Makkah. In just a couple of months, Abraham's many questions would be answered. He would again be with Hagar and Ismael! One assumes that Abraham was already experiencing the pleasure of joyful anticipation. However, part of him may have been wondering how he would be received by the wife and son he had left behind in a desolate place over a decade ago. Despite such anticipation and wondering, Abraham, as always, placed his trust in Allah.

Two months or more had probably passed since Abraham and his two servants had left Hebron. They had traveled through the wilderness from well to spring to well. Perhaps, they had occasionally shared the night and a campsite with fellow caravans along the Incense Route. However, as they entered the pass that was between the mountains at the north end of the valley of Makkah, Abraham knew that his quest was soon to be completed.

The Makkah that Abraham entered that day was quite different than the one he had left behind 11 or 12 years before. There was now abundant water flowing from the Well of Zam-zam, and perhaps this water was now supporting a nascent and rudimentary agriculture of gardens and of small fields, which were devoted to grains and to various crops of forage. Scattered tents, and perhaps even some permanent dwellings, dotted the landscape, as a testimonial to the presence of the Jorhamites, who had moved into the valley to live with Hagar and with Ismael. It was a changed scene altogether![331]

There are many speculative scenarios that one could write about the eventual reunion of Abraham with Hagar and Ismael. However, perhaps it is best merely to note the following. (1) Having been left at Makkah when Ismael was still young enough to have been nursing[332], Ismael would have had very little in the way of direct memory of his father at the time of their reunion. However, one can assume that Hagar had repetitiously told stories about his father to Ismael, and that those stories would have served Ismael as the basis for pseudo-memories of his father. (2) After so many years apart, Hagar and Abraham would probably have had to re-establish their marital relationship. (3) The three family members would have had a plethora of stories to tell each other. Many hours would have been spent in bringing each other up to date, regarding the various and sundry events in their individual lives. (4) However, one can also assume that eventually the three of them settled down to spend many joyful days together.

The Sacrifice of the Only Son: Abraham's Vision

Abraham, Hagar, and Ismael had been reunited for an undetermined

length of time, when Abraham's joy, celebration, and revelry were interrupted by a most disturbing and heartbreaking vision from Allah. Within
the confines of his vision, Abraham saw that he was to sacrifice Ismael
to Allah.[333] Abraham had waited so long for the birth of his only son,
Ismael. He had, reportedly by the command of Allah[334], been separated
from Ismael for 11 to 12 years.[335] Now, just when Abraham was reunited
with Ismael, and just when Ismael had reached the age of 13 years[336],
when Ismael was finally old enough to help his father in the serious work
of spreading the message of Allah, Abraham had received a vision from
Allah, in which Abraham was commanded to sacrifice Ismael's life for
Allah! [337]

Abraham consults Ismael

Having received this strange and terrifying vision, Abraham went to
Ismael, told his son what he had seen, and asked for Ismael's input and
reaction. Ismael, to his enormous credit, never doubted his father's vision,
and he never wavered in his own faith in Allah. Ismael was "ready to
suffer and forbear", and was willing to practice "patience and constancy"
in the face of the frightening future that now confronted him. Ismael's
verbal response was a statement reflecting total submission to Allah.
Ismael instructed his father that he should, of course, carry out any
instruction that he had received from Allah.

> So We gave him the good news of a boy ready to suffer and forbear.
> Then, when (the son) reached (the age of serious) work with him,
> he said: "O my son! I see in a vision that I offer thee in sacrifice: now
> see what is thy view!" (The son) said: "O my father! do as thou art
> commanded: thou wilt find me, if Allah so wills, one practicing
> patience and constancy!"[338]

Submission to Allah

Despite the frightening future that now confronted both of them,
Abraham and Ismael were both totally committed in their submission
to Allah. Yet, what a tangled web of emotions Abraham must have been
feeling! Despair, mourning, and grief over the impending death of Ismael
must have spread a canopy of gloom over Abraham's psyche. However,
the father's pride and joy in a son, who so totally submits to Allah,
must have incessantly burst through that canopy of gloom. To have such

pride and joy in an only son, only to know you are about to lose him! With Abraham and Ismael voicing their intention to submit to Him, Allah directed Abraham to lead Ismael, Abraham's two servants, and a donkey to a mountain, which was in the vicinity of Makkah. Along the way, they stopped to cut what wood they could, and loaded it on the back of the donkey, in order that there would be a suitable fire for the burning of Ismael's sacrificed body.[339] After they reached the foot of the mountain, Abraham and Ismael unloaded the wood from the donkey's back, and Abraham directed his two servants to remain at the foot of the mountain with the donkey. Abraham and Ismael then picked up the wood themselves, and Abraham loaded it on Ismael's back. While Ismael packed the wood on his back, and while Abraham carried the knife for the slaughtering and a burning brand for igniting the sacrificial fire, the two of them picked their way up the mountainside. Upon reaching the spot designated by Allah, the two of them laid down their burdens, and Abraham began to build an altar, upon which to sacrifice Ismael.[340]

When the altar had been erected, and after Abraham had distributed the wood around it for the eventual burning of Ismael's body[341], Abraham gently laid Ismael on top of the altar.[342] Lying there, Ismael prostrated himself before Allah, his face and forehead pressed downwards into the altar.[343] All that remained was the one sure stroke of the sharpened knife. All that remained was the incineration of the dead body with sacrificial fire. Knife poised for the final thrust, neither father nor son wavered in their faith. Their submission to Allah was complete and true.

The Ransom of Ismael

As the knife was about to descend for the deadly cut, a sudden voice stopped Abraham's hand in mid-air.

So when they had both submitted their wills (to Allah), and he had laid him prostrate on his forehead (for sacrifice), We called out to him, "O Abraham! thou hast already fulfilled the vision!"—thus indeed do We reward those who do right. For this was obviously a trial—and We ransomed him with a momentous sacrifice: and we left (this blessing) for him among generations (to come) in later times: "Peace and salutation to Abraham!" Thus indeed do We reward those who do right for he was one of Our believing servants.[344]

At the last moment, Ismael's life had been spared, and Abraham's hand had been stilled. Looking up, tears of joy probably streaming from his eyes, Abraham saw a ram caught by its horns in some nearby brush. Abraham went over to the ram, freed it from the brush, and placed it on the altar, upon which Ismael had previously submitted himself. Then, Abraham sacrificed the ram in place of his only son. Given Allah's ransoming of Ismael, Abraham reportedly named the mountain Jeruel, meaning "Allah will provide", because Allah had provided a way out of the sacrifice of Ismael, and because Allah had provided the ram for the sacrifice.[345]

A Commentary on the Site of the Sacrifice

Of note, *II Chronicles* states that Jeruel was a wilderness area, located near the end of a valley.[346] It may be noted further that the specific area around Makkah, which is associated in Islam with the sacrifice of Ismael, is known as Mina. Mina is located about four miles (six to seven kilometers) east of Makkah, and fits the description of being a wilderness area near the end of a valley. Furthermore, the Arabic word "*Mina*", which is normally translated as "a wish", has a connotation of a non-obligatory gift, i.e., something provided freely. Assuming that Minat Allah was the original name of this area, one has linguistically direct identification of Jeruel as being Mina.

The Covenant

Following Abraham and Ismael having passed their trial of faith and submission, Allah reportedly entered into a covenant with Abraham, presumably before Abraham and Ismael had left the mountain where Ismael was to have been sacrificed. The story of this covenant finds its fullest expression in a highly politicized narrative from *Genesis*.[347] Avoiding the politically charged rhetoric of this narrative, one finds the following circumstances concerning the reported covenant between Allah and Abraham.

Allah reportedly approached Abraham, asking Abraham to walk before Him and to continue being righteous, and informed him that He would enter into a covenant with Abraham. Thereupon, Abraham fell down, prostrated himself before Allah, and worshipped Allah. Presumably after Abraham had completed this act of prostration and worship, Allah reportedly then informed Abraham of the conditions, terms, clauses, and nature of this covenant.[348]

The Right of Circumcision

Upon receiving the covenant from Allah, Abraham wasted no time in acting upon it. That very day, Abraham took Ismael and the two servants, who had accompanied Abraham to Makkah, and Abraham performed the rite of circumcision on all four of them.[349] Presumably, the circumcision was carried out immediately, with the four of them still being at the site of the intended sacrifice of Ismael. As Abraham had probably brought a hatchet with him, in order to cut the wood that was to have been used to burn the sacrifice[350], and as Abraham's knife had already been contaminated with the blood of the ram, which was substituted for Ismael, it is likely that the aforementioned hatchet was the first tool, which was available to perform the rite of circumcision. As such, it is recorded in *Sahih Ahadith* that Abraham performed his circumcision with a hatchet (adze).[351]

Once Abraham was back in Hebron, one assumes that he circumcised all of his male servants and slaves, in order to comply with the covenant.[352]

Abraham's Departure for Palestine

One is not sure as to the length of Abraham's stay during this visit of his to Makkah. However, the length of his stay would have had to have been long enough to accommodate the events recounted in this chapter, and to have allowed sufficient time for post circumcision healing, before Abraham and his servants began the long and difficult trip back to Hebron. In addition, it could not have been so long as to interfere with the completion of other events in Abraham's 99th year of life, which are recounted in the next chapter, and which were awaiting him back in Palestine.

However long Abraham's stay in Makkah, it was a most remarkable and memorable one. He had been reunited with his second wife and with his only son, after what was presumably an 11 to 12 year separation. Abraham and Ismael had totally and completely submitted to Allah during the ordeal of Ismael's intended sacrifice, and they had both passed their trial. Abraham had received the covenant from Allah, and he and

Ismael had fulfilled the rite of circumcision, thus sealing their acceptance of the covenant. Now, however, it was time for the lengthy and tearful goodbye. Important events were awaiting Abraham's presence back in Palestine.

Postcript # 1 to Abraham in Makkah – II

The story of Abraham's intended sacrifice of his only son has captivated listeners and readers of this story for four millennia. It is high drama, and is a verifiable literary masterpiece. It inevitably pulls at the heartstrings of those who confront it. However, the story is not just drama, and it certainly is not fiction. There are several comments that should be made relating to the story of Abraham's sacrifice.

First, the story, which may appear to be somewhat barbaric to modern readers, needs to be understood within the context of its geographical place and of its time. Quite simply, human first-born sacrifice was not that uncommon in that place and age, and archaeological evidence for that practice has been found throughout the ancient world. Furthermore, there are numerous Biblical passages detailing human sacrifice being practiced by the ancient Semitic people, with many of those incidents involving descendants of Isaac, Abraham's second son.[353]

Second, the story must be understood within the confines of a trial of faith in Allah, a trial of obedience and submission to Allah, and a trial of fear of Allah. This point is explicit, both in the *Qur'an* and in *Genesis*. The *Qur'an* states, "for this was certainly a trial"[354], while *Genesis* has an angel saying "for now I know that you fear God, since you have not withheld your son, your only son, from me."[355] For the sake of Allah, Abraham had already sacrificed his past life and heritage, being willing to leave his homeland of Ur and his father in Harran. For the sake of Allah, Abraham had sacrificed his present life, in leaving Hagar and Ismael in Makkah some 11 or 12 years before. For the sake of Allah, Abraham was now willing to sacrifice his future and his legacy, as represented by his only son, Ismael.

Third, there is a marked contrast in the moral tone of the story of Abraham's sacrifice, as narrated in the *Qur'an*, and as narrated in *Genesis*. These contrasts go far beyond questions of which son was to be sacrificed, viz., Ismael versus Isaac, and far beyond questions of where the sacrifice was to take place, i.e., the vicinity of Makkah versus

Palestine. (A) In the *Qur'an*, Abraham is open and forthright in telling Ismael about his vision, and about his intention to sacrifice him.[356] In contrast, *Genesis* portrays Abraham as a schemer and deceiver, who is attempting to dupe and delude his son, in regard to the purpose of their journey to the spot of sacrifice.[357] (B) In the *Qur'an*, both Abraham and Ismael are being tried, and both are found to have "submitted their wills (to Allah)".[358] In contrast, *Genesis* maintains that only Abraham is being tried, and portrays Abraham's son as being an unwitting dupe, who, much against his will, has to be tied and bound, in order to be laid upon the altar.[359]

Postscript # 2 to Abraham in Makkah – II

Rather than interrupt the flow of the story of Abraham's life in Makkah II, the author passed over the story of the covenant rather quickly, noting only that the account in the *P* strand of *Genesis* of the nature, terms, and clauses of the covenant between Allah and Abraham was a highly politicized statement. However, now that the major events in Abraham's life have been covered for his second sojourn in Makkah, it is time to reflect more deeply on this account of the covenant.

The Judaeo-Christian Concept of Covenant

General Considerations: The Judaeo-Christian tradition often tends to view the concept of covenant as some divine altering of the cosmos, i.e., a major theological and paradigmatic shift, whereby different eras in the nature of the relationship between Allah and man can be identified and delineated. Covenants between Allah and man are seen as being very few and far between, and do not represent a smooth progression or evolution in the relationship between Allah and man. Rather, they represent change of cosmic proportions, typically necessitating that the very concept of covenant be presented as "Covenant", with a capital "C". Thus, the Judaeo-Christian tradition posits an initial covenant with Abraham, and a refining of that covenant with Moses, followed by a second, totally new or at least totally reformulated, covenant being ushered in with Jesus.[360]

However, by definition, a covenant is merely a contract entered into by two or more parties. Within the body of that contract, the terms and conditions applying to all parties to the contract should be specified. If any party fails to fulfill its obligations within the contract, then: (1) the contract specifies the penalties that will be brought to bear on the offending party; and/or (2) the contract has been broken, and, subject to the claim of the wronged party, is null and void. With regard to the reported covenant between Allah and Abraham, there are only a few terms and conditions listed in the *P* strand of *Genesis*, especially when it comes to the demands placed upon Abraham and his descendants. As such, one must assume that the account is an incomplete listing of the terms of the covenant. However, given the information available, the reported covenant between Allah and Abraham consisted of the following terms and clauses, which are presented below in the same order as they are listed in the *P* strand of *Genesis*.

The Contract according to *P* : (1) Allah reportedly promised Abraham the following, in the order listed here: (A) Abraham's descendants would be multitudinous; (B) Abraham's original name of Abram would be changed to Abraham; (C) Abraham's descendants would inherit the covenant; (D) Allah would remain the god of Abraham's descendants; and (E) Abraham's descendants would inherit the land of Palestine[361] (2) Abraham and his descendants were to: (A) keep the covenant; and (B) maintain the rite of male circumcision, even for their servants and slaves[362]. (3) The penalty that would fall to Abraham or to his descendants if they broke clause 2B of the covenant was that he or they would be "cut off from his people".[363] (4) Allah reportedly promised Abraham the following: (A) Sarah's original name of Sarai would be changed to Sarah; (B) Sarah would be blessed by Allah; (C) Sarah would have offspring by Abraham, and these descendants would also be multitudinous; (D) only Isaac and his descendants would inherit the covenant from Abraham; and (E) Ismael would be blessed by Allah, but would not inherit the covenant.[364]

Commentary on the *P* strand account: There are many problems with the *P* strand statement detailing the nature, terms, and clauses of the covenant. An in-depth analysis of the Abrahamic covenant according to the *P* strand of *Genesis* would necessitate its own monograph. However, a few of the problems in this account of the covenant contract are noted and briefly discussed below.

First, apart from maintaining the rite of male circumcision, there really are no demands listed for Abraham and his descendants. On the face of it, this seems most peculiar, and suggests that a fuller listing of demands and conditions in clause 2 was excised from the original account at some time. One can only wonder as to what those obligations were, the motivation behind excising them from the original story, and the penalties that were prescribed for failing to meet those obligations.

Second, the ordering of the clauses of the reported covenant appears illogical. Clauses 1 and 4 detail Allah's promises to Abraham, which are interrupted by clauses 2 and 3, which reportedly detail the obligations of Abraham and his descendants and the penalty that will be meted out for failing to meet the obligation of male circumcision. This interrupted ordering suggests that clause 4 may be a later addendum to the text.

Third, in what appears to be a highly politicized addition to the covenant story, clause 4D maintains that the covenant with Abraham would only be inherited by Isaac and his descendants, and clause 4E specifically excludes the inheritance of the covenant by Ismael and his descendants. Of note, clause 4E of the covenant appears to contradict clause 1C, in which there is no limitation on which of Abraham's descendants would inherit the covenant. Given this seeming contradiction, one cannot help wondering if this exclusivity of inheritance listed in 4D and 4E isn't merely a reflection of later Israelite ethnic prejudices, which were being propagated by the sixth or fifth century BCE author of the *P* strand account.

Fourth, this exclusivity of the inheritance of the covenant, as detailed in clause 4E, appears to be somewhat incongruous in the face of Ismael's prior submission to Allah during the intended sacrifice of Ismael. It is even more incongruous in the face of Ismael immediately fulfilling clause 2B, by undergoing circumcision at 13 years of age.[365]

Fifth, clause 4D, which details the exclusivity of the inheritance of the covenant through Isaac, specifically mentions Isaac by name, even though Isaac was not even born until the following year. Clause 4C, which reportedly predicts the future birth of Isaac, stands in sharp contrast to Abraham's and Sarah's later reaction to the prediction of Isaac's birth by angelic visitors (see Chapter 11: Abraham in Palestine–IV: The Angelic Visitors: Prediction of Isaac's Birth), where they both appear to be taken by surprise by the prediction, a reaction that would not be tenable if clause 4C and 4D had actually been presented to Abraham.

Sixth, immediately after detailing clause 4C, which promises Abraham descendants through Sarah, the compiler of the *P* strand account states that Abraham laughed.

> Then Abraham fell on his face and laughed, and said to himself, "Can a child be born to a man who is a hundred years old? Can Sarah, who is ninety years old, bear a child."[366]

These words, placed into the mouth of Abraham by the *P* strand compiler, stand in sharp contrast to the steadfast faith and belief that Abraham had demonstrated throughout his entire life up to this point. The *P* strand compiler would have the reader believe that Abraham had doubts about the promise of Allah! From where does this portrayal of Abraham come? It appears to come from two considerations. (1) The compiler of the *P* strand appears to be putting the later actions and words of Sarah onto Abraham. In that regard, note the following *J* strand material from *Genesis* concerning Sarah's reaction to the angelic announcement of her giving birth to a son, a story which is recounted in the next chapter.

> Then one said, "I will surely return to you in due season, and your wife Sarah shall have a son." And Sarah was listening at the tent entrance behind the men. Now Abraham and Sarah were old, advanced in age; it had ceased to be with Sarah after the manner of women. So Sarah laughed to herself, saying, "After I have grown old, and my husband is old, shall I have pleasure?" The Lord said to Abraham, "Why did Sarah laugh, and say, 'Shall I indeed bear a child, now that I am old?' Is anything too wonderful for the Lord? At the set time I will return to you, in due season, and Sarah shall have a son." But Sarah denied, saying, "I did not laugh"; for she was afraid. He said, "Oh yes, you did laugh." [367]

(2) In order to introduce the name of Isaac into clause 4D so that the exclusivity of the inheritance of the covenant gets established, the compiler of the *P* strand had to provide a justification for and an explanation of the name Isaac, which is literally translated as "laughter".[368]

In summary, while there is no reason to doubt that Allah covenanted with Abraham, there is every reason to doubt the specific rendition of that covenant as provided by the *P* strand of *Genesis*.

The Concept of Covenant in the *Qur'an*

General considereations: Unlike the Judaeo-Christian tradition, which posits that Allah has covenanted with man on only two or three occasions throughout history, the Islamic perspective is that covenants between Allah and man have occurred numerous times throughout history, and have not been limited to any one people. In fact, every prophet, and by extension those people following him in accepting the revelation of that prophet, has had his own covenant with Allah.

> Behold! Allah took the covenant of the prophets, saying: "I give you a book and wisdom; then comes to you a messenger, confirming what is with you; do you believe in him and render him help." Allah said: "Do ye agree, and take this my covenant as binding on you?" They said: "We agree." He said: "Then bear witness, and I am with you among the witnesses."[369]

> And remember We took from the prophets their covenant: as (We did) from thee: from Noah, Abraham, Moses, and Jesus the son of Mary: We took from them a solemn covenant.[370]

Among the prophets and people named in the *Qur'an*, who have been specifically identified as having had a covenant with Allah are the following: Adam; Abraham; Ismael; Jacob (Israel), peace be upon him, and his descendants; Jesus and his followers; Moses and his followers; Muhammad; and Noah.[371]

Viewed from this perspective, the concept of covenant is not static, but is progressive and evolutionary. Just as the Islamic perspective posits a progressive revelation from Allah over time, it also posits a progressive covenant between Allah and man. Of note, this progressive and evolutionary process may even work within the lifetime of a single prophet, and within the message delivered by that prophet. In that regard, one might note that the covenant between Allah and Abraham, as reported in the *P* strand of *Genesis* 17: 1-22, actually supersedes or abrogates an earlier covenant between Allah and Abraham, which was previously presented from the *J* strand of *Genesis* 15: 17-18 (see Chapter 7: Abraham in Palestine – II: Abraham at Hebron: The First Covenant with and the Fifth Promise to Abraham).

Obligations under a Covenant

Since the nature of covenant is progressive and evolutionary, the obligations specified for man under any given covenant with Allah are not necessarily those that were specified under a different covenant. Some obligations may have been added, some may have been deleted, and some may have been altered. As such, there is no way to look at covenants made with other prophets, and then deduce from them an exact list of the obligations of man that were in the covenant made with Abraham. However, the *Qur'an* does list a number of obligations upon mankind that were introduced under one or another covenant, and a partial listing of those obligations may be illuminating of, if not identical with, the covenant between Allah and Abraham.

1.   **Obligations to Allah** [372]
    A. Worship none but Allah (Israelite covenant);
    B. Establish regular prayers to Allah (Israelite covenant);
    C. Fear Allah, and only Allah (Israelite covenant);
    D. Worship Allah (Israelite covenant).
    E. Honor Allah's messengers, and believe in their message (Israelite covenant).
    F. Be willing to spend money for the sake of Allah (Israelite covenant).
    G. Seek Allah's help, patiently and in prayer (Israelite covenant).
    H. Do not transgress the Sabbath (Mosaic covenant).
    I.   Keep certain dietary restrictions (Mosaic covenant).

2.   **Obligations to self and to others** [373]
    A. Treat your parents and family kindly (Israelite covenant).
    B. Treat kindly the orphans and those in need (Israelite covenant).
    C. Do not make members of your own people homeless (Israelite covenant).
    D. Speak fairly to people (Israelite covenant).
    E. Practice regular charity (Israelite covenant).
    F. Do not lie or conceal the truth (Israelite covenant).
    G. Practice and enjoin right conduct (Israelite covenant).

Breaking of the Covenant and Penalties

There is obviously no way in which Allah would ever be in default on a covenant. However, the frailties and imperfections of man are such that man is often in danger of, if not actually guilty of, breaking the covenant he has made with Allah. The *Qur'an* makes several references to this occurrence, and occasionally lists penalties associated with breaking a specific covenant with Allah. The following represents a partial listing from the *Qur'an*[374] of penalties for man's breaking of the covenant contract with Allah.

1. The curse of Allah, i.e., eternal punishment and damnation.
2. Estrangement, hatred, and enmity.
3. Loss to oneself, of personal fulfillment in one's present life and of salvation in the next life.
4. Punishment from Allah.
5. Loss of all benefits described in the covenant.
6. Loss of the book of revelation from Allah.
7. The wrath of Allah, i.e., one perishes.

Summary

The basic concept of covenant differs between the Judaeo-Christian and Islamic traditions. The former tends to see a covenant as a seldom-occurring, paradigmatic shift in the basic relationship between Allah and man. As such, the very concept of covenant assumes a significance of cosmic proportions. In contrast, the Islamic tradition views covenant as a progressive and evolutionary process, in which the relationship between Allah and man was being constantly redefined up until the time of the final covenant with Prophet Muhammad.

As presented in the *P* strand of *Genesis*, the covenant between Allah and Abraham is a highly politicized document, which attempts to claim an exclusive relationship between Allah and the descendants of Isaac. In this claim of exclusivity, one sees the attempt to justify the bigotry and prejudice associated with a monoethnicentristic concept of "the chosen people", which attempts to provide an otherwise heterogeneous group of tribes with a common identity[375], and which directly or indirectly maintains that other humans are of intrinsically less worth than "the chosen people". This latter point finds direct expression in *Jubilees*, where it is maintained that out of all of Abraham's descendants, only those through

Jacob would be a "holy seed", would become "the portion of the Most High", and would be placed by Allah "above all nations".[376]

The message in this passage from *Jubilees* is clear, and no amount of later theologizing can obscure the blatant racism embedded in such concepts. "The chosen people" have become the equivalent of the Nazi "*Ubermensch*" (superman), while everyone else has become the equivalent of the Nazi "*Untermensch*" (subhuman). In this way, as recorded in numerous Biblical narratives[377], it became possible for the ancient Israelites to justify the mass genocide of non-Israelites as being the religious duty of the Israelites. In this way, the concept of "the chosen people" further paralleled Nazi ideology and practice.

In marked contrast, the Islamic tradition denies the concept of exclusivity in covenant between Allah and man, and denies any potential exclusivity in this relationship. Allah is seen as having approached each "nation", by appointing a prophet to that "nation"[378], as well as having appointed Muhammad as the "universal" prophet to the people of all nations.[379] All men, regardless of their ethnic background and affiliation, are potential inheritors of a covenant with Allah, and all men have the opportunity to enter into a personal relationship with Allah.

Chapter 11
Abraham in Palestine – IV

Abraham's second visit to Makkah had been quite momentous: he had been reunited with Hagar and Ismael; he and Ismael had submitted to and passed their trial from Allah; Allah had reportedly established a new covenant with Abraham; and Abraham and Ismael had undergone the rite of circumcision. Abraham's life had been moving quite rapidly, with one significant event following another. Much had happened to the 99-year-old prophet of Allah during the five months or so that he had been gone from Hebron.

Now, as Abraham and his two servants came into sight of their sprawling campsite near Hebron, there was much to be done, even though Abraham probably needed to rest after his long, weary journey. Abraham would need to be informed as to what had been happening with his various flocks and herds, and with his servants and slaves. Of special importance, Abraham would need to find out how Sarah had managed during his absence, would need to tell her something of his visit to Makkah without arousing her jealousies and insecurities, and would perhaps need to offer her some special reassurances about the nature of their continued relationship.

Thus, as Abraham approached his tent and his reunion with Sarah, he was aware of many obligations and duties still facing him. However, there was much more about to happen than even Abraham probably anticipated. Many more events awaited Abraham in his 99th year of life, now that he was back home in Palestine.

Sources of Information on Abraham in Palestine–IV

The *Qur'an* and the *J* strand of *Genesis* are the primary source material for reconstructing Abraham's fourth sojourn in Palestine. Additional, but secondary, information is gleaned from the *P* and *E* strands of *Genesis*, and from *Jubilees*. Finally, a helpful piece of context is gathered from a *Sahih Hadith* recorded in Imam Malik's *Al-Muwatta*.

The Angelic Visitors: Abraham as Host

Among Abraham's many virtuous character traits were his generosity and hospitality. In fact, Abraham was said to have been the first individual to practice hospitality to guests[380], and it would have been customary for Abraham to stop travelers moving past his campsite, and to invite them into his tent for rest, food, and drink. Such was the caring and concern of this prophet of Allah.

Shortly after his return from Makkah, during the heat of the day, as he sat at the entrance of his tent, which was pitched by the oaks of Mamre near Hebron, Abraham looked up and saw three strangers standing near him.[381] These strangers were angels of Allah[382], but to Abraham they looked at first like ordinary, if somewhat unusual, men.[383] Given his generosity and hospitality, Abraham's immediate response was predictable.

Despite his age, Abraham literally ran over to greet them, said "Peace" to them, and bowed solicitously to them. He invited them to sit under the shade of a tree near his tent, in order to get out of the sun's heat, and rest. Next, he suggested that they allow him to send for water, so that they could wash their feet from their dusty journey, and he invited them to stay with him for a while, and to enjoy the hospitality of his food and drink. The three accepted Abraham's invitation, and sat down under the tree. Abraham then hurried into his tent, and gave Sarah instructions to take three measures of choice flour, and to prepare cakes for the three guests. Leaving Sarah in the tent to begin her task, Abraham then ran to one of his servants, and gave him instructions to select a choice and tender calf, to slaughter the fatted calf, and to prepare and cook it in a pleasing and appetizing manner. Leaving the servant to follow these instructions, Abraham then ran to get some curds and milk to present to his guests.[384]

No doubt the preparation of the cakes and calf took some considerable measure of time, and one assumes that the angelic visitors were with Abraham most of the afternoon. Eventually, the meal was ready. Despite the hundreds of slaves and servants that were under his command, Abraham's essential humility was illustrated as he himself served his guests, and placed before them the cakes, the roasted calf, the curds, and the milk. While the angels sat before this feast, which had been prepared especially for them, Abraham stood to the side, watching attentively to see to the comfort and pleasure of his guests.[385]

However, as Abraham stood by his guests, ready to serve his guests in any way he might, he noticed that his guests made no attempt to reach for the feast in front of them. They neither ate nor drank.[386] This concerned Abraham greatly. Perhaps, the meal was somehow lacking, and he was insufficient in his role as host. Even more concerning, Abraham wondered if the three of them meant to do Abraham some harm.[387] Perhaps, they felt compelled to reject Abraham's repast, in order that they might move against Abraham freely, and unencumbered by any debts of gratitude for the meal and for Abraham's hospitality.

First Prediction regarding Sodom and Gomorrah

Sensing Abraham's discomfort, the angelic visitors sought to put Abraham at ease, by noting that their mission was directed against the inhabitants of Sodom, and not against Abraham. Hearing this statement, Sarah apparently laughed.

> But when he saw their hands went not towards the (meal), he felt some mistrust of them, and conceived a fear of them. They said: "Fear not: We have been sent against the people of Lut." And his wife was standing (there), and she laughed...[388]

Qur'anic commentators have variously attributed Sarah's initial laughter at this point to be in reaction to either: the failure of Abraham's guests to eat; or the statement made regarding the people of Sodom. In that regard, from the psychological perspective, it is noted that laughter may cover a wide range of emotional responses, including happiness, fear, release of tension, etc. In the current case, it may well have been that Sarah's laughter was an expression of fear and tension, a concern that the guests' failure to eat was indicative of some impending attack by them.

Prediction of Isaac's Birth

Perhaps not immediately comprehending the statement of the angels, and not being a fearful or reticent person by nature, Abraham directly verbalized his concern to his guests that he was now becoming afraid of them.[389] However, his guests immediately hastened to reassure him, saying: "Fear not! We give thee glad tidings of a son endowed with wisdom."[390] In this manner, Abraham received the angelic prediction of the coming birth of Isaac.

Sarah, who had long before gone through menopause, and who was apparently eavesdropping on this conversation from behind her sanctuary near the entrance to the tent, then initially and quietly laughed in derision to herself.[391] She then walked openly from the tent entrance, laughing out loud, slapped her forehead, and spoke directly for all to hear, exclaiming "a barren old woman!".[392] She then spoke again, saying:

After I have grown old, and my husband is old, shall I have pleasure?[393]

Abraham, still not recognizing his guests as angels of Allah, and thus not recognizing the prediction of Isaac's birth as coming from Allah, joined his own statement of skepticism with that of Sarah.

He said: "Do you give me glad tidings that old age has seized me? Of what then, is your good news?"[394]

Speaking to Abraham, the angels simply said that they were speaking the truth, and that Abraham should not despair.[395] The angels then turned and spoke directly to Sarah, predicting not only the birth of Isaac, but the birth of Isaac's son, Jacob, as well[396], and they said:

Even so has thy Lord spoken: and He is full of wisdom and knowledge.[397]

Having heard this, Abraham now recognized his guests as Allah's angels, and verbalized this recognition when he later questioned the angels as to their errand.[398] Also, now recognizing the angel's prediction as being a prediction from Allah, Abraham said:

And who despairs of the mercy of his Lord, but such as go astray?[399]

However, Sarah, was still not able or willing to believe what she was hearing from these visitors. Her skepticism was just too great. She could not let go of her doubts, and she was unwilling to end this conversation, into which she had so inappropriately thrust herself. As such, she sarcastically said:

Alas for me! Shall I bear a child seeing I am an old woman and my husband here is an old man? That would indeed be a wonderful thing![400]

The angels then confronted Sarah, saying:

Dost thou wonder at Allah's decree? The grace of Allah and His blessings on you, O ye people of the house! For He is indeed worthy of all praise, full of all glory.[401]

Finally, Sarah realized what was going on around her. At that point, she probably reflected on her behavior and conduct, realized the inappropriateness of her doubts and of her sarcasm, and became afraid of what she might have brought down on herself. Thus, she compounded her mistake by actively and directly denying that she had laughed derisively when she had first overheard the prediction that she would give birth to a son by Abraham.[402]

Second Prediction regarding Sodom and Gomorrah

Having heard and accepted the glad tidings that he would have a son by Sarah, and apparently dismissing Sarah from the rest of the conversation, Abraham turned and questioned the angels, asking them about the nature of their errand and of their business.[403] In answer, the angels then informed Abraham that they had been sent by Allah to destroy the cities of Sodom and Gomorrah, because of the wickedness of these cities' people.[404] Hearing this, Abraham's thoughts immediately went to his nephew, Lot, who was living in Sodom, along with the rest of Lot's family. So, Abraham, motivated by compassion, prayed to Allah, and pled for the safety of Lot, of Lot's family, and presumably of others as well.[405] Abraham was then informed that Lot and his family, excepting Lot's wife, would be saved.[406] However, Abraham was instructed not to plead anymore for the rest of the people of Sodom and Gomorrah.[407]

The Qur'anic Passages

No paraphrased rendition of the Qur'anic passages detailing the angelic visitors to Abraham can serve as an adequate substitute for the passages themselves. As such, the following English translations of the meaning of the relevant passages are quoted below.

There came Our messengers to Abraham with glad tidings. They said, "Peace!" He answered, "Peace!" and hastened to entertain them with a roasted calf. But when he saw their hands went not towards the (meal), he felt some mistrust of them, and conceived a fear of them. They said: "Fear not: we have been sent against the people of Lut. And his wife was standing (there), and she laughed: but We gave her glad tidings of Isaac, and after him, of Jacob. She said: "Alas for me! Shall I bear a child, seeing I am an old woman, and my husband here is an old man? That would indeed be a wonderful thing!" They said: "Dost thou wonder at Allah's decree? The grace of Allah and His blessings on you, o ye people of the house! For He is indeed worthy of all praise, full of all glory!" When fear had passed from (the mind of) Abraham and the glad tidings had reached him, he began to plead with Us for Lut's people. For Abraham was without doubt, forbearing (of faults), compassionate, and given to look to Allah. O Abraham! seek not this. The decree of thy Lord hath gone forth: for them there cometh a penalty that cannot be turned back!"[408]

Tell them about the guests of Abraham. When they entered his presence and said, "Peace!" He said, "We feel afraid of you!" They said: "Fear not! We give thee glad tidings of a son endowed with wisdom." He said: "Do you give me glad tidings that old age has seized me? Of what then, is your good news?" They said: "We give thee glad tidings in truth: be not then in despair!" He said: "And who despairs of the mercy of his Lord, but such as go astray?" Abraham said: "What then is the business of which ye (have come), O ye messengers (of Allah)?" They said: "We have been sent to a people (deep) in sin. Excepting the adherents of Lut: them we are certainly (charged) to save (from harm)—all—except his wife, who we have ascertained ,will be among those who lag behind."[409]

When Our messengers came to Abraham with the good news, they said: "We are indeed going to destroy the people of this township: for truly they are (addicted to) crime." He said: "But there is Lut there." They said: "Well do we know who is there: we will certainly save him and his following—except his wife: she is of those who lag behind!"[410]

Has the story reached thee, of the honoured guests of Abraham? Behold, they entered his presence, and said: "Peace!" He said, "Peace!" (And thought, "These seem) unusual people." Then he turned quickly to his household, brought out a fatted calf, and placed it before them…He said, "Will ye not eat?" (When they did not eat). He conceived a fear of them. They said, "Fear not," and they gave him glad tidings of a son endowed with knowledge. But his wife came forward (laughing) aloud: she smote her forehead and said: "A barren old woman!" They said, "Even so has thy Lord spoken: and He is full of wisdom and knowledge." (Abraham) said: "And what, O ye messengers, is your errand (now)?" They said, "We have been sent to a people (deep) in sin—"To bring on, on them, (a shower of) stones of clay (brimstone), "Marked as from thy Lord for those who trespass beyond bounds."[411]

Comparing the *Qur'an* and *Genesis*

The Qur'anic portrayal of Abraham praying to and pleading with Allah for the lives of those in Sodom and Gomorrah stands in sharp and dramatic contrast to the account as portrayed in *Genesis*. In the Qur'anic portrayal, Abraham is worshipful and moved by genuine compassion, and he humbly pleads to Allah.

When fear had passed from (the mind of) Abraham and the glad tidings had reached him, he began to plead with us for Lut's people. For Abraham was, without doubt, forbearing (of faults), compassionate, and given to look to Allah.[412]

He said: "But there is Lut there." They said: "Well do we know who is there: we will certainly save him and his following—except his wife: she is of those who lag behind!"[413]

In marked contrast to the above, the account in *Genesis* (quoted immediately below) has Abraham actively confronting Allah, appearing to question Allah's moral compass and reasoning, and haggling with Allah as though Allah were a merchant in some oriental suk! The *Qur'an* and *Genesis* present two very different pictures of Abraham, and two very different pictures of Allah!

Then Abraham came near and said, "Will you indeed sweep away the righteous with the wicked? Suppose there are fifty righteous within the city; will you then sweep away the place and not forgive it for the fifty righteous who are in it? Far be it from you to do such a thing, to slay the righteous with the wicked, so that the righteous fare as the wicked! Far be that from you! Shall not the Judge of all the earth do what is just?" And the Lord said, "If I find at Sodom fifty righteous in the city, I will forgive the whole place for their sake." Abraham answered, "Let me take it upon myself to speak to the Lord, I who am but dust and ashes. Suppose five of the fifty are lacking? Will you destroy the whole city for lack of five?" And he said, "I will not destroy it if I find forty-five there." Again he spoke to him, "Suppose forty are found there." He answered, "For the sake of forty I will not do it." Then he said, "Oh do not let the Lord be angry if I speak. Suppose thirty are found there." He answered, "I will not do it, if I find thirty there." He said, "Let me take it upon myself to speak to the Lord. Suppose twenty are found there." He answered, "For the sake of twenty I will not destroy it." Then he said, "Oh do not let the Lord be angry if I speak just once more. Suppose ten are found there." He answered, "For the sake of ten I will not destroy it."[414]

The Destruction of Sodom and Gomorrah: The Angels meet Lot

Ever the good host, Abraham escorted his angelic visitors out of his campsite. The angels then left Abraham, and journeyed on by their own means to Sodom, arriving at the gateway into Sodom as evening was falling. Sitting at the gate, they met Lot, who rose to greet them, and who bowed to them in salutation. Having apparently learned his hospitality from Abraham, Lot invited the strangers to stop and wash their feet at his house, to eat a meal with him, and to spend the night at his house. The angels initially declined Lot's hospitality, saying that they would simply spend the night in the central square of the city. However, Lot was most insistent, and eventually they accepted his proffer of hospitality, and accompanied Lot to his home.[415]

Lot's Mission to Sodom

Now, Lot had apparently been preaching the *Tawheed* to the inhabitants of Sodom ever since he had separated from Abraham some 16 or 17 years before. Yet, despite the length of his ministry, he had acquired no converts, other than the members of his own household, and Sodom had remained deeply rooted in sin and in sexual perversion.[416]

We also (sent) Lut: he said to his people: "Do ye commit lewdness such as no people in creation (ever) committed before you? For ye practice your lusts on men in preference to women: ye are indeed a people transgressing beyond bounds."[417]

However, despite the directness of Lot's message, the people of Sodom had refused to heed his warning.[418] They had mocked this prophet of Allah, and the message that he had brought to them from Allah. They had even threatened to drive Lot and his family from their town, if Lot did not cease his preaching.

(We also sent) Lut (as a messenger): behold, he said to his people: "Do ye do what is shameful though ye see (its iniquity)? Would ye really approach men in your lusts rather than women? Nay, ye are a people (grossly) ignorant!" But his people gave no other answer but this: they said, "Drive out the followers of Lut from your city: these are indeed men who want to be clean and pure!"[419]

Despite such setbacks and threats, Lot had continued his mission to the people of Sodom. He had attempted to assure them that he was after no personal gain or financial reward. He had continued preaching to them, and his voice had not been stilled. Yet, he had worried about his own family being repeatedly exposed to the behavioral patterns of the inhabitants of Sodom, and he had prayed to Allah that his family would not be influenced by such exposure.

The people of Lut rejected the messengers. Behold, their brother Lut said to them: "Will ye not fear (Allah)? I am to you a messenger worthy of all trust. So fear Allah and obey me. No reward do I ask of you for it: my reward is only from the Lord of the worlds. Of all the creatures in the world, will ye approach males, and leave those whom Allah has created for you to be your mates? Nay, ye are a people transgressing (all limits)!" They said. "If thou desist not O Lut! thou wilt assuredly be cast out!" He said: "I do detest your doings: O my Lord! deliver me and my family from such things as they do!"[420]

Nonetheless, the inhabitants of Sodom had continued their pattern of sodomy, homosexual rape, and highway hijackings. They had even paraded their homosexual sex lives in the midst of their own public assemblies, apparently engaging in mass public orgies. They had continued to mock Lot and the message, which he had brought. They had taunted him, and they had dared him to bring down the justice of Allah on their perverse community.

> And (remember) Lut: behold, he said to his people: "Ye do commit lewdness, such as no people in creation (ever) committed before you. Do ye indeed approach men, and cut off the highway?—and practice wickedness (even) in your councils?" But his people gave no answer but this: they said: "Bring us the wrath of Allah if thou tellest the truth." He said: "O my Lord! help Thou me against people who do mischief!"[421]

The Destruction

Given the background of Lot's mission to the people of Sodom, it is quite understandable that Lot had feared for the safety of the strangers, who had arrived at the city gate. No doubt, this was one reason that he was so insistent that the strangers not camp out in the central square of the city, but that they should accompany him to his home, where he could try to hide them and to protect them. Like Abraham, he had not immediately recognized them as angels of Allah, but he certainly had noticed something different about them.[422]

The story of the angels' stay in Lot's home, and of the eventual destruction of Sodom and Gomorrah, is referred to or told in numerous passages in the *Qur'an*.[423] However, the following represents two of the more complete narrations:

> When our messengers came to Lut, he was grieved on their account and felt himself powerless (to protect) them. He said: "This is a distressful day." And his people came rushing towards him, and they had been long in the habit of practicing abominations. He said: "O my people! Here are my daughters: they are purer for you (if ye marry)! Now fear Allah, and cover me not with shame about my guests! Is there not among you a single right-minded man?" They said: "Well dost thou know we have no need of thy daughters: indeed thou knowest quite well what we want!" He said: "Would that I had power to suppress you or that I could betake myself to some powerful support." (The messengers) said: "O Lut! we are

messengers from thy Lord! By no means shall they reach thee! Now travel with thy family while yet a part of the night remains, and let not any of you look back: but thy wife (will remain behind): to her will happen what happens to the people. Morning is their time appointed: is not the morning nigh?" When our decree issued, we turned (the cities) upside down, and rained down on them brimstones hard as baked clay, spread, layer on layer—marked as from thy Lord: nor are they ever far from those who do wrong! [424]

At length when the messengers arrived among the adherents of Lut, he said: "Ye appear to be uncommon folk." They said: "Yea we have come to thee to accomplish that of which they doubt. We have brought to thee that which is inevitably due, and assuredly we tell the truth. Then travel by night with thy household, when a portion of the night (yet remains), and do thou bring up the rear: let no one amongst you look back, but pass on whither ye are ordered." And We made known this decree to him, that the last remnants of those (sinners) should be cut off by the morning. The inhabitants of the city came in (mad) joy (at news of the young men). Lut said: "These are my guests: disgrace me not: but fear Allah and shame me not." They said: "Did we not forbid thee (to speak) for all and sundry?" He said: "There are my daughters (to marry), if ye must act (so)." Verily by thy life (O Prophet), in their wild intoxication, they wander in distraction to and fro. But the (mighty) blast overtook them before morning, and We turned (the cities) upside down, and rained down on them brimstones hard as baked clay.[425]

Lot's Escape

Before the dawn of the new day, Lot and the members of his household, excluding only Lot's wife, made their escape out of Sodom.[426] They crossed out of the Valley of Siddim and out to the edge of the plains. Finally, they arrived at the city of Zoar, which was nestled on the edge of the plains, near the hill country south of Sodom.[427] In all, they had traveled about eight miles (13 kilometers), moving south from Sodom to Zoar. However, that distance provided the margin of difference between life and death.

Commentary: A Comparison of the *Qur'an* and *Genesis*

In most respects, the account in *Genesis*[428] of the destruction of Sodom and Gomorrah parallels the two Qur'anic passages quoted above. In all these statements: (1) the men of Sodom gather around the house of Lot, demanding access to the strangers within it; (2) Lot begs the populace to leave his guests alone; (3) Lot offers his unmarried daughters as substitutes for his guests; and (4) Lot's offer of his daughters is rejected. Further, the *Qur'an* and *Genesis* agree that: (5) the men of Sodom are blinded and wander aimlessly around[429]; (6) Lot and his family flee the city of Sodom before morning or as dawn breaks[430]; (7) Lot's wife is destroyed[431]; and (8) the city of Sodom is destroyed by objects (variously described as being brimstone, sulfur, and fire) falling from the sky.[432] However, *Genesis* adds a couple of details not mentioned in the *Qur'an*.

Firstly, it is stated in *Genesis* that when the men of Sodom rejected Lot's offer of his daughters as potential wives, the men of Sodom became infuriated with Lot for once again preaching to them, and for once again daring to judge their sexual behavior and proclivities. They then threatened Lot with the same homosexual rape, which they were planning for Lot's guests, and they actually began to move physically against Lot. However, at this moment, the angels intervened, opened the door to the house, and pulled Lot back inside into the safety of the house.[433]

Secondly, *Genesis* claims that both of Lot's daughters were engaged to be married, that Lot warned his prospective sons-in-law to flee with them, and that these young men thought that Lot must be jesting, implying, although never directly stating, that they did not heed Lot's advice.[434] However, if one rejects the implication that these young men did not escape from Sodom with Lot and his daughters, the Qur'anic implication that more than just Lot and his two daughters escaped becomes explained.[435]

Thirdly, readers of the *Qur'an* and of *Genesis* typically assume that the destruction was limited to Sodom, or to Sodom and Gomorrah. However, *Genesis* clearly states that Allah destroyed all the cities of the plain, excepting Zoar[436], which would have necessitated the destruction of four cities: Sodom; Gomorrah; Admah; and Zeboiim.

Fourthly, *Genesis* maintains that Abraham viewed the destruction of Sodom and Gomorrah from a hill in the vicinity of Hebron[437]. The distance between Hebron and the presumed site of Sodom is about 36 to 37 miles (58 to 60 kilometers), which would normally be too far of a distance to accommodate Abraham witnessing the destruction. However, it is quite possible that the nature of the destruction of Sodom and Gomorrah has been minimized by readers of both the *Qur'an* and *Genesis*. This point is elaborated below.

The Earthquake

Prior to the destruction of Sodom and Gomorrah, the area, in which they were located, was described as being a rich and fertile plain.

> Lot looked about him, and saw that the plain of the Jordan was well watered everywhere like the garden of the Lord, like the land of Egypt, in the direction of Zoar; this was before the Lord had destroyed Sodom and Gomorrah.[438]

However, it was also the case that the area contained bitumen pits and oil pools.[439] Furthermore, the area was located directly over a major seismic fault line, which is variously known as the Great Rift Valley, the East African Rift Valley, and the Afro-Arabian Rift Valley. (A rift is an elongated trough in the earth's crust, which is formed by a geologic fault between two tectonic plates, which tend to be separated from or are pulling away from each other. Frequently, rift valleys are associated with a high potential for volcanic activity, especially during times of tectonic movement.)

The eastern branch of the Great Rift Valley extends from the Jordan River, through: the Dead Sea; the land between the Dead Sea and the Gulf of 'Aqaba; the Red Sea; the Denakil Plain in Ethiopia; Lakes Rudolf, Naivasha, and Magadi in Kenya; the Zambesia River in Tanzania; and the Shire River valley and Mozambique Plain to the coast of the Indian Ocean near Beira, Mozambique. It measures about 4,000 miles (6,500 kilometers) in length, and averages about 30 to 40 miles (49 to 65 kilometers) in width. The Great Rift Valley is a sunken block confined by two parallel geologic faults, of which the eastern extends along the edge of the Moab Plateau in Jordan, and of which the western extends along the Judaean hills in Palestine.

As noted previously, the Jordan River valley and the Dead Sea comprise the northern portion of the Great Rift Valley. The Dead Sea is situated between the Judaean hills to the west and the Jordanian plateaus to the east. As currently formed, the Dead Sea is about 50 miles (81 kilometers) long, has a maximum width of 11 miles (18 kilometers), covers an area of 394 square miles (1,040 square kilometers), and consists of a northern and a southern basin. These two basins are demarcated by the Al-Lisan ("the tongue") Peninsula extending into the Dead Sea from the Jordanian plateau on the east, and by Mount Sedom (Sodom) on the west. The northern basin consists of 75% of the Dead Sea's total surface, and reaches a depth of 1,300 feet (400 meters). In marked contrast, the depth of the southern basin averages less than 10 feet (three meters).

With this background in mind, it is time to examine the clues afforded by *Genesis* and by the *Qur'an*, with regard to the specifics of the destruction of Sodom and Gomorrah. In presenting the destruction of Sodom and Gomorrah, *Genesis* notes: (1) sulfur and fire raining down on the cities from the sky; (2) that Allah "overthrew" the cities; and (3) that smoke rose from the cities, like smoke rising from out of a furnace.[440] Whereas the statement that Allah "overthrew" the cities is ambiguous and is subject to varied interpretation, the comments about sulfur, fire, and smoke are rather straightforward and clear.

The *Qur'an* variously refers to Sodom being destroyed by: (1) a shower or rain of brimstone; (2) a shower of evil; (3) stones of clay; (4) a shower of stones; (5) a violent tornado; and (6) being turned upside down.[441] In regard to the statement of Sodom being turned literally upside down, some commentators have advanced the story that the angel Gabriel: took his wing; inserted his wing under the land, on which was located Sodom; lifted up the land into the air; turned it completely over; and then dropped it back down upon itself.[442]

The physical and natural mechanics of an event corresponding to Gabriel's reported action are clear. A major seismic event would have occurred along the Great Rift Valley fault line, with an epicenter located around the Dead Sea. There would have been a pronounced upward movement of one of the earth's tectonic plates, which would have thrust the cities of the plain skyward. As the plates slipped back, the land, on which had stood the cities of the plain, would have flipped over on itself and fallen back down. Thus, Sodom and Gomorrah would have been buried at an elevation far below and far beneath where they had once stood. As the earth settled back down, a permanent break apparently occurred in the natural land barrier extending from Mount Sedom to the Al-Lisan Peninsula. This break would have allowed the onrushing waters of the northern basin of the Dead Sea to cover what had once been the fertile plain hosting the cities of Sodom and Gomorrah. As such, the southern basin of the Dead Sea was formed, covering what had been the area comprising the flourishing cities of the plain. Further, a seismic event of this magnitude would have probably unleashed tremendous volcanic and geothermal energy, hurling magma, various ashes, burning oil, and bitumen far into the sky, before they fell back down to earth. A smoking, desolate ruins would have been all that was left.

It's worth noting that a description of a similar and catastrophic seismic event appears in the archaeological record, dated to around 1,900 BCE. Given the inevitable slippage involved in the archaeological dating of ancient events, this is a good fit with the current estimate of the destruction of Sodom and Gomorrah occurring about 2,067 BCE.[443] Furthermore, the archaeological record supports the claim that the area around Sodom and Gomorrah had been a rich and fertile bastion of agriculture, before this major earthquake forever changed the terrain and landscape of the area. Prior to this earthquake, the Dead Sea would have been much smaller, and may have contained water, which was far more usable than that of today. Judging by this latter point, it should be noted that it is quite likely that prior to this earthquake, and in the times of Lot, the River Jordan continued southward from the Dead Sea, and emptied into the Gulf of 'Aqaba, making the Dead Sea a large freshwater lake. As a freshwater lake, the Dead Sea would have provided an abundant source of irrigation water to the surrounding plains, and would have contributed to the agricultural fertility of the area in that bygone and ancient era.

It is gratifying to see how all of the descriptors concerning the destruction of Sodom and Gomorrah, whether found in *Genesis* or the *Qur'an*, are so explicitly accounted for by this major seismic event. Indeed, Abraham, standing some 36 or 37 miles (58 to 60 kilometers) away, would not only have seen the smoke from this major destruction, but he would have probably also felt the ground tremble under his feet.

Abraham moves to between Kadesh and Shur

Within a couple of weeks after the destruction of Sodom and Gomorrah, Abraham reportedly moved from the vicinity of Hebron to deep in the

Negeb, to a place between Kadesh and the Wilderness of Shur.[444] This would have necessitated a move of about 85 miles (138 kilometers) to the southeast from Hebron. Reportedly, Abraham only stayed in this area for about one month, before moving to the vicinity of Beersheba.[445] Thus, Abraham moved about 62 miles (101 kilometers) back to the northwest, settling only about 24 miles (39 kilometers) southeast of Hebron.

There is no report in any of the information sources to explain this back and forth movement of Abraham and Sarah, of Abraham's servants and slaves, and of Abraham's considerable herds and flocks. Further, there is no report detailing any significant event that happened in Abraham's life during his one-month stay between Kadesh and the Wilderness of Shur. One is reduced to informed speculation about Abraham's back and forth movement, and about the reasons for it. Fortunately, the temporal sequence of events provides a basis for informed speculation. Within less than a two-month period, one is confronted by the following sequence of events: (1) Sodom and Gomorrah are destroyed by Allah, in what appears to have been a massive seismic event, with subsequent volcanic eruptions; (2) Abraham moves from Hebron, which was located about 36 to 37 miles (58 to 60 kilometers) northwest of Sodom, to an area about 85 miles (138 kilometers) southwest of Hebron and about 85 miles (138 kilometers) west southwest of Sodom; and (3) Abraham moves again, going about 62 miles (101 kilometers) back to the northeast, settling at Beersheba, which was about 40 miles (65 kilometers) west of Sodom.

The aftermath from the major earthquake that destroyed Sodom and Gomorrah, and the distribution of volcanic ash during the subsequent volcanic activity, were presumably sufficient to disrupt the grazing and care of Abraham's herds and flocks in the vicinity of Hebron. Pasture areas may have been destroyed by volcanic ash near Hebron. Wells and springs may have collapsed and been destroyed during the repeated aftershocks. Both ash and aftershocks may have disrupted the normal breeding and birthing cycles of Abraham's livestock. Accordingly, he packed up, and moved to temporary quarters between Kadesh and Shur. Abraham stayed there about a month, which may have been enough time for the aftershocks and volcanic activity to cease. Abraham then moved back to the northeast, settling near Beersheba, where the distribution of volcanic ash may not have destroyed available pasture areas, and where the seismic activity may not have adversely affected the wells and springs.

Abraham at Beersheba: Sarah conceives

Within a month of moving over to the vicinity of Beersheba, Sarah conceived.[446] After approximately 50 years of marriage, after having long since passed through menopause[447], and after turning 89 years of age, Sarah was finally with child. There are probably no words that can adequately describe the joy and elation, which Sarah must have felt when she first realized that she was pregnant. The angel's prediction of two months before had been realized. Sarah's earlier skepticism, sarcasm, and laughter had been sorely misplaced. Sarah was at long last to be a mother of her own child!

Abraham and Sarah had hardly settled down at Beersheba before Sarah conceived. There were so many things to do after they moved to their new location, especially when one considers all the overbearing responsibilities that Abraham had. Moving was not merely a matter of pitching one's tent in a new location. There were relationships to establish, to define, and to develop with new neighbors, some of whom were quite powerful. There were new grazing schedules and locations to be created for Abraham's many herds and flocks. Most importantly, there were water rights to be determined, and wells to be dug. Indeed, Abraham had a lot to do. Nonetheless, one assumes that this prophet of Allah made time to celebrate, and to give repeated thanks to Allah for Sarah's pregnancy.

The Birth of Isaac

Nine months after conceiving, during the early harvest season, Sarah gave birth to Abraham's second son.[448] She was 90 years old at the time, and Abraham was 100 years old.[449] The son was named Isaac, meaning "laughter". The *E* strand of *Genesis* attempts to associate Isaac's name with the fact that his birth brought Sarah pleasure and laughter.[450] Undoubtedly, after so many years of waiting for a child, Isaac did bring Sarah much pleasure and laughter. How she must have doted on this child of her old age! However, it appears more probable that Isaac's name was derived from the earlier *J* strand incident, in which Sarah derisively laughed when the angels predicted this birth.[451] On the eighth day after being born, Isaac was reportedly circumcised by Abraham.[452]

The Well of the Oath[453]

Background: The city of Gerar was located about 18 miles (29 kilometers) northwest of Beersheba, about 12 miles (19 or 20 kilometers) southeast of Gaza, and about 15 miles (24 kilometers) southeast of the Mediterranean coast. The king of Gerar was Abimelech, whose name in Hebrew means "my father, the king", and Abimelech's military commander was Phicol. Gerar's suzerainty apparently extended far enough from Gerar to have included Beersheba and its vicinity within the domain of his rule. It is unknown whether Abimelech was a Canaanite or an Amorite.[454]

(While *Genesis* identifies Abimelech as being a Philistine[455], this is a rather obvious anachronism, as the Philistine's did not inhabit the area around Gerar until several centuries after Abraham's era.[456])

Apparently, some time prior to the present incident involving the Well of the Oath, Abraham had been required by Abimelech to enter into a covenant with him, in order for Abraham to remain within the lands ruled by Abimelech. Such a demand would have been imminently practical for a secular ruler like Abimelech. After all, why should he have allowed an alien to reside in his lands, if that alien were unwilling to take some kind of loyalty oath to him. The demand would have been even more insistent for someone of Abraham's wealth, military prowess, and manpower. According to the account given in *Genesis*, this oath of loyalty was a rather simple affair, involving Abraham swearing that he would only deal loyally, never falsely, with Abimelech and with Abimelech's descendants. Likewise, Abimelech swore to deal loyally and justly with Abraham. Apparently, this oath was sealed with Abraham bestowing on Abimelech a gift of some sheep and oxen.[457]

When Abraham and his household of servants and slaves had first settled Abraham's large flocks and herds in the vicinity of Beersheba, it would have been necessary for Abraham to have many wells dug, in order to have provided water for his livestock and household. Water supplies in the vicinity of Beersheba were limited, and Abraham's demand for water would have been great. As such, Abraham apparently had his men dig a succession of wells in the area, one of which was at Beersheba.[458]

The Dispute: At some point after Abraham had these wells constructed, servants of Abimelech, apparently without Abimelech's knowledge, seized the well at Beersheba. Abraham then complained to Abimelech, who professed his innocence of any knowledge of the event. Given this initial response from Abimelech, Abraham separated out seven female lambs from his flock, and approached Abimelech with this gift. Accepting this gift, Abimelech, who had come to Beersheba with his army, perhaps fearing an insurrection from Abraham, then ruled that the well in question belonged to Abraham. Immediately thereafter, Abimelech and Abraham renewed their covenant with each other at Beersheba. Upon renewal of this covenant, Abimelech, Phicol, and the army of Abimelech returned to Gerar.[459]

Significance: The story of the well at Beersheba has etymological significance in explaining the name of the city, which later grew up in this area. "*Beer*" is the Hebrew for "well", and "*Sheba*" could refer either to "seven" or to "oath".[460] In the former case, Beersheba refers to the well of the seven, i.e., the seven female lambs Abraham gave to Abimelech. In the latter case, Beersheba refers to the Well of the Oath, referring to the oath taken between Abraham and Abimelech. The latter is the more typical etymological rendition.

The Weaning of Isaac

Isaac apparently was healthy, and grew without difficulty throughout his infancy. Presumably, around two years of age, Isaac was weaned. In celebration of Isaac having completed this rite of passage, Abraham reportedly gave a large feast.[461]

Postscript to Abraham in Palestine – IV

Abraham now had two sons: Ismael, living with his mother and with the Jorhamites in far off Makkah; and Isaac, living with Sarah and Abraham in the vicinity of Beersheba. Both sons were close to Abraham's heart, he entrusted both sons to the care of Allah, and he reportedly sought refuge for both sons with Allah by reciting:

> O Allah! I seek refuge with Your perfect words from every devil and from poisonous pests and from every evil, harmful, envious eye.[462]

Chapter 12
Abraham in Makkah – III

Three separate trips by Abraham to Makkah are presented in this chapter. As per the available historical chronicle, these three trips constitute Abraham's third, fourth, and fifth trips to Makkah. While it is not impossible that Abraham made additional trips to Makkah, the designations of third, fourth, and fifth trips will be used throughout this book for referring to the three trips discussed in this chapter. *Sahih Ahadith* provide the primary information concerning Abraham's third and fourth trips. In contrast, information regarding the fifth trip is provided by numerous sources, including the *Qur'an, Sahih Ahadith,* and *Al-Tabari.*

Abraham's Third trip to Makkah

It appears as though at least seven years had passed since Abraham had last visited Makkah, and Abraham was now somewhere between 106 and 136 years of age.[463] During the prior visit, Abraham and Ismael had passed the enormous trial that Allah had placed in front of them. Abraham and Ismael had both totally submitted to Allah, during the difficult trial of the sacrifice. Abraham's submission had been his acceptance of Allah's decree that Ismael should be sacrificed, while Ismael's submission had been his willing acceptance of being the sacrificial victim. Once they both had submitted, Allah had intervened to save Ismael, and a ram had been sacrificed in place of Ismael. Allah had then entered into a covenant with Abraham, and Abraham and Ismael had both fulfilled part of their obligations under that covenant, by undergoing the rite of circumcision.

As Abraham approached Makkah, near the completion of his nearly two-month journey down the Incense Route from Beersheba, there would again be many changes confronting him. Much had happened in Makkah since Abraham had last been there. The Jorhamite settlement at Makkah had continued to grow and prosper, and was rapidly becoming more of a permanent town and urban center. Houses were replacing tents, doors were replacing tent flaps, and Ismael was now living in a house. Hagar had died at some unknown time since Abraham's second trip, and perhaps Abraham was to learn of the death of his second wife only when he arrived in Makkah for the third time. In addition, Abraham now had a daughter-in-law, as Ismael had married a woman from the Jorhamite tribe. Clearly, there had been many changes.[464]

Ismael's First Wife

Abraham arrived in Makkah to discover the community growing and thriving. He probably began his activities by asking questions of the first Jorhamites whom he encountered. From them, if he did not already know, he would have learned of Hagar's death, and of Ismael's marriage. Thus, it is likely that grief and joy fused inharmoniously in Abraham's heart shortly after he entered Makkah. Setting aside his emotions, perhaps with some difficulty, he continued his questioning. At that point, he might also have been informed that Ismael was not presently in Makkah. Whether or not he received that last piece of information, he acquired directions to Ismael's home, and quickly traced his steps to his son's dwelling.[465]

Arriving at Ismael's home, Abraham was confronted by a Jorhamite woman, who identified herself as Ismael's wife. Not identifying himself to his daughter-in-law, Abraham inquired about Ismael, and was informed that Ismael was away on a hunting trip. Abraham, still not identifying himself, then asked about how things were for his daughter-in-law. She immediately responded with a long harangue, in which she complained that she and her husband were living in a state of near destitution. She was miserable, her life was filled with one hardship after another, and she was more than willing to verbalize her numerous complaints.[466]

Clearly, Ismael's wife was dissatisfied with her lot in life, with her present marriage, and with the level of her current lifestyle. Moreover, she apparently had no qualms about telling anyone, including a total stranger, all about her numerous complaints and dissatisfactions. Abraham had heard more than enough. However, how was Abraham going to convey his impressions to his older son? Abraham knew that Ismael's hunting trip might last for several weeks, or even for a month or more. It simply wasn't feasible for Abraham to remain idly by in Makkah for that length of time. Yet, he needed to convey his impressions to his son. Abraham needed to give some warning to Ismael about his wife's behavior.

As Abraham prepared to leave, he turned to his daughter-in-law. Still not having identified himself, he asked her to convey two messages to Ismael. First, she was to convey his greetings to Ismael. Second, she was to tell Ismael that his visitor had advised him to change the threshold to his door or gate. Having conveyed these two messages for his son, Abraham left Ismael's home.[467]

Abraham had a long trip awaiting him back to Beersheba, and there was no point in delaying his departure. He had not seen his older son, Ismael. If he had not already known it, he had discovered that Hagar was dead. He had also discovered that Ismael's wife was quite a bit less of a person, than Abraham would have wanted for his son. Now, he could but trust in Allah that his two messages to Ismael would be delivered. In the meantime, Sarah and Isaac awaited his return at Beersheba.

Postscript

At some point after Abraham's departure, Ismael returned to his home from his hunting trip. He naturally inquired of his wife about what had happened in her life while he had been gone. She told him of the solitary visitor who had arrived at their doorstep, and she described the visitor to her husband. Recognizing the description as being that of his father, Ismael inquired if the visitor had left any message for him. Ismael's wife then told him of the visitor's salutation to him and of the visitor's strange statement about his needing to change the threshold to his gate or door. Hearing those words, Ismael immediately understood to what Abraham was referring. Ismael turned to his wife, told her that the visitor had been his father, informed her that Abraham's message to him had instructed him to divorce his wife, and soon thereafter proceeded to carry out his father's instructions.[468]

Abraham's Fourth trip to Makkah

Sometime after Ismael divorced his first wife, he remarried. Tradition says that Ismael's new wife was also a Jorhamite, and that she was known as Al-Sayyidah, the daughter of Madad, the son of 'Amr[469]. Her father, Madad, was reportedly the sheykh of the Jorhamite tribe[470], suggesting that he was a person of considerable influence, prestige, and power. Whether or not news of this new marriage reached Abraham in Beersheba is unknown. However, at some point after this marriage, Abraham again took leave of Sarah and of Isaac, in order to journey to Makkah and to attempt to visit Ismael.[471] (Given that the round trip between Beersheba and Makkah could easily have taken four months, it is probable that Abraham's fourth trip to Makkah was at least a year after his third trip.)

Ismael's Second Wife

Arriving in Makkah, and already knowing his way to Ismael's home, Abraham probably wasted no time in arriving at Ismael's doorstep. However, once again, Ismael was not there to greet his father. Instead, it was Ismael's new wife, who greeted Abraham. Abraham, without identifying himself, asked for Ismael, and was informed that Ismael was again out hunting. Probably seeing a look of disappointment on Abraham's face, Ismael's wife invited the weary traveler to sit and to rest, and she volunteered to fix a meal for him. Abraham then inquired as to how she and Ismael were doing in life. She quickly responded by saying that she and her husband were prosperous and doing well, and in so saying, she gave thanks to Allah. Abraham then inquired about their sustenance, and Ismael's wife happily told him that they had the meat from Ismael's hunting trips, and that they had the water from the Well of Zam-zam. Her sustenance was limited to meat and to water, and she was content, happy, and satisified with the sustenance that Allah provided through Ismael. What more could she possibly want? Abraham then invoked the name of Allah, and said, "O Allah! bless their meat and water." [472]

One assumes that Abraham was deeply moved by the attitudes, values, piety, and faith, which he saw exhibited in his new daughter-in-law. Here was a woman, who appeared to have the same uncomplaining trust in Allah, which Hagar had so beautifully demonstrated when Abraham had initially left Hagar and Ismael in Makkah so many years before. Here was a woman, who appeared to be equal to the difficult challenge of being a prophet's wife. How great is a father's joy and celebration, when his son has chosen wisely, and has found a wife and helpmate, of whom the father can be justifiably proud!

Again, it was not feasible for Abraham to wait some unknown length of time for Ismael to return from his hunting trip. As such, Abraham prepared to leave. However, before leaving, he asked his daughter-in-law to convey two messages to Ismael. First, she was to convey the greetings of this unidentified traveler to Ismael. Second, she was to tell Ismael that the traveler advised Ismael to keep the threshold of his gate or door exactly as it was. After giving those words of greeting and of advice, Abraham departed from Makkah.[473]

Postscript

When Ismael later returned from his hunting foray, his wife quickly informed him of the visitor that had stopped by their house. She described Abraham in detail to Ismael, noting that the visitor had been a good-looking, old man, with praiseworthy character and behavior. She volunteered that Abraham had inquired about Ismael, and that she had answered his questions. She further volunteered that Abraham had asked about their livelihood, and that she had told him that she and Ismael were doing quite fine, thanks be to Allah. Ismael then inquired of his wife, whether or not the visitor had left any message for him. Ismael's wife quickly informed him that the visitor had left his greetings for Ismael, and that the visitor had advised Ismael to keep the threshold of his gate or door exactly as it was. At that point, Ismael identified the visitor to his wife as having been his father, Abraham, and joyfully told her that Abraham's message about the threshold had been his father's way of telling Ismael that Abraham fully approved of Ismael's wife.[474]

One assumes that Ismael's marriage to Al-Sayyidah was long and joyful, each being content with the other, and both being content with the life, which Allah provided to them. Tradition maintains that the marriage produced at least 13 children, including: Nabit or Nabaioth; Qaydar or Kedar; Adabil or Adbal or Adbeel; Mabasha or Mabasham or Mibsam; Masma' or Mishma; Duma or Dhuma or Dumah; Mas or Masa or Massa; Adad or Haddad or Hadad; Watur or Yatur or Jetur; Nafis or Naphish; Tuma or Taym or Tema; Qaydaman or Qadaman or Kedemah; and Basmah or Mahalath, who later was to become the wife of Esau, the elder son of Isaac.[475]

Abraham's Fifth trip to Makkah (The Building of Ka'ba)

Sahih Ahadith clearly date this trip as occurring after Abraham's fourth trip to Makkah, and before the death of Sarah.[476] If one were to assume that Abraham did not make this trip in the same year that he made the fourth trip, given that each round trip may have taken up to four months, this would probably place this fifth trip somewhere between Abraham's

108th and 137th year of life. Unlike the third and fourth trips, which were motivated by Abraham's desire to see Ismael, this fifth trip was in direct response to an ordinance from Allah.[477]

The Reunion

Abraham arrived in Makkah to find Ismael sitting under a tree, which was located behind the Well of Zam-zam. There, Ismael was sharpening and mending his arrows, perhaps preparing for another extended hunting foray, in order to provide the meat that was the primary provision for his table. In that regard, it is worth noting that Ismael had already acquired quite a reputation as an archer of some considerable repute and distinction.[478]

Twice before, Abraham had made the approximately 700 mile (1,200 kilometer) journey from Beersheba to Makkah, only to fail in his quest to visit Ismael. Each time, Abraham's round trip had taken him about 1,400 miles (2,400 kilometers), and had cost him about four months of his life. Each time, Abraham had failed to find Ismael at home. Now, the reunion was complete. Father and son were together again, after a separation of perhaps as much as nine years or more. One can only assume that the embraces were warm and strong, and that the tears of joy flowed freely.

Probably, Ismael would have immediately walked his father back to Ismael's home, with father and son walking arm in arm. Arriving at his home, Ismael would have had the pleasure of introducing his father to Al-Sayyidah, Ismael's virtuous wife, whom Abraham had met during his fourth trip to Makkah. Possibly, there were other introductions to be made, as well.[479] Quite possibly, Ismael's first son, Nabit, had already been born. Perhaps, Ismael's second son, Qaydar, had also been born. It is even conceivable that there were more than two of Ismael's 13 children waiting to greet their grandfather. If the author's assumption is correct, Abraham was not only reunited with his elder son and with his daughter-in-law, but was also meeting some of his grandchildren for the first time. There would have been so many greetings to make and make again, so many stories to share, so much catching-up-on to do, and perhaps even grandchildren to cuddle, tickle, and bounce on the knee.

Finally, however, Abraham broached the reason behind his unexpected visit. Abraham informed Ismael that Allah had ordered Abraham to journey to Makkah, and to build a permanent sanctuary at Makkah, at which mankind could worship Allah. Such was the faith of Ismael, that he immediately put aside all thoughts of continuing this joyful reunion between himself and his father, and he advised his father to begin the task immediately. Abraham then either asked for Ismael's help, or told Ismael that Allah had ordered that Ismael should help Abraham in constructing this sanctuary. In either case, Ismael was the ready volunteer.[480]

The Building of the Ka'ba

One does not just build a structure for worship. There are site preparation issues to be solved, foundation lines to be laid out, stones to be cut and shaped, and perhaps mortar to be prepared. The task of building is not something that is accomplished in a leisurely afternoon, but is a prolonged project requiring time, effort, determination, and a great deal of hard, manual labor. Nonetheless, Abraham and Ismael wasted no time on needless preliminaries, and rose immediately to begin the task that confronted them. Approaching the Well of Zam-zam, Abraham pointed to a slight rise in elevation close by the well, and informed Ismael that this was the site, which Allah had selected for His sanctuary.[481]

With the site of the Ka'ba previously chosen by divine selection, Abraham and Ismael proceeded along the lines of a simple, but effective, division of labor. Ismael would prepare and gather the requisite stones, and would bring them to Abraham. Meanwhile, Abraham would lay out the foundation lines of the sanctuary (Ka'ba), and would be in charge of placing the stones once Ismael had brought them to him. Having divided their labor accordingly, Abraham and Ismael began to pray, by chanting the following words.[482]

Our Lord! accept (this service) from us: for Thou art the all-hearing, the all-knowing.[483]

Thus, they proceeded, hour after strenuous hour, and, presumably, day after arduous day. With their backbreaking work and personal sacrifice, the structure, which they were building for Allah, began to rise slowly into the air, one stone after another.

Of the various stones used in the construction of the Ka'ba, two stones deserve particular comment. First, one particular stone was identified as having descended from paradise. Given this description, perhaps it was originally part of a meteorite, which landed near Makkah.

However, whatever its origin, its color was reportedly a pure white, which was whiter than milk. This stone was placed near the eastern corner of the Ka'ba. Tradition holds that this stone gradually became black, as a result of being touched by sinful men, and has since become famous as the black stone (*Al-Hajar Al-Aswad*).[484]

Second, when eventually the walls of the structure became too high for Abraham to place the stones another level up, Ismael brought a certain, particular stone, on which Abraham could stand (known to later generations as the Station of Abraham), so that Abraham could reach up just one more level. Throughout it all, Abraham and Ismael humbly continued their prayerful chant.[485]

> Our Lord! accept (this service) from us: for Thou art the all-hearing, the all-knowing.[486]

A Qur'anic interlude

The story of Abraham and Ismael building the Ka'ba is referred to in several passages in the *Qur'an*. English translations of the meaning of some of these passages are quoted below.

> And remember that Abraham was tried by his Lord with certain commands, which he fulfilled: He said: "I will make thee an Imam to the nations." He pleaded: "And also (Imams) from my offspring!" He answered: "But My promise is not within the reach of evildoers." Remember We made the house a place of assembly for men and a place of safety; and take ye the Station of Abraham as a place of prayer; and We covenanted with Abraham and Isma'il, that they should sanctify My house for those who compass it round, or use it as a retreat, or bow, or prostrate themselves (therein in prayer). And remember Abraham said: "My Lord, make this a city of peace, and feed its people with fruits—such of them as believe in Allah and the last day." He said: "(Yea), and such as reject faith—for a while will I grant them their pleasure, but will soon drive them to the torment of fire—an evil destination (indeed)!" And remember Abraham and Isma'il raised the foundations of the house (with this prayer): "Our Lord! accept (this service) from us: for Thou art the all-hearing, the all-knowing. Our Lord! make of us Muslims, bowing to Thy (will), and of our progeny a people Muslim, bowing to thy (will); and show us our places for the celebration of (due) rites; and turn unto us (in

mercy); for Thou art the oft-returning, most merciful. Our Lord! send amongst them a messenger of their own, who shall rehearse Thy signs to them and instruct them in scripture and wisdom, and sanctify them: for Thou art the exalted in might, the wise."[487]

Say: "Allah speaketh the truth: follow the religion of Abraham, the sane in faith; he was not of the pagans. The first house (of worship) appointed for men was that at Bakka; full of blessing and of guidance for all kinds of beings: in it are signs manifest; (for example) the Station of Abraham; whoever enters it attains security; pilgrimage thereto is a duty men owe to Allah—those who can afford the journey; but if any deny faith, Allah stands not in need of any of His creatures.[488]

Behold! We gave the site, to Abraham, of the (sacred) house, (saying): "Associate not anything (in worship) with Me; and sanctify My house for those who compass it round, or stand up, or bow, or prostrate themselves (therein in prayer).[489]

Abraham's Prayer

There is no way known to the author of determining how long it took Abraham and Ismael to build the Ka'ba, and there is no known record of Abraham's length of stay during his fifth trip to Makkah. One assumes that after the completion of the building of the Ka'ba, Abraham would have taken some additional time to enjoy the company of Ismael and his family. Finally, however, it would have been time to return to Sarah and to Isaac in Beersheba. As such, Abraham eventually prepared to leave. There would have been food, water, and supplies to pack. Donkeys would have been loaded for the long trip ahead. Long and tearful good-byes would have been said.

As Abraham then left Makkah, for what is believed to be the last verifiable time, he apparently stopped to offer up a prayer to Allah. In this prayer, he made several specific requests. He asked for a special blessing upon Makkah[490], and for Allah to protect him and his family from falling into false worship. He asked for Allah to bless Ismael and his descendants, for Allah to instill in the descendants of both Ismael and of Isaac the practice of proper prayer, and for Allah to forgive Abraham, his parents[491], and all believers.

Remember Abraham said: "O my Lord! make this city one of peace and security: and preserve me and my sons from worshipping idols. O my Lord! they have indeed led astray many among mankind; he then who follows my (ways) is of me, and he that disobeys me—but Thou art indeed oft-forgiving, most merciful. O our Lord! I have made some of my offspring to dwell in a valley without cultivation, by Thy sacred house; in order, O our Lord, that they may establish regular prayer: so fill the hearts of some among men with love towards them, and feed them with fruits: so that they may give thanks. O our Lord! truly Thou dost know what we conceal and what we reveal: for nothing whatever is hidden from Allah, whether on earth or in heaven. Praise be to Allah. Who hath granted unto me in old age Isma'il and Isaac: for truly my Lord is He, the hearer of prayer! O my Lord! make me one who establishes regular prayer, and also (raise) such among my offspring O our Lord! And accept Thou my prayer. O our Lord! cover (us) with Thy forgiveness—me, my parents, and (all) believers, on the day that the reckoning will be established!"[492]

Proclaiming the *Hajj*

The Ka'ba had now been built. However, Abraham's relationship with the Ka'ba was not yet over. As Abraham left Makkah, Allah had one more instruction for him regarding the Ka'ba. Abraham was to proclaim the message that the Ka'ba had now been built, and that it was now a religious obligation upon every believer in the Oneness of Allah to make the *Hajj* or pilgrimage to Makkah and to the Ka'ba. Furthermore, this obligation was to be binding upon every believer who had the physical and financial resources to complete the journey.[493]

"And proclaim the pilgrimage among men: they will come to thee on foot and (mounted) on every kind of camel, lean on account of journeys through deep and distant mountain highways; that they may witness the benefits (provided) for them, and celebrate the name of Allah, through the days appointed, over the cattle which He has provided for them (for sacrifice): then eat ye thereof and feed the distressed ones in want. Then let them complete the rites prescribed for them, perform their vows, and (again) circumambulate the ancient house." Such (is the pilgrimage): whoever honours the sacred rites of Allah, for him it is good in the sight of his Lord. Lawful to you (for food in pilgrimage) are cattle, except those mentioned to you (as exceptions): but shun the abomination of idols, and shun the word that is false—being true in faith to Allah, and never assigning partners to Him: if anyone assigns partners to Allah, he is as if he had fallen from heaven and been snatched up by birds, or the wind had swooped (like a bird on its prey) and thrown him into a far-distant place. Such (is his state): and whoever holds in honour the symbols of Allah, (in the sacrifice of animals), such (honour) should come truly from piety of heart. In them ye have benefits for a term appointed: in the end their place of sacrifice is near the ancient house.[494]

Postscript # 1 to Abraham in Makkah – III

The Ka'ba, as constructed by Abraham and Ismael, was a quite different structure than that seen by modern pilgrims as they complete their rites of *Hajj* and/or of *'Umrah* in contemporary Makkah. The Ka'ba was totally rebuilt in the early seventh century CE by the Quraysh tribe of Makkah, and in that rebuilding its form was greatly altered.[495] In that regard, a direct comparison of the contemporary Ka'ba with the prior Ka'ba is quite instructive.

As it presently stands, the Ka'ba is a stone building, which is about 49 feet (15 meters) high, and which is covered with a roof, which rests on six interior pillars. Two parallel sides, one of which houses the famous black stone, are approximately 32 to 33 feet (10 meters) in length. The other two parallel sides are approximately 39 feet (12 meters) in length. There is a single door, which is situated about six feet (two meters) above ground level.

The corners of the Ka'ba roughly correspond to the four points of the compass. Using the above information and the Yemeni corner of the Ka'ba as a guide, this corner can be identified as the southern point on the compass. Moving then to the northeast, one travels along the southeastern wall, which is approximately 32 to 33 feet (10 meters) in length, and which contains the black stone just before its eastern corner. Turning the corner, and beginning to move to the north, one immediately passes the elevated door to the Ka'ba, as one travels the 39 feet (12 meters) along the northeastern wall, before arriving at the northern corner. The north-western side of the Ka'ba, which is approximately 32 to 33 feet (10 meters) in length, is adjacent to the semi-circular area known as the Hijr of Ismael, which prevents one from walking directly beside the north-western wall. The Hijr of Ismael ends at the western corner of the Ka'ba. One then travels approximately 39 feet (12 meters) down the southwest-ern wall of the Ka'ba, before again reaching the Yemeni corner. The Well of Zam-zam is located just a few hundred feet southeast of the Ka'ba, and the hill of Safa is located just a little further southeast of the Well of Zam-zam, with the hill of Marwa located northeast of the Ka'ba.

Having described the current construction of the Ka'ba, one can now turn to what the Ka'ba was like before its rebuilding in the early seventh century BCE. In this context, the following specific changes can be identified. (1) Prior to its rebuilding, the Ka'ba had no roof. (2) Prior to its rebuilding, the height of the Ka'ba was no more than: about a little taller than a man's height, the more probable estimate, given that Abraham merely had to stand on a stone to lift additional stones to the top of the Ka'ba; or about 20 feet (6.3 meters). (3) Prior to its rebuilding, the northeastern and southwestern walls were considerably longer than currently, and extended far enough northwestward to have included the Hijr of Ismael within its walls. As such, before its rebuilding, the Ka'ba was much more rectangular, and less square-shaped, in appearance. (4) Prior to its rebuilding, the door to the Ka'ba was not elevated above ground level.[496]

Postscript # 2 to Abraham in Makkah – III

Abraham was instructed by Allah to "proclaim the pilgrimage"[497] of the rites of *Hajj*, as a religious obligation owed by mankind to Allah. While this modest postscript cannot begin to encompass a thorough discussion of the *Hajj*, it is instructive to note how many of the rites and traditions of *Hajj* commemorate events from the life of Abraham, and from the lives of his family. (1) After completing the *Tawaf* (circumambulation) of the Ka'ba, one prays two *Rakat* behind the Station of Abraham, the stone upon which Abraham stood in completing the building of the Ka'ba. (2) After saying this prayer, one drinks water from the Well of Zam-zam, thus commemorating the miracle of the digging of that well by Gabriel, the event which saved the lives of Hagar and of Ismael. (3) The rite of

Sa'ee, i.e., walking back and forth between Safa and Marwa for a total of seven one-way trips, commemorates Hagar's desperate search for help, when she and Ismael were first left alone in Makkah. (4) The sacrifice at Mina commemorates Abraham's intended sacrifice of Ismael, and Allah's substitution of a ram in place of Ismael. (5) The stoning of the three pillars at Mina commemorates Abraham rejecting any temptation, which he might have encountered, not to sacrifice Ismael.

Chapter 13
Abraham in Palestine –V

This chapter reviews the known events in the last 41 years of Abraham's life, e.g., from Abraham's 134th to his 175th years of life. The sources of information for these events are primarily Biblical, and consist of information from *Genesis*. However, some additional information is obtained from *Jubilees* and from *A-Tabari*.

Abraham Moves to Hebron

Abraham had moved to Beersheba when he was 99 years old[498], having resided in the vicinity of Hebron for the 16 or 17 years before that[499]. As noted previously, Abraham may have relocated from Hebron to Beersheba, because of the possible disruption in available pasture and water caused by the destruction of Sodom and Gomorrah. Now, at the age of 134 years, Abraham moved his family from Beersheba, and returned to Hebron.[500] The available source material gives no explanations or reasons for this move back to the Hebron area. It is possible that Abraham had always intended to move back to Hebron, and that it simply took 35 years for the Hebron area to return back to normal after the destruction of Sodom and Gomorrah. However, this hypothesis must be considered speculative.

The Death of Sarah

Sarah Dies: Three years after returning to Hebron, Sarah died, having lived to the age of 127 years.[501] She and Abraham had been married for about 88 years at the time of her death[502], and they had experienced many trials, tribulations, and celebrations together. She had been with Abraham since the days of persecution in Ur, had moved with him to Harran, to Palestine, to Egypt, and then back to Palestine. Sarah had lived to give birth to Isaac, and she had been able to watch him grow and mature through the first 37 years of his life.[503] Her life had been full and complete.

One may assume that Abraham experienced considerable grief at the loss of Sarah[504], and that Abraham and Isaac spent time mourning for Sarah, and in comforting each other. Abraham and Isaac still had each other, but, more importantly, they still had their devotion to and faith in Allah, which had to have been their greatest comfort and reassurance at this time of loss. However, as is usually the case at the time of a loss of a loved one, one's grief has to give way to such practical matters as preparing the body, arranging for burial, etc.

The Burial of Sarah: In Abraham's situation, one immediate issue, with which he had to deal quickly, was the fact that he did not own any land. He had always lived a somewhat nomadic existence as a tent-dwelling shepherd, and had apparently never bothered to acquire title to any piece of real estate. As such, he had no land that could serve as a burial plot, in which to place Sarah's body. This was a pressing issue, which had to be handled immediately and decisively.

According to *Genesis*, Abraham attempted to resolve this issue of securing a burial spot for Sarah by announcing his need to the indigenous population of Hebron, probably when they called upon Abraham to offer their condolences. The assembled men from Hebron quickly reassured Abraham, telling him that they regarded him as being a prince among them, and suggesting that he simply let them know which piece of property he wanted for Sarah's grave. Hearing this response, Abraham reportedly bowed in appreciation, and then requested that these men entreat on his behalf with Ephron, the son of Zohar. This Ephron apparently owned a particular field of land, which was well planted with trees. The field was near Hebron, and was located east of the oaks of Mamre. At the end of this field, there was a cave, which was called Machpelah, which was also owned by Ephron. Abraham asked that Ephron be approached by these men, in order to see if Ephron would sell just the cave of Machpelah to Abraham, so that Abraham could use this cave as a tomb for Sarah. In making this request, Abraham stated that he would pay the full purchase price that Ephron requested.[505]

Now, Ephron was actually sitting in the midst of these men of Hebron, who were gathered around Abraham. Hearing Abraham's words, Ephron rose to his feet, and reportedly said:

> No, my lord, hear me; I give you the field, and I give you the cave that is in it; in the presence of my people I give it to you; bury your dead.

Abraham then reportedly replied:

> If you only will listen to me! I will give the price of the field; accept it from me, so that I may bury my dead there.

To this comment from Abraham, Ephron reportedly responded, by saying:

> My lord, listen to me; a piece of land worth four hundred shekels of silver—what is that between you and me? Bury your dead.

Hearing this response, Abraham immediately weighed out the 400 pieces of silver, and handed them over to Ephron. The transaction completed, Abraham placed Sarah's body in the cave of Machpelah, which was to serve as her tomb.[506]

Commentary on the Burial of Sarah

There are several background points, which need to be made regarding the story of Abraham's acquisition of the cave of Machpelah. Without a proper understanding of these background points and context, important aspects of the transaction may well be lost to the reader. These contextual and background points are elucidated below.

(1) Abraham had most likely seen Ephron among the group, and had probably even greeted him at some point in time before Abraham made his general statement, in which he asked the assembled men to entreat Ephron on his behalf. Yet, Abraham did not address Ephron directly about the matter of purchasing the cave. In considering Abraham's approach, one can perhaps glean some additional insight into Abraham's virtuous character. Even though Abraham was in the midst of dealing with his own grief at Sarah's death, he was still concerned about the feelings of others. He probably did not want to put Ephron on the spot or in a difficult position. What if Ephron really didn't want to sell this cave? Maybe Ephron would feel pressured by the context of the situation, e.g., by Abraham's grief and by so many of his neighbors witnessing what was transpiring, and thus agree to sell that which he didn't really want to sell. Given Abraham's approach, Ephron could remain sitting quietly, and could simply not respond. In this manner, Ephron would have a way out of the whole situation. What a tribute to Abraham's caring and concern, that, at this most difficult of times, he was still thinking of others, before thinking of his own needs and wants.

(2) Ephron's immediate response was to stand up, and publicly say that Abraham could have the cave and the field, to which the cave was attached, for nothing. At first glance, this might appear to be a generous offer. In reality, it was anything but that. By appearing to be so gracious and giving, Ephron was actually staking out his negotiating position. By making the offer that Abraham take the cave and the field for nothing, Ephron was setting up a situation, which he knew Abraham would have to refuse. Once Abraham refused to accept the cave and the field as a gift, Abraham was put into a position of basically having to ask Ephron to name a price. Ephron then suggested 400 shekels of silver by weight, which he referred to as being a trifle, i.e., "what is that between you and me". However, in reality, that was an exorbitant price for the place and times, being equal to 10 lbs. of silver at a time when silver was more precious than gold. This move by Ephron left Abraham in a position of either: haggling over the price in public at the very time Abraham was grieving Sarah's loss; or simply paying this grossly inflated price. Abraham chose the latter alternative.

(3) Abraham had requested that he be allowed to purchase only the cave of Machpelah. However, Ephron had insisted that Abraham also purchase the adjoining field. This maneuver by Ephron resulted in two pecuniary benefits to Ephron. First, Abraham now had to pay for additional land, which Abraham really didn't need or want, thus driving up the purchase price. Second, and perhaps more importantly, the legal codes operating at that place and time specified that a land owner had certain feudal responsibilities and obligations for the people who worked that land. Not only was Ephron making Abraham buy more property than Abraham wanted, and not only was Ephron thereby driving up the purchase price, Ephron was also saddling Abraham with the financial responsibility for caring for the workers and families who tended that field.

In summary, there is a most educational contrast in character studies, between that of Abraham's virtuosity and that of Ephron's greed and self-interest, which is being subtly illuminated by *Genesis*.

The Marriage of Isaac

At some point in time, Abraham had received word about his family back in Harran. Among whatever other things he may have learned, Abraham found out that the marriage of Nahor II (Abraham's brother) and Milcah (Sarah's sister) had resulted in numerous children, including eight sons: Uz; Buz; Kemuel; Chesed; Hazo; Pildash; Jidlaph; and Bethuel. Moreover, whether Abraham had been told it or not, Kemuel was now the father of Aram (the eponymous ancestor of the Aramaeans), and Bethuel was the father of Rebekah. In addition, Nahor II had four children out of his concubine, Reumah, including: Tebah; Gaham; Tahash; and Maacah.[507]

Three years had passed since Sarah's death, and Isaac was now 40 years old.[508] Despite his age, Isaac had yet to marry, although he was no longer living with Abraham at Hebron. At some unknown time previously, Isaac had moved to Beerlahairoi in the Negeb[509], the site of the well at which the pregnant Hagar stopped on her flight from Sarah.[510] As such, Isaac was now living about 75 to 80 miles (122 to 130 kilometers) south of Abraham.

Whether it was because of Isaac's age, whether it was that Isaac was now living so far removed from Abraham, or whether it was for some other reason, Abraham apparently decided it was time for Isaac's single status to end. However, for whatever reason, Abraham was reportedly somewhat hesitant for Isaac to marry a local Canaanite or Amorite woman, preferring that Isaac marry someone from Abraham's own family and kin. As such, Abraham summoned a faithful, but unnamed, servant, supposedly the one who had been longest in Abraham's service, to undertake a special task.[511]

The Servant's Task

When the servant presented himself in Abraham's presence, Abraham explained his wishes to him. He reportedly told the servant that he did not want Isaac marrying from among the local Canaanites or Amorites, and that he wanted Isaac to marry someone from Abraham's own family back in Harran. Abraham was entrusting this task of finding a wife for Isaac to this old and faithful servant, who would have to travel to Harran, in order to make the arrangements. Having explained his wishes to the servant, Abraham then asked the servant to swear that he would carry out Abraham's wishes and instructions as best he could, and presumably to the extent that Allah allowed. However, before making this oath to Abraham, the servant had one question. What if he found a wife for

Isaac from among Abraham's kin in Harran, but the woman would not agree to leave Harran, and would not agree to relocate to Palestine. Should the servant then take Isaac back to Harran to live? Abraham answered in the negative, maintaining that Isaac should remain in Palestine, which had been bequeathed to Abraham's descendants by Allah. If the woman refused to accompany the servant back to Palestine, in order to marry Isaac and to reside in Palestine with Isaac, then the servant was free of the oath. Upon hearing this, the servant reportedly put his hand under Abraham's thigh, and swore to carry out Abraham's wishes, presumably to the extent that Allah allowed. The servant then prepared a small caravan to make the long journey from Hebron to Harran. Numerous choice gifts were packed to be distributed among Abraham's family back in Harran, as well a dowry for the intended bride.[512]

Having packed the donkeys[513] for the journey, the servant set off, apparently accompanied by other servants of Abraham.[514]

Abraham's servant would have probably traveled north-northwest from Hebron to Aleppo (Syria), and then would have moved northwest to Harran (Turkey). In all, he would have journeyed about 450 miles (731 kilometers), and the trip would have taken a good month or more, given the need to graze and water his donkeys. Finally, he approached the well of water by the edge of Harran.[515] What should he do now? He had arrived at Harran, but where should he go to find Abraham's family? It had been 65 years since Abraham had left Harran[516], and the servant would have had no way of knowing where Abraham's family now resided. What should he do?

The servant of Abraham now entrusted his task to Allah, and he reportedly prayed as follows.

> O Lord, God of my master Abraham, please grant me success today and show steadfast love to my master Abraham. I am standing here by the spring of water, and the daughters of the townspeople are coming out to draw water. Let the girl to whom I shall say, "Please offer your jar that I may drink," and who shall say, "Drink, and I will water your (donkeys)"—let her be the one whom you have appointed for your servant Isaac. By this I shall know that you have shown steadfast love to my master.[517]

Rebekah

Before the servant was even done saying his prayer, a young woman named Rebekah was approaching the well, carrying her water jug on her shoulder. Although the servant had no way of knowing it, Rebekah was the virgin daughter of Bethuel, the son of Nahor II, the brother of Abraham. However, the faithful servant could see for himself that Rebekah was quite lovely. He watched her fill her jug with water at the well, and then watched as she began to walk away. At that point, he hurried up to her, and asked for a drink of water. Rebekah lowered the jar from her shoulder, and allowed the old servant to drink his fill. Once he was done drinking, Rebekah immediately volunteered to draw water from the well, so that the old man's donkeys could be watered. Allah had answered the prayer of Abraham's servant![518]

As soon as the donkeys were done drinking, the servant removed a gold nose ring, weighing half a shekel (about .2 ounces), and two gold bracelets, weighing ten shekels (about four ounces), from where they had been packed, and handed them to Rebekah. He then inquired about Rebekah's name and family, and asked if her family might have some spare room where he could spend the night. He was informed that she was Rebekah, the daughter of Bethuel, the son of Nahor II and of Milcah. Rebekah, furthermore informed him that her family had a place where he might stay, and that they had spare fodder for his donkeys. The old servant then praised and gave thanks to Allah. While the servant was thus worshipping Allah, Rebekah ran ahead to her family's home, and informed them about the old man and his donkeys.[519]

Arriving at her home, Rebekah told her "mother's household" about the old man, whom she had encountered at the well. Hearing this news, and seeing the gold his sister was now wearing, Laban, Rebekah's brother, ran out to the well at the edge of town. There, Laban greeted Abraham's servant, and guided him and his companions back to Laban's house. Reaching his home, Laban helped unload and feed the donkeys, and then invited the servants of Abraham into his house. Water was presented for the washing of feet, and food was placed in front of the men.[520]

However, at that point, Abraham's old and faithful servant announced that he would not eat anything, until he had explained his trip to Harran to Laban. Laban told the servant to proceed, and Abraham's servant then identified himself for the first time as being the servant of Abraham. He explained that Allah had greatly blessed Abraham, and that Abraham had grown exceedingly wealthy in flocks, herds, silver, gold, slaves, and donkeys. He further explained that Sarah had finally given Abraham a son, Isaac, who stood to inherit from Abraham's extensive estate. Recently, Abraham had delegated the servant to travel to Harran, and to find a wife for Isaac among the women of Abraham's family. The servant had complied, and had reached Harran that evening. Arriving at Harran, the servant had set up the trial of water for the young women coming to the well, and Rebekah had passed that trial. Having completed his tale, Abraham's servant then asked for Rebekah to be the bride of Isaac.[521]

Having heard the servant's story, Bethuel[522] (the father of Rebekah and of Laban) and Laban gave their blessing to the proposed marriage, and entrusted Rebekah into the care of Abraham's servant, in order that he might escort Rebekah back to Isaac. Hearing this, Abraham's servant distributed gifts of silver, gold, and clothing to Rebekah, with such gifts probably being her dowry from Abraham. In addition, Abraham's servant gave costly presents to Laban and to the mother of Laban and Rebekah. The formalities of marriage having been arranged, the meal was eaten, and people then retired for the night.[523]

Rising the next morning, Abraham's servant immediately asked Laban's leave to depart with Rebekah for distant Palestine. However, Laban and his mother were in no hurry to have Rebekah leave them, and suggested that the trip back to Palestine be put off for at least 10 days. Abraham's servant wanted no part of this suggestion, as he was anxious to complete the task, which Abraham had assigned to him. He had acquired a bride for Isaac, but he had yet to deliver that bride back to Isaac in Palestine. As such, he again asked Laban's permission to leave immediately with Rebekah. At this second request, Laban basically said that he would leave it up to Rebekah. Rebekah was now called into the room to meet with Abraham's servant, with Laban, and with the mother of Rebekah and Laban. The situation was explained to her: Abraham's servant wanted to leave immediately for Palestine; while Laban and his mother wanted at least a 10 day delay. It was now up to Rebekah. After considering the issues involved, Rebekah said that she was prepared to leave immediately. As such, Rebekah and her nurse were hurriedly packed up, joined the small caravan of Abraham's servant, and began the trip back to Palestine.[524]

Rebekah in Palestine

Presumably, Rebekah had lived her entire life in Harran. She had always before been in the company of her family, and she had always been cared for by her mother, and by her brother, Laban. Now, she was beginning a great adventure, which would take her some 450 miles (731 kilometers) from her family, and from the only home that she had ever known. Accompanied only by her nursemaid, Rebekah would be forced to encounter many changes. She was exchanging her mother and her brother, whom she might never see again, for a husband she had never met. She was exchanging the urban life of Harran for the life of a shepherd's wife. There were so many changes, which she had to anticipate and overcome.

Change, whether for the better or for the worse, is a stressful event in the normal course of human life. Even positive change requires the recipient to adapt, and adaptation is seldom easy. Stress always accompanies the need for adaptation. The greater the change that one experiences, the greater the stress that accompanies it. As the caravan slowly made its way out of Harran (Turkey), southwest to Aleppo (Syria), south to Damascus (Syria), and south into Palestine, Rebekah would have been under a great deal of stress, and there would only have been Rebekah's nursemaid, with whom Rebekah could talk about her anxieties and concerns. Granted, there was the thrill and excitement of all that she was seeing for the first time in cities such as Aleppo and Damascus. At such times, she may well have been caught up in the whirlwind of new sights and sounds. But there was also the long and tedious hours spent on the back of a donkey. Such time would have given Rebekah more than enough opportunity to stew over a myriad of different questions and concerns. What had she gotten herself into? What was going to happen? What was Isaac like? How would Isaac treat her? As such, one assumes that it was a somewhat stressed and anxious Rebekah, who rode through the hill country of Palestine.

As Beerlahairoi lies 75 to 80 miles (122 to 130 kilometers) south of Hebron, and as the caravan would have had to pass near by Hebron on its journey south to Beerlahairoi, one assumes that Abraham's servant stopped at Abraham's campsite near Hebron. Here, Abraham and Rebekah would have met, and would have been introduced to each other. At long last, great uncle and great niece had met for the first time. For her part, Rebekah must have found Abraham's character and personality most assuring. Just meeting Abraham, some of Rebekah's stress must have been alleviated. For his part, Abraham apparently found his niece an acceptable life-partner for Isaac. Having reassured himself on that account, one imagines that Abraham had question after question for his great niece. He had a lot of family business, on which he needed to come up to date. What had happened with his father, Azar? What could Rebekah tell him about Nahor II, about the children of Nahor II, about Milcah, etc.? How had Harran changed? What was happening there now? It must have been quite a conversation.

One doesn't know how long Rebekah stayed at Abraham's campsite. However, the caravan packed up eventually, and began moving to the south, and into the Negeb. Approaching Beerlahairoi, the members of the caravan saw a solitary figure walking in a field. Knowing that they were close to Beerlahairoi, and seeing the man in the distance, Rebekah dismounted from her donkey, and asked Abraham's servant about the man in the distance. The servant replied that it was Isaac, who was coming to greet them. Upon hearing that news, Rebekah veiled herself, in preparation to meet her husband. When the caravan and Isaac finally met, Abraham's servant informed him of all that had transpired. Thereupon, Isaac took Rebekah into his tent as his wife. Isaac grew to love Rebekah, and he found Rebekah to be a great comfort.[525]

Abraham Marries Keturah

Isaac was now married to Rebekah. One assumes that Abraham made visits to Beerlahairoi to see Isaac and Rebekah, and one assumes that Isaac and Rebekah returned those visits. As such, Abraham would have had the opportunity to see the joy that Rebekah had brought into Isaac's life. If Isaac could find this kind of marital happiness, was it possible that Abraham might also enjoy the comfort of a wife and of marriage once again? That thought may have begun to tease at the corners of Abraham's consciousness. In any event, within about a year of Isaac's marriage to Rebekah[526], Abraham married for the third time.

Abraham's third bride was Keturah, who is variously identified by *Al-Tabari* as being: Qantura, the daughter of Maftur; and Qaturah, the daughter of Yaqtan. *Jubilees* states that Keturah was the daughter of one of Abraham's household servants, while *Al-Tabari* states that she was a

Canaanite. The two statements are not mutually exclusive, and both may be correct. In any case, over a 14-year time span, Keturah bore Abraham either six or seven sons. *Genesis* lists six sons, including: Zimran; Jokshan; Medan; Midian; Ishbak; and Shuah. *Al-Tabari* lists a seventh possible son, i.e., Basar. At least two of these sons of Abraham and Keturah left recorded offspring. (1) Jokshan was the father of Sheba and of Dedan, the latter of whom was the eponymous ancestor of the Dedanites, who later lived in the Hijaz (western Saudi Arabia), north of Madinah. In turn, Dedan was the father of Asshurim, Letushim, and Leummim. (2) Midian was the eponymous ancestor of the Midianites (Madyan), and was the father of Ephah, Epher, Hanoch, Abida, and Eldaah. *Al-Tabari* lists a sixth son for Midian, namely Thabit, who reportedly was the father of 'Anqa, the father of Safyun, the father of Shu'ayb, peace be upon him.[527]

Abraham Marries Hajur

Al-Tabari reports a fourth marriage by Abraham, and identifies Abraham's fourth wife as being Hajur, the daughter of Arhir. If one accepts the historical accuracy of this report, this marriage would probably have occurred between Abraham's 141st and 150th years of life. *Al-Tabari* anachronistically identifies Hajur bint Arhir as having been an Arab, and he lists five sons resulting from this marriage: Kaysan; Shawarukh; Amin; Lutan; and Nafis.[528]

The Birth of Isaac's sons

After 20 years of marriage to Isaac, and after Isaac's repeated prayers that Allah might grant children to Isaac and Rebekah, Rebekah finally gave birth, producing twin sons. The pregnancy was apparently quite difficult and painful for Rebekah, reportedly causing her to question why she bothered to continue living. However, one imagines that all such thoughts of discomfort and pain were banished upon the joy of birth. The firstborn was quite reddish in complexion and was also quite hairy, and was thus called Esau. Esau was also known as Edom ("red", because of his ruddy complexion), and Esau is thus associated with being the eponymous ancestor of the Edomites. Reportedly, Esau was also called Seir, the name of the land that the Edomites would later inhabit. Born second, and reportedly clutching onto Esau's heel, was Jacob, whose name is associated with the noun for "heel" and with the verb for "overreach", thus implying someone who is overreaching for first place.[529]

The birth of Esau and Jacob was no doubt a joy to Abraham, who was apparently in his 160th year of life.[530] However, Abraham had his own children from his third and fourth marriages, and one assumes that these children kept Abraham quite active and happy.

The Death of Abraham

Shortly before the death of Abraham, Ismael had journeyed north to visit Isaac in the Negeb, apparently at Beersheba, where Isaac was reportedly living at that time. Following that visit, the two brothers had traveled together to Hebron, in order to visit their father.[531]

It was now Abraham's 175th year of life. Apparently, in celebration of the presence of Ismael and of Isaac, Abraham had gathered his other sons, those from Keturah and those from Hajur, and he had divided his estate among them, and he had imparted to them his last words and blessings. Shortly after that, while Ismael and Isaac were both with him, Abraham died. He was buried by Ismael and by Isaac in the cave of Machpelah, next to his first wife, Sarah.[532]

Postscript # 1 to Abraham in Palestine – V

Genesis uses the occasion of Abraham's division of his estate to make a political statement about the preference of Isaac over the other sons of Abraham. In doing so, *Genesis* claims that Abraham passed off some gifts on Ismael and on the sons of Keturah, and presumably on the sons of Hajur although they are not directly mentioned in the account. Supposedly, Abraham then sent these sons away from him, while keeping Isaac at his side, and bestowing his entire estate on Isaac. This passage in *Genesis* then attempts to justify this reported disparity in the way Abraham treated his sons, by claiming that only Isaac was the son of Abraham's wife, while all the rest of Abraham's sons were out of Abraham's concubines.[533]

This account has to be rejected on at least three counts. Firstly, this rendition is an obvious political ploy to help justify the notion of the "chosen people". Secondly, this account is morally offensive in its portrayal of blatant injustice and unfairness, and in its attribution of such behavior to a prophet of Allah. Thirdly, *Genesis* elsewhere refers to Hagar as having been Abraham's wife[534], as it does in referring to Keturah.[535] In short, the account in *Genesis* of Abraham's last wishes and actions must be rejected.

Postscript # 2 to Abraham in Palestine – V

This modest biography of Abraham has now come to a close. Abraham's life has been traced from Ur to Harran, from Harran to Palestine, from Palestine to Egypt, from Egypt to Palestine, and then back and forth between Palestine and Makkah. Throughout Abraham's wanderings and relocations, two themes have emerged with frequent repetition. Firstly, Abraham was confronted with a series of successive trials, all of which he passed with faith and with honor. Secondly, no matter where he was, and no matter the risk involved, Abraham practiced *Da'wa*. He preached by word and by example to the Akkadians of Ur, to the Horites of Harran, to the Canaanites and Amorites of Palestine, and to the Egyptians in Egypt.

> And remember that Abraham was tried by his Lord with certain commands, which he fulfilled: He said – "I will make thee an Imam to the nations."[536]

Truly, Abraham was *Khalil-ul-Allah,* the Friend of God.[537]

Appendices

Appendix I
Sources of Information

Five general types of sources of information have been used in this book in attempting to construct a biographical sketch of the prophet Abraham. Each type is noted below.

The *Qur'an* and *Sahih Ahadith*

The *Qur'an*

Throughout the Muslim world, the *Qur'an* is honored as the actual words of Allah, revealed by the angel Gabriel (Jibril) to Prophet Muhammad, who then recited those words verbatim to the early Muslims. These revelations were then immediately memorized, and written down by the early Muslim community. As such, for Muslims, there can be no higher authority.

From a secular, historical perspective, the *Qur'an* can be traced in unbroken provenance to the first half of the seventh century CE. The steps in that line of unbroken provenance can be briefly summarized as follows. (1) Prophet Muhammad recited the revelation of Allah, delivered through the angel Gabriel, directly to the early Muslim community. (2) These recitations were memorized verbatim by Muhammad and by others in the Muslim community, and many early Muslims committed the whole of the *Qur'an* to memory. These memorizers of the entire *Qur'an* were known by the title "*Hafez*". (3) In addition, yet during the lifetime of Muhammad, numerous passages of the *Qur'an* were written down on whatever writing material was available, e.g., date leaves, white stone, deer skin, paper, etc. (4) Within about a year of Muhammad's death, i.e., around 633 CE, Abu Bakr, the first Caliph (ruled 632-634 CE), appointed Zayd b. Thabit, a *Hafez* and one of the primary secretaries of the deceased prophet, to produce a written form of the entire *Qur'an*, which was then compiled from the various fragmentary writings and from the *Hafez* in the community. (5) This written copy of the entire *Qur'an* was kept by Abu Bakr until his death in 634 CE, at which time it came into the possession of 'Umar b. Al-Khattab, the second Caliph (ruled 634-644 CE). (6) 'Umar entrusted this copy to his daughter,

Hafsah, the widow of Prophet Muhammad. (7) Utilizing the written *Qur'an* that had been entrusted to Hafsah, a final recension of the *Qur'an* was made by Zayd b. Thabit during the caliphate of 'Uthman b. 'Affan, i.e., 644-656 CE. This final recension was basically a matter of standardizing minor differences in dialect among the various Arabic-speaking Muslims of the time.

Sahih Ahadith

An *Hadith* is a recorded saying or action of Prophet Muhammad, or occasionally of one of Muhammad's immediate companions. A *Sahih Hadith* is one judged by competent *Hadith* scholars to have the highest level of historical authenticity. Such judgments regarding authenticity are based on a variety of factors, including: provenance (the chain of transmission of the oral *Hadith*); the memory skills of those transmitting the *Hadith*; the honesty and integrity of those transmitting the *Hadith*; and the *Hadith*'s consistency with the *Qur'an* and with the principles of Islam. As a source of religious information, Muslims rank *Sahih Ahadith* as second in authority only to the *Qur'an*.

However, it must be acknowledged that numerous bogus *Ahadith* were fabricated throughout time for various reasons. In order to minimize the possibility of utilizing a fabricated *Hadith*, the *Hadith* sources utilized in background research were limited to the collections of Al-Bukhari, Muslim, Abu Dawud, Al-Tirmidhi, and Malik. Malik's collection was compiled in the latter half of the eighth century CE, while Al-Bukhari's, Muslim's, Abu Dawud's, and Al-Tirmidhi's were compiled in the ninth century CE. Of course, all five are based on oral and written traditions reliably tracing to Prophet Muhammad, and to the first half of the seventh century CE, as determined by rigorous scholarly analysis.

Torah

Within the context of Judaeo-Christian scriptures, stories concerning the history of Abraham are basically confined to the *Torah*. Jews, Christians, and Muslims agree that the *Torah* was the book originally revealed by Allah to Prophet Moses. However, a distinction needs to be made between the original *Torah*, i.e., the book revealed to Moses, and the received *Torah*, i.e., the book which has come down to readers at the present time. As presently constituted, the received *Torah* consists of five component parts, which are known in the Christian canon of scriptures as the *Pentateuch*, i.e., the books of *Genesis, Exodus, Leviticus, Numbers,* and *Deuteronomy*. Within the received *Torah*, the story of Abraham is basically confined to the book of *Genesis*.

Compilation of the *Torah*

Literary Strands in *Genesis*: The book of *Genesis* is a later editorial compilation of several, earlier written sources. On the basis of numerous easily identifiable and distinct literary characteristics, formal Biblical scholarship has consistently identified three of these sources as being: (1) *J* (the Yahwistic source; composed about 950 BCE; and characterized by referring to Allah as Yahweh, to Isaac's second son as Israel, to Mount Sinai instead of Mount Horeb, to northern Mesopotamia as Aram-naharaim, to the inhabitants of Palestine as Canaanites, to the first person with the pronoun "*Anokhi*" not "*Ani*", etc.); (2) *E* (the Elohist source; composed around 750 BCE; and characterized by referring to Allah as Elohim, to Isaac's second son as Jacob, to Mount Horeb instead of Mount Sinai, to the inhabitants of Palestine as Amorites, etc.); and (3) *P* (the priestly source; composed between 539 and 400 BCE; and characterized by referring to Allah as Elohim, to northern Mesopotamia as Paddan-aram, to Mt. Sinai instead of Mt. Horeb, to the first person with the pronoun "*Ani*" not "*Anokhi*", etc.) *J, E,* and *P* were probably each based on earlier oral traditions. Additional source material has also been identified in *Genesis*, e.g., chapter 14, but such material is not as easy to characterize as *J, E,* and *P*.[538]

The *D* Strand of *Deuteronomy*: Further, a fourth source, i.e., *D*, can be identified in non-*Genesis* material of the *Torah*, and is the primary source material utilized in *Deuteronomy*. The *D* strand is typically dated by Biblical scholars to the seventh century BCE.[539]

Combining the Strands: The various literary strands identified within the *Torah* were gradually integrated by unknown editors over the centuries. The first such integration appears to have taken place in the eighth century BCE, and involved the integration of the *J* and *E* strands. However, *J, E, D,* and *P* were first compiled into a single written work, i.e., the *Torah*, only around 400 BCE, and it is only to this time that one can date *Genesis* as a composite book.[540]

Versions of the *Torah* [541]

The above discussion may make it appear that what is presently called the *Torah* can be dated back to around 400 BCE. This would be, however, a premature and erroneous conclusion. In that regard, it is noted that at least four different versions of the *Torah* can be demonstrated to have existed by at least the time of Jesus. These four versions include: (1) the proto-Masoretic text of the *Torah*; (2) the Samaritan version of the *Torah*; (3) an Alexandrian version of the *Torah*; and (4) a Palestinian version of the *Torah*.

The Proto-Masoretic Text: The proto-Masoretic text of the *Torah* appears to be heavily influenced by the traditions of those Jews, who were returning to Palestine from their Babylonian exile, between the fifth and fourth centuries BCE. It was this text, which was later perpetuated by the Pharisees, after the fall of Jerusalem in 70 CE, and which evolved into the Masoretic text, which is the Hebrew text used by Jews today. It is interesting to note that the Masoretic text was not fixed into its final form until the evolution of the Tiberian system of vowel markings between 780 and 930 CE. The oldest extant manuscript of the Masoretic text is the Cairo Prophets, written and punctuated by Moses b. Asher in Tiberias, Palestine, in 895 CE.[542] As such, in terms of a written record, the Masoretic text of the *Torah* is actually almost 300 years newer than the *Qur'an*.

The Samaritan Text: The Samaritan version of the *Torah* can probably be dated no earlier than the fourth century BCE, at the time of schism between the Samaritans and the Jews. However, scholars suggest that a more realistic origin for this version of the *Torah* might be in the second century BCE. Unfortunately, most extant manuscripts of the Samaritan version are from the 13th century CE or later. It may be noted that the Samaritan version of the *Torah* differs from the Masoretic text in some 6,000 places, dramatically illustrating the non-standard nature of the *Torah*! In about 2,000 of these places, the Samaritan text agrees with the Alexandrian text.[543]

The Alexandrian Text: The Alexandrian version of the *Torah* was the Hebrew text translated into Greek, which created the Greek *Septuagint* around 280 BCE. The original text of the *Septuagint* no longer exists. Further, numerous revisions of the *Septuagint* were made over the first millennium of its existence, all of which differ in some important details from other versions of the *Torah*. In addition, these different versions of the *Septuagint* also differ among themselves.

The Palestinian Text: The Palestinian version of the *Torah* is known today only through surviving fragments found at Khirbet Qumran on the Dead Sea, which comprise part of the so-called *Dead Sea Scrolls*. These surviving fragments document that the Palestinian version differed in places from the proto-Masoretic text, from the Samaritan version, and from the *Septuagint*.

Summary

Dating the *Torah*: As can be seen, dating of the *Torah* is a precarious enterprise, and in no way can the *Torah* of today be equated with the original book of revelation given to Moses. While some of the oral traditions embedded in the *Torah* go back before the 10th century BCE, the earliest written strand within the *Torah*, i.e., *J*, can be dated no earlier than around 950 BCE. Further, *Genesis*, as a whole, did not exist before the late fifth century BCE. By the time of Christ, at least four different versions of the *Torah* were in use, each differing from the others in many places. Further, the Masoretic text may not have been finalized until almost the 10th century CE, the current Samaritan text appears to exist only in manuscripts dating to the 13th century CE, the *Septuagint* can be shown to have evolved throughout the first 1,000 years of its existence, and the Palestinian version exists only in fragments.

Given the above concerns, it is noted that the present book utilizes *The Holy Bible: New Revised Standard Version* as the most authoritative reconstruction and translation of what was probably the original reading of the original Hebrew version of *Genesis*. However, this must be seen as being an obviously inferior substitute for the original *Torah*.

The *Genesis* Strands: Given the previous discussion on the origins of the received *Torah*, and especially given the discussion of the literary strands within the book of *Genesis*, it should be clear that anyone attempting to use *Genesis* as historical data must follow the following procedure: (1) divide the *Genesis* account into its various literary strands, i.e., *J, E, P,* and unknown; (2) examine each strand separately; and (3) contrast each strand with the other strands. The necessity of this approach can be illustrated by two examples.

Firstly, consider *Genesis* 12: 10-20 (*J* strand material) with *Genesis* 20: 1-17 (*E* strand material). The former narrative details the story of the pharaoh of Egypt taking Sarah from Abraham, after Abraham had allegedly falsely claimed that Sarah was his sister. The latter narrative details a story of Abimelech, king of Gerar, taking Sarah from Abraham, after Abraham had allegedly falsely claimed that Sarah was his sister. If one does not separate the *Genesis* account into its component literary strands, the reader concludes that Abraham twice past off his wife as being his sister, first with the pharaoh, and then subsequently with Abimelech. However, by dividing the *Genesis* story into its literary strands, and then looking at each strand separately, one easily sees that the *E* account of Abraham and Abimelech is merely a variation of the *J* account of Abraham and the pharaoh.

Secondly, because the original compiler cut and spliced information from *J, E,* and *P,* in order to create *Genesis* as a single literary work, failure to separate the narrative material of *Genesis* into its component parts runs the risk of grossly misinterpreting the sequence of events in Abraham's life. In that regard, consider the following hypothetical sequence of narrative material in *Genesis: J1; E1; J2; P1; J3; P2;* and *E2.* If the reader of *Genesis* does not divide the material into its component literary strands, the obvious conclusion to be drawn by that reader is that the *J1* precedes *E1,* which precedes *J2,* which precedes *P1,* which precedes *J3,* which precedes *P2,* which precedes *E2.* However, as soon as one separates the *Genesis* account into its literary strands, one realizes that the most that can be concluded regarding sequence of events is that: (1) *J1* precedes *J2,* which precedes *J3;* (2) *E1* precedes *E2;* and (3) *P1* precedes *P2.*

Other Canonical Jewish Scriptures

At times in this book, the author has made use of canonical Jewish scripture, which is technically not part of the *Torah.* In that regard, it is briefly noted here that canonical Jewish scripture has traditionally been divided into three main categories: (1) the *Torah*[544], i.e., the law, also known as the *Pentateuch* in the Christian *Old Testament* of the *Bible*; (2) the *Nevi'im*[545], i.e., the prophets; and (3) the *Ketuvim*[546], i.e., the writings. The following chart lists the Jewish scripture from the *Nevi'im* and the *Ketuvim* that have been used in this book.

Table 4
Referenced Books from the *Nevi'im* and *Ketuvim*

Book	Composition
Ezekiel	Sixth century BCE or later [547]
Isaiah	Eighth century BCE or later [548]
Jeremiah	Sixth century BCE [549]
Joshua	Seventh or sixth century BCE [550]
Judges	Seventh or sixth century BCE [551]
Micah	Eighth to sixth century BCE [552]
Nehemiah	Fourth century BCE [553]
Psalms	Cannot be reliably dated [554]
I Chronicles	Fourth century BCE [555]
II Chronicles	Fourth century BCE [556]
I Kings	Sixth century BCE [557]
II Kings	Sixth century BCE [558]
I Samuel	Sixth century BCE [559]

Non-Canonical Jewish Scripture

After the end of the Jewish canon of scripture, a large body of Jewish religious writing was developed in the last two centuries BCE. This literary corpus has been traditionally divided into the *Apocrypha* and the *Pseudepigrapha*. The word "pseudepigrapha" is from the Greek, and means "false writings". This corpus of literature gets its name from the fact that the authorship of the various books comprising the *Pseudepigrapha* was falsely attributed by their writers to famous Biblical characters, who had died centuries or even millennia before the books were actually written, e.g., *The Books of Adam and Eve, I Enoch, The Testaments of the Twelve Patriarchs, The Assumption of Moses, II Enoch, The Psalms of Solomon*, etc. Within the *Pseudepigrapha*, there is one book in particular that purports to report narrative material concerning Abraham, specifically including a great deal of chronological information. This is the book of *Jubilees*, also known as *The Little Genesis* and *The Apocalypse of Moses*.

Traditionally, it has been believed that *Jubilees* was written by a member of the Pharisaic branch of Judaism, at some point in the last half of the second century BCE, i.e., during the reign of Hyrcanus as Jewish high priest, but with much of its material coming from earlier oral and written sources, e.g., *I Enoch* and *The Book of Noah*. However, more recent analysis, based primarily on the prevalence of *Jubilees* among the *Dead Sea Scrolls*, suggests an origin in the third century BCE.[560] The authorship of *Jubilees* was falsely attributed to Moses, who was supposedly writing down information dictated to him by an angel. While the narrative material within *Jubilees* appears to have a rather weaker historical provenance than that of the received *Torah*, the chronological data, while substantially more complete than that found in the *P* strand of *Genesis*, is often supported by the *P* strand of *Genesis*. As such, the author does make occasional use of this chronological information from *Jubilees*.

A second book from the *Pseudepigrapha*, which was utilized solely for providing information on the marriage of Prophet Lot, was the *Genesis Apocryphon*, which dates to the second or third centuries BCE.[561] The *Genesis Apocryphon* survives only as a preserved fragment in the so-called *Dead Sea Scrolls*.

Archaeology and Middle Eastern History

Unfortunately, it must be reported that the sciences of archaeology and ancient Middle Eastern history have so far uncovered nothing that can be definitely identified with Abraham. However, these sources are used in the current book to provide context regarding Abraham's life, and to serve as a springboard for speculation as to the time of Abraham.

Priority of Sources

Having spent some time describing the sources of information used in this book, it is incumbent upon the author to delineate the manner in which such sources are being utilized. As a Muslim, the author accepts the *Qur'an* as the literal and revealed words of Allah. As such, in all matters pertaining to this book, the *Qur'an* is taken as the final, authoritative source. However, the author acknowledges that it is unrealistic to expect that the *Qur'an* would include all historical information about a person, even about a prophet. As such, *Sahih Ahadith* and the information contained in *Genesis* are used to supplement the information contained within the *Qur'an*. Occasionally, information from other Jewish scripture, from *Jubilees*, and from certain historical texts is also utilized. In this way, the goal is to arrive at a synthesis of information, especially the information contained in the Islamic and Judaeo-Christian traditions, which is still consistent with, and in no way contradicts, the *Qur'an*. The sciences of archaeology and ancient Middle Eastern history are then utilized in constructing a general framework, and in providing specific, contextual detail.

Appendix II
Chronology

Any attempt to present a biography of Abraham must wrestle with the issue of chronology. When did Abraham live? What was going on in the world around him at that time? By reviewing the information available from various sources, the following attempts to provide an answer to those questions.

The *Qur'an* and *Sahih Ahadith*

Neither the *Qur'an* nor *Sahih Ahadith* provide any firm chronological dating for the life of Abraham. However, there may be a chronological clue in *Surah Al-Baqarah* of the *Qur'an*, the relevant portion of which is quoted immediately below:

> Hast thou not turned thy vision to one who disputed with Abraham about his Lord, because Allah had granted him power? Abraham said: "My Lord is He Who giveth life and death." He said: "I give life and death." Said Abraham: "But it is Allah that causeth the sun to rise from the east: do thou then cause him to rise from the west?" Thus was he confounded who (in arrogance) rejected faith. Nor doth Allah give guidance to a people unjust.[562]

If one could identify this unnamed and arrogant despot who disputed with Abraham, then perhaps the historical and archaeological records could identify the time of Abraham by cross-reference to Abraham's antagonist. While neither the *Qur'an* nor the *Sahih Ahadith* utilized in this book provide direct identification, several Muslim commentators and authors have speculated that this individual is Nimrod (Nimrud or Namrud), a king of ancient Mesopotamia, whose name in Hebrew means "we will rebel" or "let us rebel". Likewise, Jewish *aggadic* tales identify the king who was Abraham's antagonist as being Nimrod. Who was Nimrod? There are no archaeological records that identify any king of ancient Mesopotamia named Nimrod. However, through two different chains of transmitters[563], *Al-Tabari* notes that Nimrod was said to have been one of the three or four kings in history to have ruled the whole world. One understands from the *Al-Tabari* material that Nimrod was said to have ruled the entire known world of his time.[564]

The speculation regarding Abraham's antagonist being Nimrod draws some indirect support from the Judaeo-Christian scriptures, where Nimrod's name occurs four times.

> Cush became the father of Nimrod; he was the first on earth to become a mighty warrior. He was a mighty hunter before the Lord; therefore it is said, "Like Nimrod a mighty hunter before the Lord." The beginning of his kingdom was Babel, Erech, and Accad, all of them in the land of Shinar. From that land he went into Assyria, and built Nineveh, Rehobothir, Calah, and Resen between Nineveh and Calah; that is a great city.[565]

> Cush became the father of Nimrod; he was the first to be a mighty one on the earth.[566]

> They shall rule the land of Assyria with the sword, and the land of Nimrod with the drawn sword; they shall rescue us from the Assyrians if they come into our land or tread within our border.[567]

Cush is used in two ways in the *Torah*. On the one hand, Cush can refer to the region now known as Ethiopia. On the other hand, Cush (used for Kassite) can refer to Mesopotamia. As such, all three Biblical references can be read as referring to Nimrod as a Mesopotamian leader of renown. Perhaps more importantly, the 10th century BCE *J* strand material of *Genesis*, the earliest of the Biblical references to mention Nimrod, specifically links Nimrod with the Sumerian (Shinar) and Akkadian (Accad) Empires, a point which will become increasingly important as we attempt to identify the chronological dates to be associated with Abraham.

The *Torah* and Biblical References

The *Torah* and other Judaeo-Christian scripture provide three points of departure for attempting to date the life of Abraham. First, there is the issue of where Abraham initially lived. Second, there is the issue of contemporaries of Abraham mentioned in the *Torah*. Third, there is genealogical information that can be combined with other dating methods. In what follows, each method is considered in turn.

Abraham's initial Residence

In order to make the tenth century BCE *J* strand closely harmonize with the *P* strand of the sixth or fifth century BCE, it was maintained in a later gloss of or editorial insertion into the *J* strand of *Genesis*, that the original home of Abraham was "Ur of the Chaldeans"[568], an area in southern Mesopotamia (southern Iraq). This can be seen as a later insertion simply by considering the fact that: (A) the *J* strand traces to the 10th century BCE; and (B) the Chaldeans were not in possession of Ur until the 8th century BCE.   Ur is also mentioned as the original home of Abraham in the *P* strand of *Genesis*.

> Terah took his son Abram and his grandson Lot son of Haran, and his daughter-in-law Sarai, his son Abram's wife, and they went out together from Ur of the Chaldeans to go into the land of Canaan; but when they came to Haran, they settled there.[569]

Ur is also mentioned as the original home of Abraham in Judaeo-Christian scripture that is not found in the *Torah*, but which is heavily associated with the *P* strand of the *Torah*.

> You are the Lord, the God who chose Abram and brought him out of Ur of the Chaldeans and gave him the name Abraham...[570]

Disregarding later editorial insertions and glosses, the *J* strand of *Genesis* basically associates Abraham with Harran, an area in northern Mesopotamia in what is now southeastern Turkey. However, the *J* strand picks up the story of Abraham as an adult man, and there is nothing in the *J* strand, which specifically contradicts Ur as being the original home of Abraham. As such, the author accepts the *Genesis* account of Abraham originating in southern Mesopotamia, in the vicinity of Ur, and as having migrated as an adult man to Harran. This fixes the quest for the historical Abraham to Mesopotamia, when looking for archaeological and historical markers to provide a chronological dating for his life.

Associates of Abraham

Few personal names are mentioned in the *Torah* in association with Abraham. Individuals such as Lot, Sarah, Hagar, Ismael, Isaac, Keturah, and Midian present one with the same dating problems as does Abraham. Other individual names associated in the *Torah* with Abraham are basically confined to the 14th chapter of *Genesis*, which, as noted before, does not conform to *J, E,* or *P* narrative material.[571] These names are basically a king list, and are listed in Table 5.

Table 5
The Associates of Abraham

King's Name	Land or City
Amraphel	Shinar (Sumeria)
Arioch	Ellasar
Chedorlaomer	Elam
Tidal	Goim
Bera	Sodom
Birsha	Gomorrah
Shinab	Admah
Shemeber	Zeboiim
Melchizedek	Salem (Jerusalem)

Unfortunately, there is no way to identify the Canaanite kings on the above list with any known historical figures. While attempts have been made to identify the non-Canaanite kings in this list, e.g., Amraphel with Hammurabi, Aroich with Arriwuku (a king of the city of Mari on the middle Euphrates), Ellasar with Larsa in lower Mesopotamia or with the Hurrian city of Alziya, Chedorlaomer with the Elamite name Kudur-Lagamar, and Tidal with Tudhalias (a Hittite king), these identifications are tenuous at best, and frequently mutually exclusive.

In short, the associates and contemporaries of Abraham mentioned in the Judaeo-Christian scriptures are of little or no assistance in dating the life of Abraham.

Genealogy and Dating

A somewhat more promising strategy is to combine genealogical information from the *Torah* with other dates mentioned in the Judaeo-Christian scriptures. In order to utilize this procedure, one needs a firm anchoring point, from which one can begin the chronological process. One such anchoring point would appear to be the reign of King Solomon, peace be upon him.

Establishing the reign of King Solomon: Almost all scholars place the 40-year reign of King Solomon as occurring in the 10th century BCE, although there is some minor disagreement as to the exact dates involved. Various estimates of the Solomonic reign have included 992-952 BCE, 977-937 BCE, 973-933 BCE, 971-931 BCE, 970-931 BCE, 965-926 BCE, 962-922 BCE, and 961-922 BCE. As can be seen, all but one of the estimates are within a 16-year margin of error. For purposes of this discussion, the author will assume that Solomon began his reign in 970 BCE.

Establishing the dates for the sojourn in Egypt: Having established the start of the reign of King Solomon, one can begin working backward in the chronological sequence, utilizing information found in the *Torah* and in other Judaeo-Christian scripture. In that regard, the following chronological reference from *I Kings* is noted:

> In the four hundred eightieth year after the Israelites came out of the land of Egypt, in the fourth year of Solomon's reign over Israel, in the month of Ziv, which is the second month, he began to build the house of the Lord.[572]

If one were to assume the dating process from this passage is at least approximately correct, the Israelite exodus from Egypt would have been around 1,446 BCE. If the exodus from Egypt began around 1,446 BCE, then the following chronological reference from *Exodus* becomes important.

> The time the Israelites had lived in Egypt was four hundred thirty years.[573]

Again, assuming that this dating is at least approximately accurate, this would place the start of the Israelite sojourn in Egypt at about 1,876 BCE.

Establishing the time of the Patriarchs: According to *Genesis*, the Israelite sojourn in Egypt began during the second year of the great famine. Further, *Genesis* states that eight years before the start of the Israelite sojourn in Egypt, Joseph, peace be upon him, had became vizier of Egypt at age 30. As such, it would appear that Joseph was born about 1,914 BCE. Now, according to *Genesis*, Jacob lived in Egypt for 17 years before dying at age 147. Assuming Jacob entered Egypt in 1,876 BCE, i.e., at the start of the Israelite sojourn in Egypt, he would have been born around 130 years earlier, i.e., around 2,006 BCE. Continuing on, *Genesis* notes that Jacob was born when Isaac was 60 years old, placing the birth of Isaac around 2,066 BCE. Finally, *Genesis* states that Abraham was 100 years old when Isaac was born, suggesting that Abraham was born around 2,166 BCE.[574]

Summary

The above chronology is a succession of "if-then" statements, with the accuracy of each such statement contingent upon the approximate accuracy of the dates given in the *Torah* and in *I Kings*. Having stated this caution, and using these dates as approximates, Table 6 summarizes the current findings.

Table 6

The Chronology

Event	Date
Start of temple	966 BCE
Start of Solomon's reign	970 BCE
The exodus from Egypt	1,446 BCE
Start of sojourn in Egypt	1,876 BCE
Joseph becomes vizier	1,884 BCE
Joseph is born	1,914 BCE
Jacob is born	2,006 BCE
Isaac is born	2,066 BCE
Abraham is born	2,166 BCE

Given a margin of error of 100 years either way, it would thus appear that Abraham was born sometime between 2,266 and 2,066 BCE. Similar estimates have been suggested by others, too.[575]

Archaeological and Historical Records

Having identified lower (Ur) and upper (Harran) Mesopotamia as the regions in which one needs to make the initial search for the Abraham of history, one needs to consider the history of this region in some detail. However, before beginning this discussion, a word of caution is in order.

Problems exist in providing firm archaeological and historical dates for Mesopotamia prior to the middle of the second millennium BCE. For example, one finds estimates of the time of start of the Akkadian dynasty ranging from 2,800 to 2,334 BCE, and even to 2,264 BCE. Differences of similar magnitude can be shown for dating other events in ancient Mesopotamia. For example, the reign of Hammurabi has been variously estimated as 2,130-2,088 BCE, 1,792-1,750 BCE, as around 1,750 BCE, and as beginning around either 1,700 BCE or 1,565 BCE.[576] Generally speaking, as archaeological evidence has mounted over time, the dating of events in ancient Mesopotamia has been pushed ever more recently in time. Thus, the accumulation of archaeological evidence over time allows for refinement of, if not actual correction of, prior dating systems. Nonetheless, it must still be recognized that archaeological dating of events in ancient Mesopotamia is not fixed, and is not absolutely certain.

With the above caution in mind, it should be noted that the present book reports the chronological estimates of Edzard et al.[577] for events in ancient Mesopotamia. However, Rohl's dating of Hammurabi[578], would suggest that the Edzard et al. dates may be placing events about 200 years before they actually occurred.

Having urged due caution in blindly accepting any one chronological system for dating events in ancient Mesopotamia, and having stated the chronological system being used in this book, it is time to turn to a general overview of the history of ancient Mesopotamia. In doing so, this book will focus on successive chronological periods.

The Ubaidians

The area of southern Mesopotamia known as Sumer was first settled by the Ubaidians. Little is known about this people. However, it is known that they were a non-Semitic people, who moved into Sumer between 4,500 and 4,000 BCE. They established a village at Al-Ubaid, drained the marshes for agricultural production, developed a trade network, and established such cottage industries as weaving, leatherwork, metalwork, masonry, and pottery.

This era can be categorically rejected as the time of Abraham. First, the Ubaidian period is much too early to accommodate Abraham. Second, Abraham was a Semite, as illustrated by: (A) *Genesis*[579], which identifies Abraham as a descendant of Shem, the son of Noah; and

(B) linguistic evidence, which illustrates that Abraham's descendants spoke Semitic languages (Hebrew for the descendants of Isaac, and Arabic for the descendants of Ismail). However, during the Ubaidian period, the Semites had yet to enter southern Mesopotamia.

The Sumerians

About 3,300 BCE, the non-Semitic Sumerians arrived in southern Mesopotamia, probably coming from Anatolia (Turkey). They gave their name to that region of southern Mesopotamia known as Sumer, and the Sumerian language became the primary language of the area, in part due to the fact that the Sumerians apparently invented writing. By the start of the third millennium BCE, the Sumerians had established at least 12 city-states in southern Mesopotamia, including Kish, Erich, Ur, Sippar, Akshak, Larak, Nippur, Adab, Umma, Lagash, Bad-tibira, and Larsa. Each of these city-states was defended by walls, and ruled over surrounding villages and land. Etana, a king of Kish during its first dynasty (about 2,800 BCE), was the first person to unite the separate city-states of Sumer under a centralized rule. Following the first dynasty of Kish, various of the Sumerian city-states established successive dynasties that ruled over southern Mesopotamia.

The Sumerians left a profound legacy in southern Mesopotamia. This legacy outlived the Sumerian people, who ceased to exist as a separate ethnic group after the Amorite invasion of southern Mesopotamia around 1,900 BCE. The Sumerian legacy included: cuneiform writing and epic narratives; architectural innovations (the column, arch, vault, and dome); increased specialization of the work force (sculptors, seal engravers, smiths, carpenters, shipbuilders, potters, and workers in reeds and textiles) and agricultural irrigation; etc. The Sumerian era ends with their being first conquered by the Elamites (around 2,530-2,450 BCE), and subsequently conquered by the Akkadians (around 2,334 BCE).

The Sumerian period must also be rejected as a setting for the historical Abraham, both because the period appears to be a little too early in time, and because the Sumerians were a non-Semitic people.

The Akkadians

The Akkadians were a Semitic people, who originated in the Arabian Peninsula, who spoke a Northern Peripheral Semitic language, and who migrated into southern Mesopotamia by at least the early years of the third millennium BCE. Originally, they were a nomadic, pastoral people, whose way of life was based on the herding of sheep and goats, which defined their nomadic lifestyle as one of frequent changes in pasture areas, without ever being more than one day's travel from water. Over time, the Akkadians, or at least a substantial portion of them, became urbanized, and adopted the Sumerian cuneiform writing system.

While some of the kings of the first dynasty of Kish may have had Akkadian names, the Akkadians first rose to real prominence in Mesopotamia when they established their dynasty at Akkad (Accad or Agade) around 2,334 BCE. The Akkadian dynasty, while lasting only about 200 years, represented the first true empire in Mesopotamia. Of note, this empire stretched from the Persian Gulf on the south, to Asia Minor in the north, and included Iraq, Syria, Lebanon, and parts of Turkey and Iran. (It may also have included, or at least had in its sphere of influence, Egypt, Ethiopia, and Cyprus.) This empire was at its zenith under its first five kings: Sargon I (ruled 2,334-2,278 BCE), Rimush, Manishtusu, Naram-Sin, and Shar-kali-sharri (ruled 2,217-2,193 BCE). Thereafter, the dynasty of Akkad continued to exist for another 39 years, but its power as an empire had been broken.

Two kings of Akkad are specially noteworthy, because they are candidates for identification with Nimrod, reportedly the first king to rule the entire known world[580], and the possible antagonist of Abraham mentioned in *Qur'an* 2: 258.[581] These two kings are Sargon I (died 2,278 BCE) and his grandson, Naram-Sin (died 2,217 BCE). These two kings are reviewed in turn.

Sargon I (ruled 2,334-2,278 BCE) was said to have had humble origins, having been abandoned as a baby, and having been raised by a common gardener. Nonetheless, through his own efforts, he rose in rank to being the cupbearer of the king of Kish. When Lugalzaggisi, the last king of the third dynasty of Uruk, who had managed to unite the city-states of Sumer under his control, was finally defeated, Sargon I somehow managed to gain control of southern Mesopotamia. He renamed himself Sargon (*Sharru-kin* = rightful king; Sargon's actual name is unknown), began a vigorous military campaign that eventually created the Akkadian Empire, and built a new capital city (Akkad, Accad, or Agade, since destroyed and never uncovered by archaeologists). The magnitude of his empire has already been mentioned above. However, over and above his actual empire holdings, it is noted that he established regular trade and commercial activities with such far-flung areas as the Indus Valley, the coast of Oman, Cappadocia, Crete, and Greece.

Sargon obviously had a direct and personal interest in the temple of the Akkadian moon god, i.e., Sin, at Ur, as he appointed his daughter, Princess Enheduanna, to be the high priestess there. In doing so, he was the first of the Mesopotamian rulers to make his daughter the high priestess of Sin at Ur. Sargon later added to Enheduanna's duties, by giving her an additional appointment as high priestess of the temple of Anu, the Akkadian god of the sky, at Warka (Ereck or Uruk). Throughout her appointment at the temple of Sin at Ur, Enheduanna devoted her energies to elevating the perceived status of Ishtar (the goddess of Venus) in the Akkadian pantheon, and eventually succeeded in having Ishtar seen as the consort of Anu. Enheduanna was also a poet, and her poem *Nin-Me-Sar-Ra* (*The Mistress of All Divine Codes*) is one of the oldest poems, which has ever been discovered, which bears the name of its author. This poem is a tribute to Ishtar (known as Inanna in the Sumerian language), and excerpts of it are quoted below.

> The invocation of Inanna.
> Oh, my lady, the Inanna, the great, great gods,
> Fluttering like bats, fly off from before you to the clefts.
> They, who dare not walk in your terrible glance,
> who dare not proceed before your terrible countenance.
> Who can temper your raging heart?
> Your malevolent heart is beyond tempering.
> Lady (who) soothes the reigns, lady (who) gladdens the heart,
> Lady supreme over the land, who has (ever) denied (you) homage? [582]

The fourth emperor of Akkad, Naram-Sin, is also of some special interest. While ruling over the vast Akkadian Empire, he took the royal titles of "king of the four quarters of the earth" and "god of Akkad". Following the example of his grandfather, Sargon, he made his daughter, Enmenanna, the high priestess of the moon god, i.e., Sin, at Ur, which continued to be one of the major cult cities in ancient Mesopotamia for the worship of the moon. His pride and arrogance apparently knew no bounds, and the epic poem *The Fall of Akkad* attributed the eventual end of the Akkadian dynasty to events stemming from these personality defects in Naram-Sin. Naram-Sin died around 2,217 BCE.

The Akkadian period is a very viable candidate for being the historical period in which Abraham lived. Issues favoring the Akkadian period include the following facts: (A) the Akkadians were a Semitic people, as was Abraham; (B) the period of Akkadian rule (approximately 2,334-2,154 BCE, or perhaps up to around 200 years later) compares favorably with the previous, Biblical-based estimate of the year of Abraham's birth (2,166 BCE); and (C) both Sargon I and Naram-Sin appear to be candidates to be identified with Nimrod, the possible antagonist of Abraham mentioned in *Qur'an* 2:258. Of the two candidates to be identified with Nimrod, Naram-Sin provides a slightly better chronological match with the Biblical-based estimate of Abraham's year of birth. In addition, Naram-Sin's personality traits of overbearing pride and arrogance are a good fit with the description of Abraham's antagonist given in *Qur'an* 2: 258. Further, Naram-Sin's royal title of "king of the four quarters of the earth" and the geographical extent of his empire fit well with the *Al-Tabari* material claiming that Nimrod was the first king to rule the entire known world. Finally, Naram-Sin's appointment of his daughter, Enmenanna, as priestess of the moon god temple at Ur, indicates his close association with an astral polytheism utilizing idols, i.e., the very type of worship specifically rejected by Abraham, presumably at Ur.

> So also did We show Abraham the power and the laws of the heavens and the earth that he might (with understanding) have certitude. When the night covered him over, he saw a star: he said: "this is my Lord." But when it set, he said: "I love not those that set." When he saw the moon rising in splendor, he said: "This is my Lord." But when the moon set, he said: "Unless my Lord guide me, I shall surely be among those who go astray. When he saw the sun rising in splendor, he said: "This is my Lord; this is the greatest (of all)." But when the sun set, he said: "O my people! I am indeed free from your (guilt) of giving partners to Allah. For me, I have set my face, firmly and truly, towards Him Who created the heavens and the earth, and never shall I give partners to Allah."[583]

It must be admitted that the following are all speculations: (A) Abraham was born around 2,166 BCE; (B) Abraham's antagonist was

Nimrod; and (C) Nimrod was Naram-Sin (rule ending between 2,217 and 2,017 BCE).[584] Nonetheless, it is the province of the historian to offer informed speculation, so long as that speculation is clearly marked as such. Given current information, such speculation appears to be feasible, and there appears to be no reason to reject the earlier Biblical-based estimate that Abraham was born around 2,166 BCE, which time is believed to have corresponded with the actual chronology of the reign of Naram-Sin of Akkad.

Ur–III

Separating the Akkadian period from the Amorite period is the third dynasty of Ur (2,112-2,004 BCE). Five kings ruled during this period, including Ur-Nammu (the first king to take the title of "king of Sumer and Akkad"), Shulgi (the first king to revive Naram-Sin's title of "king of the four quarters of the earth"), Amar-Su'ena, Shu'Sin, and Ibbi-Sin. The population of southern Mesopotamia during this time continued to be predominantly that of Sumerian and Akkadian, although some Amorites had moved into the area.

The time of the third dynasty of Ur is not inconsistent with the Biblical-based estimate for the time of Abraham. However, despite the title taken by Ur-Nammu and the title revived by Shulgi, the third dynasty of Ur was a far cry from a sprawling empire. In fact, the third dynasty of Ur was basically confined to southern and middle Mesopotamia. Quite simply, within the five kings of the third dynasty of Ur, there does not appear to be a suitable candidate to be identified with Abraham's antagonist as mentioned in the *Qur'an* 2:258.

The Amorites

Like the Akkadians before them, the Amorites (Amurru) were a Semitic people, who originated in the Arabian Peninsula. However, unlike the Akkadians, who spoke a Northern Peripheral Semitic language, the Amorites spoke a Northern Central Semitic language, which was more similar to Canaanite, Ugaritic, Pheonician-Punic, Aramaic, Moabite, and Hebrew, than it was to Akkadian or to Arabic (a Southern Central Semitic language).

Migrating out of the Arabian Peninsula, the Amorites originally moved north into Palestine and Syria, where they displaced non-Semitic cave dwellers starting around the 23rd century BCE. It was only after stabilizing their hold on Palestine and Syria, that they later began a migration into northern Mesopotamia, and then down into southern Mesopotamia. Because they came into Mesopotamia from the west, they were called Amorites, i.e., Westerners.

The Amorites were present in southern Mesopotamia by at least the end of the Akkadian period, although they would have formed a small, nomadic minority of the population. During the third dynasty of Ur (2,112-2,004 BCE) some Amorites had become urbanized, and were already in administrative positions in Ur, although it is likely that a majority of them were still leading their nomadic, pastoral lifestyle.

By about 2,000 to 1,800 BCE, the Amorites were dominant throughout Mesopotamia, and helped overthrow the third dynasty of Ur. They established the ancient Babylonian dynasty, which finally unified all of Mesopotamia under their sixth king, Hammurabi (1,792-1750 BCE). Hammurabi's kingdom included southern and northern Mesopotamia, Syria, and parts of Palestine. His kingdom was large, but certainly not as large as the prior Akkadian Empire. The Babylonian dynasty fell by about 1,600 BCE.

The Amorite period appears to be a little late to accommodate the birth of Abraham. However, there have certainly been scholars who have argued for this late date for Abraham, in part because of two linguistic considerations. The first linguistic argument for Abraham having originated in the Amorite period is that the names Abamram (a variant of Abraham) and Jacob-el (a variant of Jacob) were known to be in use in southern Mesopotamia during the mid-20th century BCE. The second linguistic argument is that Amoritic, being a Semitic language of the Northern Central Group, is more similar to Hebrew, than is Akkadian, which is in the Northern Peripheral Group of Semitic languages.

However, there are counter arguments to both of the above linguistic arguments for Abraham having lived in the Amorite period. (1) While it is true that variations of the names of Abraham and Jacob can be shown to have been common in the Amorite period, their occurrence was early enough in the Amorite period that it was still quite possible that the bearers of those names were Akkadians. Further, it is also the case that some names associated with the immediate family of Abraham, e.g., Jacob's later name of Israel, can be found in the Akkadian period of

Sargon I.[585] (2) The greater similarity between Amoritic and Hebrew, than between Akkadian and Hebrew, need not be given much significance. Hebrew did not evolve into a separate Northern Central Group language until about the 13th century BCE. Assuming that Abraham spoke Akkadian, and that he was born around 2,166 BCE, allows almost 900 years for the original Akkadian of Abraham, and of his descendants through Isaac, to have been either: (A) replaced by the Amoritic or Canaanite languages, which are North Central Group languages similar to Hebrew; or (B) so influenced by Amoritic and Canaanite as to have evolved into Hebrew.

In short, notwithstanding the circumstantial, linguistic evidence noted above for Abraham to have lived during the Amorite period, the linguistic evidence is hardly definitive. The Amorite period appears to be too late in time to accommodate Abraham, and the Amorite period does not provide a viable candidate to accomodate Abraham's antagonist as portrayed in *Qur'an* 2:258.

Summary and Conclusions

Given the available information derived from the *Qur'an* and *Sahih Ahadith,* from the *Torah* and Biblical references, and from archaeological and historical records, it appears likely that Abraham was born during or slightly before the reign of Naram-Sin, the fourth king of Akkad. This would place Abraham at Ur during the middle of the 22nd century BCE. While the above is far from a certainty, the information and reasoning justifying that selection have been previously presented, and that selection has been the working hypothesis throughout this book.

Appendix III
The People or Tribe of Abraham

Within this treatise, Abraham has previously been identified as being the son of Azar of the clan of Terah, and as being a Semite. However, no tribal identification for Abraham has been determined, other than to state that Abraham was a Semite. Assuming that Abraham was a Semite, five different tribal affiliations have been suggested.

The Hebrew Hypothesis

At least one passage in *Genesis* identifies Abraham as having been a Hebrew (Habiru or Apiru).[586] However, the question remains as to what is meant by "Hebrew"? Is it an actual tribal identification? Does it signify something else? To answer these questions, we must examine the origin of the word "Hebrew". In that regard, at least three etiologic possibilities have been posited. We will examine each of these three theories in turn.

Eber as the Eponym of the Hebrews

Traditional interpretation of *Genesis* has identified the Hebrew people as being all of the descendants of Eber[587], with Eber being identified as the son of Shelah and the father of Peleg and Joktan (Qahtan).[588] In this way, Eber becomes an eponym for an entire people. With *Genesis* identifying Peleg as a son of Eber, one can quickly trace through *Genesis* to find Peleg being the father of Reu, the father of Serug, the father of Nahor, the father of Terah, the father of Abraham.[589] Thus, if one accepts the identification of Eber as being the father of the Hebrews, and if one accepts the account in *Genesis* of the genealogy between Eber and Abraham, Abraham can be said to be a Hebrew.

However, before too readily accepting the identification of Eber as being the father of the Hebrews, one needs to consider two factors. Firstly, Hebrew did not even evolve into a separate Semitic language of the North Central Group until the 13th century BCE.[590] Was there an ethnic Hebrew group over 900 years before there was a Hebrew language? Secondly, *Genesis* identifies Eber as being the father of Joktan (Qahtan), as well as of Peleg.[591] As *Genesis* further identifies Joktan (Qahtan) as being the father of the southern Arab peoples[592], one is left with both the 'Adnani (via Ismael, the son of Abraham) and Qahtani (via Joktan) Arab peoples as being Hebrews. In short, the Hebrew tribe becomes so broadly defined as to include both great roots of the Arab people, meaning that all Arabs are Hebrews. Clearly, given such a consideration, the identification of the Hebrew people with the descendants of Eber becomes so overly inclusive that it renders this presumption meaningless. One is thus forced to look for other explanations for the term "Hebrew".

To Cross the River

It has been suggested that the word "Hebrew" is derived from the word "*Eber*" ("*Ever*"), meaning "the other side". Given this derivation, it has been maintained that the word "Hebrew" refers to the person from the other side of the Euphrates River, and thus originally referred to Abraham when he crossed the Euphrates River in the course of his migration through the Fertile Crescent from east to west. The problem with this formulation is that the word "Habiru" appears too early and in too many places in the archaeological record to be derived from Abraham himself. Further, if the word "Hebrew" were to have its origin with Abraham, it then gives us no information as to Abraham's actual tribal identification. Again, one is forced to look elsewhere.

Hebrew as a non-ethnic term

There is a third hypothesis about the derivation of the word "Hebrew". It is based upon the derivation of "Hebrew" from "'*Abhar*", meaning "to move or to pass"[593]. However, unlike the second hypothesis, this formulation posits that the word "Hebrew" was applied to a whole class of people, regardless of ethnic derivation. In short, the Hebrews were any nomadic, wandering people, i.e., anyone who would be considered foreign, uncouth, an outsider, and uncivilized in the eyes of the speaker. This is the majority hypothesis among contemporary Biblical scholars.

Given the above, the word "Hebrew" can be seen as a derogatory and contemptuous term implying: a low socio-economic status; a landless class of people; a foreigner; an uncouth and uncivilized people; and nomadic wanderers. A few traces of this pejorative meaning can still be discovered in the *Torah*.

> They served him by himself, and them by themselves, and the Egyptians who ate with him by themselves, because the Egyptians could not eat with the Hebrews, for that is an abomination to the Egyptians.[594]

In the above verse, the Egyptians would not even consider eating with Joseph, the son of Jacob, even though he was vizier over them.

Conclusions

Current evidence suggests that the term "Hebrew" did not originally imply ethnic or tribal affiliation. Rather, it was a term of contempt, which was applied to a whole class of people, which did not share any ethnic heritage. It was only many centuries after Abraham lived and died that the word "Hebrew" came to be specifically associated with the members of the tribes of Israel. As such, one must reject the ethnic or tribal designation of Abraham being a Hebrew.

The Akkadian Hypothesis

Having dispensed with the Hebrew hypothesis, one can turn next to the hypothesis that Abraham was an Akkadian. This hypothesis has sometimes been presented in terms of Abraham being a Sumerian. However, as already noted in Appendix II, the Sumerians were a non-Semitic people, who were displaced in Mesopotamia in the third millennium BCE by the Semitic Akkadians. Thus, the actual hypothesis should be stated in terms of Abraham being an Akkadian.

Background information regarding the Akkadians was previously presented in Appendix II, where the chronological evidence suggested that Abraham's birth was during the Akkadian reign in Mesopotamia. While it must be admitted that the first Amorites to migrate into southern Mesopotamia were already present during the late Akkadian Empire, they would have comprised a very small portion of the population, compared to the Akkadians. As such, on a purely statistical level, the odds heavily favor the argument that Abraham was an Akkadian, rather than an Amorite.

The Amorite Hypothesis

The background of the Amorite people was also presented in Appendix II. As noted there, there is some circumstantial, linguistic evidence suggesting that Abraham may have been an Amorite. However, it was also noted in Appendix II that such linguistic evidence is far from being definitive. In the final analysis, chronological factors appear to contradict the hypothesis that Abraham was an Amorite.

The Aramaean Hypothesis: Introduction

Like the Akkadians and the Amorites before them, the Aramaeans were a Semitic people, who originated in the Arabian Peninsula. Their original migration northward out of the Arabian Peninsula appears to have taken them northward into an area extending from the upper Euphrates and Balikh rivers to Damascus and northern Transjordan, where they appear to be well established by the end of the Hittite Empire (about 1,500 BCE).

Here, they originally led the nomadic lifestyle of a wandering tribe. They tended goats and sheep, moving nomadically with the demands of their flocks for available water and pasture. Hunting was probably also part of their sustenance. Some of them may have become robber clans, haunting travelers, key caravan routes, and villages.

Over time, they began to establish city-states in the Euphrates-Balikh region, such as Beth-eden and Bit-adini. These city-states were in the general region known as Paddan-aram or Aram-naharaim, which also housed the city of Harran. (As noted previously, Harran is closely associated with the lives of Abraham, Isaac, and Jacob.[595]) Eventually, around the end of the second millennium BCE, the Aramaeans began to expand down into Mesopotamia. The first non-Biblical reference to the Aramaeans occurs in inscriptions of Tiglath-pileser I (about 1,100 BCE), where they are called Akhlami-aramaya, i.e., Aramaean Bedouin.

The Aramaean Hypothesis

Many Biblical scholars have concluded, or at least implied, that Abraham was an Aramaean. Their conclusion appears to be primarily based on the following Biblical passages and traditions. The late seventh century author of *Deuteronomy*, which is one of the five books comprising the contemporary *Torah* or *Pentateuch*, appears to be referring either to Abraham or to Jacob, when he states that "a wandering Aramean was my ancestor."

...you shall make this response before the Lord your God: "A wandering Aramean was my ancestor; he went down into Egypt and lived there as an alien, few in number, and there he became a great nation, mighty and populous..."[596]

Furthermore, *Genesis* consistently refers to Rebekah, the wife of Isaac, and Rachel, the wife of Jacob, as having Aramaean fathers.

...and Isaac was forty years old when he married Rebekah, daughter of Bethuel the Aramean of Paddan-aram, sister of Laban the Aramean.[597]

Then Isaac sent Jacob away; and he went to Paddan-aram, to Laban son of Bethuel the Aramean, the brother of Rebekah, Jacob's and . Esau's mother.[598]

This becomes relevant when one considers that: (1) Bethuel was the father of Rebekah and of Laban, and Laban was the father of Rachel; and (2) Bethuel was the son of, and Laban was the grandson of, Nahor II, the brother of Abraham.

Now after these things it was told Abraham, "Milcah also has borne children, to your brother Nahor: Uz the firstborn, Buz his brother, Kemuel the father of Aram, Chesed, Hazo, Pildash, Jidlaph, and Bethuel. Bethuel became the father of Rebekah... [599]

Arguments against the Aramaean Hypothesis

However, there are more than enough reasons to reject the identification of Abraham as having been an Aramaean. (1) The Aramaic language, one of the Northern Central Group of Semitic languages closely allied with Hebrew, did not evolve into a separate language before the 14th century BCE.[600] Were there Aramaeans so many centuries before there was an Aramaic language? (2) The Aramaeans were not well established in the vicinity of Harran until about the 15th century BCE, some six or seven centuries after Abraham appears to have lived there. (3) The sixth or fifth century BCE *P* strand material of *Genesis* lists Aram, the eponym of the Aramaeans as being a son of Shem, the son of Noah[601], while listing Abraham as being a descendant of Aram's brother, Arpachshad.[602] By definition, if the Aramaeans were the descendants of Aram the brother of Arpachshad, and if Abraham were a descendant of Arpachshad, then Abraham could not have been an Aramaean. (4) The 10th century BCE *J* strand of *Genesis* lists Aram, the eponym for the Aramaeans, as being the son of Kemuel, the son of Nahor II, the brother of Abraham[603], suggesting that the Aramaeans came after Abraham, not before him. Further, if the Aramaeans descended from Aram, the son of Kemuel, the son of Nahor II, and if Rebekah were the daughter of Bethuel, the son of Nahor II, then Rebekah, and by extension Rachel, could not have been Aramaeans. (5) The *D* strand (seventh century BCE) material of *Deuteronomy* and the *P* strand (sixth or fifth century BCE) material of *Genesis*, which are being used by some authors to claim that Abraham was an Aramaean, were written approximately 15 or more centuries after the life of Abraham.

Conclusions

In the final analysis, the Aramaean people emerged on the scene of Middle Eastern history at far too late a date to be identified as the parent tribe of Abraham, and there are far too many genealogical problems in trying to maintain that Abraham was an Aramaean.

The Arab Hypothesis

Arab Muslims occasionally advance the hypothesis that Abraham was an Arab. It is certainly the case that Abraham was one of the grandfathers of the Arab people. This can be demonstrated through several lines of descent, e.g., (1) from Ismael through 'Adnan[604], establishing one of the two main roots ('Adnani as opposed to Qahtani) of the Arab people; (2) from Midian through the Midianites[605]; (3) from Dedan through the Dedanites[606]; and (4) from Isaac through Esau through the Edomites and possibly the Amalekites[607]. Further, it is certainly the case that Abraham was a member of one of the ethnic groups that contributed to the formation of the Arab people, whether that group be Akkadian, Amorite, or Aramaean. However, the sum total of the above does not make Abraham an Arab, although it certainly establishes him as one of the ancestors of the Arabs.

Etymology of "Arab"

In marshaling the arguments that contradict the Arab hypothesis, it may be profitable to begin by examining the origin of the word "Arab". As was the case with the word "Hebrew", philologists have advanced numerous theories regarding the etymology of the word "Arab".

Firstly, a few linguists have attempted to derive the word "Arab" from a Semitic root that may be translated as "west". Linguistically, it is difficult to see how this proposed etymological transformation and evolution might have taken place. Further, Arab-as-west implies a geographic relationship, in which Arabs would be left describing themselves as being a people west of some other people, and thus adopting the perspective of the other people in describing themselves. Secondly, "Arab" may have been derived from the Hebrew "'*Arabha*", which may be translated as "dark land" or "steppe land", and which may imply a nomadic people. Thirdly, "Arab" may have evolved from the Hebrew "'*Erebh*", which may be translated as "mixed" or "unorganized", which might again imply a nomadic lifestyle. Fourth, "Arab" may have evolved from "'*Abhar*", i.e., "to move" or "to pass", which again implies a nomadic lifestyle, and which is the same root word from which "Hebrew" evolved. Fifth, some have suggested that "Arab" derives from the Arabic verb meaning "to express" or "to enunciate". The problem with this formulation is that it is likely a post hoc explanation that reverses the actual process of derivation, i.e., the Arabic verb probably derives from the word "Arab", and not vice versa.[608]

Regardless of the exact etymology of the word "Arab", the above discussion demonstrates that, like the word "Hebrew", the origin of the word "Arab" was probably independent of any specific ethnic or tribal identification, being instead tied to the concept of a nomadic people. On this basis alone, one would have to reject the notion that Abraham's ethnic or tribal affiliation could be encapsulated with the word "Arab".

History of "Arab"

Regarding the chronology of Abraham's life, i.e., around the 22nd century BCE, it becomes clear that the use of the term "Arab" to describe Abraham is a blatant anachronism. This can be demonstrated by reviewing the history of the use of the word "Arab": first, by the indigenous population of the Arabian Peninsula; and second, by others.

The first known use of the word "Arab" by the indigenous population of the northern portion of the Arabian Peninsula occurs in the early fourth century CE in the Namara Epitaph. This inscription refers to Imru'l-Qais as "King of all the Arabs". The first use of the word "Arab" by the indigenous population of the southern rim of the Arabian Peninsula can be dated no earlier than slightly before the time of Jesus. However, the context of these latter inscriptions makes clear that the term "Arab" was used to delineate the Bedouin, as opposed to sedentary people.[609]

Outside of the Arabian Peninsula, the use of the word "Arab" can be traced through many stages of history. (1) The use of the term "Arabia" as a place name occurs in the Greek of Aeschylus's *Prometheus*. (2) The term "Arabaya" appears in Persian cuneiform documents dating to around 530 BCE. (3) Between the ninth and sixth centuries BCE, the terms "Arabi", "Arabu", and "Urbi" occur with some frequency in Assyrian and Babylonian inscriptions. (4) However, the earliest known use of the word "Arab" occurs in an Assyrian inscription dating to 853 BCE. This inscription records the victory of King Shalmaneser III over various others, including "Gindibu the Aribi".[610]

The word "Arab" or "Arabs" occurs in nine places in the Judaeo-Christian scriptures that are included in the *Old Testament* of the *Bible*[611]: (1) three times in the fourth century BCE book of *Nehemiah*; (2) four times in the fourth century BCE book of *II Chronicles*; (3) once in the late seventh or early sixth century BCE book of *Joshua*, where it appears as the name of a town; and (4) once in the eighth century BCE or later book of *Isaiah*.[612] The word "Arabia" appears five times in the *Old Testament*[613]: (1) once in the fourth century BCE book of *II Chronicles*; (2) twice in sixth century BCE or later book of *Ezekiel*; (3) once in the sixth century BCE book of *I Kings;* and (4) once in the sixth century BCE book of *Jeremiah*.[614]

It is possible that there is one earlier use of the word "Arabs" in the *Torah*. The 10th century BCE *J* strand of *Exodus* 12:38 refers to the "mixed crowd", a translation of the Hebrew word "*Erev*". However, early Hebrew had no vowel markings. If the Hebrew word were actually "*Arav*", then the correct translation would be "Arabs".[615]

The above clearly illustrates that the use of the word "Arab" or "Arabs", to describe an identified ethnic group of people, cannot be dated earlier than the 10th century BCE, and cannot be reliably dated earlier than the ninth century BCE. Further, the use of the word "Arabia" cannot be dated earlier than the sixth century BCE. As such, it is clearly anachronistic to use the word "Arab" to describe someone living in the late third millennium BCE.

Linguist considerations

Arab Muslims, in casual conversation, sometimes advance the argument that Abraham spoke Arabic as proof that Abraham was an Arab. Quite simply, there was no Arabic language at the time of Abraham. Classical Arabic is a middle stage evolution of the Southern Central Group of Semitic languages, and dates to the first millennium BCE. Likewise, the South Arabic Group of dialects (Sabaean, Minaean, Qatabanian, and Hadramawtian) of the Southern Peripheral Group of Semitic languages, while an ancient to middle stage evolution, is still dated to the first millennium BCE.[616]

Eponymous Considerations

Some might argue that "Arab" refers to any descendant of Ya'rub, the son of Qahtan (Joktan), making Ya'rub the eponymous ancestor of the Arabs. The genealogy of Ya'rub as either a son or a grandson of Qahtan is well documented[617], and Ya'rub certainly lived several generations prior to Abraham[618]. However, Abraham's descent is recorded as being through Peleg, the son of Eber[619], not through Qahtan, the son of Eber[620]. Thus, the argument for Ya'rub being the eponymous ancestor of the Arabs would specifically exclude Abraham from being an Arab.

Final Considerations

If Abraham were an Arab, then via descent through Isaac and Jacob, the 12 tribes of Israel all become Arabs. This is a conclusion that would be unacceptable to most Arabs, especially in light of geopolitical claims made about Palestine being an Arab land. Are 20th century Israelis merely Arabs returning to an Arab land? Quite obviously, most Arabs would adamantly answer in the negative. Consistency and logic then demand that Abraham not be considered an Arab.

Summary

While Abraham was clearly one of the ancestors of the Arab people, and while Abraham clearly belonged to a Semitic people, which contributed to the evolution that resulted in the Arab people, it would be a gross historical anachronism to claim that Abraham was an Arab. Support for this conclusion is found in the linguistic sciences concerning the evolution of the Semitic languages. Further, appeals to eponymous considerations involving Ya'rub, the son of Qahtan, merely reinforce the inescapable conclusion that Abraham was not an Arab. In short, the appellation of Arab (and of Hebrew in any ethnic sense) to Abraham is a gross historical anachronism of the sort mentioned in the *Qur'an*, where the designations of Jew and Christian are rejected as terms applying to Abraham.

> Ye People of the Book! Why dispute ye about Abraham, when the Law and the Gospel were not revealed till after him? Have ye no understanding?…Abraham was not a Jew nor yet a Christian; but he was true in faith, and bowed his will to Allah's, (which is Islam), and he joined not gods with Allah.[621]

In his commentary on the above verses, 'Ali specifically draws attention to rejection of the anachronistic element that is present in labeling Abraham as being a Jew or a Christian.

> Abraham was a true man of God, but he could not be called a Jew or a Christian as he lived long before the Law of Moses or the Gospel of Jesus were revealed.[622]

Conclusions

After careful consideration, one must reject the hypothesis that Abraham was an ethnic Hebrew, as the use of the word "Hebrew" to imply ethnic meaning is clearly anachronistic when applied to the time of Abraham. Likewise, it is anachronistic to describe Abraham as being an Arab. The Biblical suggestions that Abraham was an Aramaean are soundly contradicted by: (1) chronological considerations; and (2) genealogical considerations. While it cannot be ruled out that Abraham was an Amorite, the Amorite period in Mesopotamia appears to be a little late for the time of Abraham. Given available information, it appears most likely that Abraham was an Akkadian.

Appendix IV
Sequential Events in Abraham's life

Major Markers in the life of Abraham

There are certain events within the life of Abraham, about which the Islamic and Judaeo-Christian traditions are in complete agreement, both with regard to the occurrence of those events as well as their relative sequencing. These events, and their relative sequencing, serve as major markers in any attempt to construct the totality of the sequential events in the life of Abraham. The following formulations state those events and their relative sequencing.

1. Abraham married Sarah prior to the acquisition of Hagar.
2. Hagar was acquired prior to the birth of Ismael.
3. Ismael was born prior to Isaac.
4. Angels visited Abraham, foretold the birth of Isaac, and destroyed Sodom and Gomorrah prior to the birth of Isaac.
5. Isaac was born prior to Abraham's death.

Having established these major markers, one next considers geographical markers in the life of Abraham. If one can establish the sequence of geographical locations in the life of Abraham, one can then use those geographical locations as secondary markers of sequential events, and can then group individual events into the life of Abraham according to geographical location.

Events in Ur

With the above sequential outline of major markers in place, one turns to the birth of Abraham. As already noted in Appendix II, there is Biblical support for the birth of Abraham having taken place in or near the vicinity of Ur in southern Iraq.[623] With the geographical location of Ur now in place for Abraham's early years, it is noted that Abraham married Sarah while he was still residing in Ur.[624] From this, one can hypothesize that Abraham remained in Ur from his birth until at least young adulthood, i.e., marriageable age.

Abraham destroys the idols

Given the above, one now turns to the Qur'anic evidence that suggests that Abraham destroyed the idols of the temple while he was yet a youth (i.e., *Fta*)[625], suggesting that Abraham's destruction of the temple idols occurred in Ur, and before he was married to Sarah. Unless one is willing to suggest that Abraham's assault on the temple idols was merely vandalism and juvenile delinquency, then one is forced to assume that Abraham had embraced monotheism or the *Tawheed* at some time prior to the destruction of the temple idols. This then dates Abraham's contemplation of the course of the sun, moon, and star[626], by which process he embraced monotheism, prior to his destruction of the idols.

Abraham embraces Monotheism

Now the type of abstract reasoning employed by Abraham in reaching his monotheistic conclusion requires the development of formal operational thought, a process that typically does not occur prior to around age 13. Thus, it would appear that Abraham first contemplated the heavens, then reasoned to the *Tawheed*, and only somewhat later destroyed the temple idols while still in his early teens, thus fulfilling the dual requirements of: the onset of formal operational thought around age 13; and the destruction of the temple idols while still a youth. Of note, this reasoning finds support in *Jubilees*, where it is maintained that Abraham became a monotheist at age 14.[627]

Abraham and *Da'wa*

Further, common sense suggests, and the *Qur'an* implies[628], that Abraham began his preaching and exhortation about the *Tawheed* immediately after his monotheistic realization, which was based upon the observation of the natural course, movement, and order of the astral bodies. As such, one places the beginning of Abraham's preaching immediately after his acceptance of the *Tawheed*, and before his destruction of the temple idols.

Abraham's Trial and Sentence

Having destroyed the temple idols at the cult temple of Ur, which was dedicated to the Akkadian moon god, Sin[629], it is likely that Abraham came to the immediate attention of the emperor, Naram-Sin, who has previously been suggested as Abraham's antagonist in *Qur'an* 2:258.

That Naram-Sin would have wasted no time dealing with Abraham's destruction of the idols in the temple of Sin is suggested by two considerations: Naram-Sin's own name incorporates the name of the Akkadian moon god, i.e., Sin, thus indicating his close identification with the cult temple of Sin in Ur; and Naram-Sin's own daughter, Enmenanna, was the high priestess of that very temple.[630] Thus Abraham's confrontation with his antagonist is placed shortly or immediately after the destruction of the temple idols.

It seems reasonable to conclude that the Qur'anic account[631] of Abraham being thrown into a fire would have transpired as a direct result of the confrontation between Abraham and Naram-Sin, and of Abraham's destruction of the temple idols. As such, one then places the attempt to kill Abraham next in sequence, but still during his early teens. Of note, the conclusion, which is drawn from this reasoning, is consistent with *Al-Tabari*'s information that Abraham was 16 years old when he was thrown into the fire.[632]

Conversion of Lot and Marriage to Sarah

At least partially as a result of Abraham's miraculous escape from the attempt to kill him by fire, Abraham's nephew, Lot, accepted monotheism. This event can apparently be placed at some point prior to the migration from Ur to Harran, given that upon his acceptance of the *Tawheed*, Lot specifically stated his willingness to immigrate for the sake of Allah.[633] As such, this is placed next in sequence. One then hypothesizes Abraham growing to marriageable age in Ur, and then marrying Sarah. Finally, *Jubilees* states that Abraham was 49 years old when he married Sarah.[634]

Abraham leaves Ur

At some point after the marriage of Abraham, one then places the migration of Abraham, Sarah, Lot, and others from Ur to Harran.[635] In that regard, *Jubilees* places the migration to Harran as occurring when Abraham was 60 or 61 years old, and as being secondary to the somewhat questionable report of Abraham having burned the temple of Sin to the ground.[636]

Summary

Given the sum total of the above, the following sequence of events can reasonably be posited for Abraham's life in Ur.

1. Abraham is born in or near Ur in southern Iraq.
2. While in his early teens, Abraham:
    a. Uses natural observation of the astral bodies to arrive at conceptual monotheism – perhaps at age 14;
    b. Begins his preaching and exhortation;
    c. Destroys the temple idols;
    d. Is brought before Naram-Sin;
    e. Is condemned to death by fire; and
    f. Miraculously escapes death by fire – perhaps at age 16.
3. Lot converts to the monotheistic religion of Abraham.
4. Abraham marries Sarah – perhaps at age 49.
5. Abraham, Sarah, Lot, and others migrate from Ur to Harran – perhaps at age 60 or 61.

Events in Harran

There are so few known events from Abraham's life in Harran, and those that are known are so obvious in sequence, that there is no need to discuss the sequence of events in any detail. As such, the following statement of sequence will suffice.

1. Abraham arrives in Harran with Azar, Sarah, Lot[637], and probably with Nahor II and Milcah[638] – perhaps at age 61.[639]
2. Abraham continues his preaching and exhortation.
3. Abraham finally breaks from his father.[640]
4. Abraham leaves Harran with Sarah, Lot, and other believers – probably at age 75.[641]

Events in Palestine – I

The *Qur'an* and *Sahih Ahadith* are silent concerning any events specifically identified as occurring during Abraham's first sojourn in Palestine. Likewise, the *P* and *E* strands of *Genesis* report no material for this period of Abraham's life. However, both the *J* strand of *Genesis* and the book of *Jubilees* suggest an itinerary for Abraham during this time period. Fortunately, the sequence of events reported by these two sources is totally and mutually consistent, with *Jubilees* supplying some additional detail about Abraham's movements, as he journeyed from Bethel to Egypt. As such, the following statement of sequential events can be listed.

1. Abraham arrives at Shechem and builds an altar.
2. Abraham moves to between Bethel and Ai, and builds a second altar.
3. Abraham moves in stages to the Negeb:
   a. First to Hebron for two years; and
   b. then to Bealoth.
4. Abraham moves from the Negeb to Egypt.[642]

Events in Egypt: Introduction

There are only four significant events reported about Abraham's sojourn in Egypt. The first is that Abraham and Lot became rich and prosperous while in Egypt.[643] The second is that Lot married an Egyptian woman.[644] The third is that Abraham continued his mission of *Da'wa* while in Egypt.[645] The fourth is the taking of Sarah by the pharaoh of Egypt. *Jubilees* places this fourth event as happening five years after Abraham entered Egypt.[646]

Problems with the *E* strand

However, there are several different versions of this fourth event that can be considered. The *J* strand of *Genesis* 12: 10-20 tells the story, clearly placing the event in Egypt. In contrast, the *E* strand of *Genesis* 20: 1-17 appears to be telling the same story, but placing the event in Gerar, and making Abraham's and Sarah's antagonist Abimelech, the king of Gerar. This discrepancy between the *J* and *E* strands can be resolved by considering the *J* strand of *Genesis* 26: 6-11, where a story is told about Isaac and Rebekah, in which Isaac tells Abimelech, king of Gerar, that Rebekah is Isaac's sister. When these three narratives are contrasted with each other, keeping in mind that the first and third are both from the *J* strand while the second is from the *E* strand, it becomes obvious that the author of the *E* strand has confabulated two different *J* strand stories, one involving Abraham and the other involving Isaac, into a single story about Abraham. If one removes the events and circumstances of the *J* strand narrative of *Genesis* 26: 6-11, which involves Isaac, from the *E* strand story of *Genesis* 20: 1-17, which is about Abraham, one is then theoretically left with the residual *E* strand story about Abraham and Sarah in Egypt.

Contrasting this *E* strand residual with the *J* strand of *Genesis* 12: 10-20 story of Abraham, Sarah, and the pharaoh, one discovers that the *E* strand information does add two pertinent facts, i.e., that the pharaoh was somehow personally and physically afflicted by his proximity to Sarah[647], and that the pharaoh sent Sarah back to Abraham with gifts.[648] These additional pieces of information square quite nicely with the story as portrayed in *Sahih Ahadith*[649], which serve as a second source of information about Abraham's sojourn in Egypt. Finally, we have the events as reported in *Jubilees* 13: 11-15 as a third source of information.

The above illustrates quite clearly how even contaminated documentation can at times be utilized successfully in building the biography of an individual, but only if that documentation is correctly analyzed. The helpful results from this process are twofold. Firstly, one can now simply and totally disregard the *E* strand story of *Genesis* 20: 1-17 supposedly involving Abraham, Sarah, and Abimelech during the time after they returned from Egypt. Secondly, the residual from the *E* strand story of *Genesis* 20: 1-17 (after removing the *J* strand story of *Genesis* 26: 6-11, which is about Isaac,) provides important corroboration of the *Sahih Ahadith* stories of the pharaoh being personally and physically afflicted by his proximity to Sarah, and of the pharaoh bestowing gifts, including Hagar, on Abraham and Sarah.

Summary

With the above in view, the chronology of events for Abraham's sojourn in Egypt can be summarized as follows.

1. Abraham, Sarah, and Lot enter Egypt during a time of famine.
2. Abraham and Lot grow rich and prosperous during five years of living in Egypt.
3. Lot marries an Egyptian woman.
4. Abraham continues his mission of *Da'wa* while in Egypt.
5. Pharaoh takes Sarah from Abraham, assuming that Sarah is Abraham's sister, instead of his wife.
6. Pharaoh is physically afflicted by his proximity to Sarah.

7. Pharaoh returns Sarah, and bestows gifts on Abraham and Sarah, with such gifts including the servant Hagar.
8. Pharaoh orders Abraham, Sarah, and Lot out of Egypt.[650]

Events in Palestine – II

Information regarding Abraham's second sojourn in Palestine is basically dependent upon Biblical sources, primarily the *J* strand of *Genesis*. By isolating them from the rest of the text of *Genesis*, and then recombining the pieces of the *J* strand of *Genesis*, one obtains an overall sequence of events for this second sojourn in Palestine. These events may be sequenced as follows:

1. Abraham, Sarah, and Lot enter the Negeb and move to Bethel.
2. Abraham and Lot separate, and Lot moves to Sodom.
3. Allah promises the land of Palestine to Abraham's descendants.
4. Abraham moves to the oaks of Mamre at Hebron, and builds an altar there.
5. Allah promises Abraham an heir.
6. Abraham sacrifices to Allah.
7. Allah makes a covenant with Abraham.
8. Abraham takes Hagar as his second wife.
9. The pregnant Hagar flees from conflict with Sarah.[651]

To this basic outline from *J*, one can add a few details from *P, E,* and *Jubilees*, most notable of which is the *P* account of the birth of Ismael after Hagar returns to Abraham and Sarah.[652]

Events in Makkah – I: Introduction

There is only one known event marking Abraham's first recorded visit to Makkah, and *Sahih Ahadith* are the primary source material for the narration of that event. From the *Sahih Ahadith*, one can conclude that Ismael was less than two years old, because he was reportedly still nursing from Hagar.[653] As such, the one event comprising Abraham's first sojourn in Makkah can be reliably placed within the first two years of Ismael's life, which corresponds to Abraham being 86 to 88 years old.[654] This one event was that Abraham left Hagar and Ismael in Makkah, secondary to renewed conflict between Sarah and Hagar, and secondary to the command of Allah.[655]

More problems with the *E* strand

Having stated the above, it must be noted that the *E* strand of *Genesis* gives a variant account[656] of Abraham having sent Hagar and Ismael out from his home. In this variant account, the wanderings of Hagar and Ismael supposedly take place in the wilderness by Beersheba, in the area known as the Negeb. Further, in this variant account, an unsuccessful attempt is made to place the events in question as occurring when Ismael was about 16 years old.[657] Before proceeding further with the discussion of this variant *E* strand account, it should be remembered that it was previously shown in this appendix (Events in Egypt) that the *E* strand account of *Genesis* 20:1-17 was a confabulated merging of two different *J* strand stories, one related in *Genesis* 12:10-20 and one in *Genesis* 26: 6-11. With regard to these two *J* strand stories, the former pertained to Abraham, while the latter pertained to Isaac.

A detailed analysis of this *E* strand account of *Genesis* 21: 8-21, in which it is maintained that Abraham merely sent Hagar and Ismael out to wander in the Negeb, reveals that it is a confabulated combination of: (1) the earlier *J* strand account of *Genesis* 16: 5-8,11-14, which reported Hagar's desperate escape from Sarah; and (2) the story of Abraham leaving Hagar and Ismael at Makkah, as reported in *Al-Bukhari* 4:582-584, which story presumably was originally reported in the *J* strand narration before being excised at the time of the combination of the *J* and *E* strands into a single document in the eighth century BCE. This confabulation is illustrated in Table 7 below, which shows the parallels among the *J* strand of *Genesis* 16: 5-8,11-14, the *E* strand of *Genesis* 21: 8-21, and *Al-Bukhari* 4:583-584 (listed as *B* in Table 7).

Table 7

J, E, and *Hadith* parallels

A. Those making the journey include:

    J: only Hagar;

    E: only Hagar and Ismael;

    B: Abraham, Hagar, and Ismael.

B. This journey is to:

    J: the south into the Negeb, i.e., Kadesh;

    E: the south into the Negeb, i.e., Beersheba;

    B: Makkah.

C. Age of the child:

J: no children involved;

E: Ismael is supposedly 16, but is still young enough to be carried on Hagar's shoulder (verse 14) and young enough for Hagar physically to place him under a bush (verse 15), indicating that Ismael is actually a very young child;

B: Ismael has not yet been weaned from nursing.

D. The bush or tree:

J: there is no mention of a bush or tree;

E: Hagar places Ismael under a bush;

B: Abraham has Hagar and Ismael sit under a tree.

E. What Abraham gave to Hagar:

J: Nothing;

E: Bread and a skin of water;

B: Dates and a skin of water.

F. Does Hagar run out of water:

J: There is no such account;

E: Yes;

B: Yes.

G. An angel speaks to Hagar:

J: Yes;

E: Yes;

B: Yes.

H. The angel promises Hagar that Ismael will have a multitude of descendants:

J: Yes;

E: Yes:

B: No.

I. The angel makes a comment about Allah hearing, thus providing an explanation of Ismael's name.

J: Yes;

E: Yes;

B: No.

J. The well existed prior to Hagar's arrival:

J: Yes;

E: Unclear, but probably;

B: No.

An examination of Table 7 clearly indicates that with respect to: (1) point A, the *E* strand attempts to bridge two different stories, respectively told in *J* and in *Al-Bukhari;* (2) points B, H, I, and J, *E* parallels *J*, but not *Al-Bukhari;* (3) points C, D, E, and F, *E* parallels *Al-Bukhari*, but not *J*; and (4) point G, all three sources are in agreement. In and of itself, these parallels would be strong evidence that the *E* strand account of *Genesis* 21: 8-21 is a confabulation of two different stories, one told in the *J* strand account of *Genesis* 16: 5-8, 11-14 and one told in *Al-Bukhari* 4: 583-584. However, there is yet one other consideration, which appears to clinch the argument that the *E* strand account is a confabulation, namely that the *E* strand account cannot keep the age of Ismael straight. *E* places its account at the time of the weaning of Isaac, which would make Ismael about 16 years old at the time.[658] However, *E* maintains that Hagar carried Ismael on her shoulder when leaving Hebron (verse 14), and that Hagar was able physically to place Ismael under a bush (verse 15). It is a little beyond belief that Hagar would carry her 16-year-old son on her shoulder when she set out on a trip, and this blatant inconsistency necessitates that the *E* strand account be seen as a contaminated and confabulated narrative.

Given the sum total of the above, the *E* strand account of *Genesis* 21:8-21 is seen as a confabulation of two discrete stories, only one of which is relevant to Abraham's first sojourn in Makkah. Obviously, any use of the confabulated *E* strand account must be quite cautious, and must make sure that all elements of the *J* strand story of *Genesis* 16: 5-8, 11-14 have been eliminated from it.

Summary

Thus said, it becomes clear that: Abraham's first sojourn in Makkah must be placed during the first two years of Ismael's life; and the only significant event concerning Abraham's first sojourn in Makkah is the following.

1. Abraham leaves Hagar and Ismael at Makkah.

Events in Palestine – III: Introduction

Chapter 14 of *Genesis* stands outside and independently from the main literary strands (*J, E, P,* and *D*) that comprise the rest of the *Torah*. As such, the dating of this chapter as a written literary work is quite difficult, although the post-exilic (sixth to fourth century BCE) glosses, which have been identified within the chapter, suggest that the core of the chapter may be quite ancient. Within this 14th chapter of *Genesis*, two basic stories are narrated. The first story recounts Abraham's rescue of Lot, after invading kings from Iraq and Iran had sacked the city of Sodom, where Lot had been living. The second story reports on the nature of the relationship between Abraham and a certain king of Salem (Jerusalem), a story which is inserted into the first story, and which is thus associated with the events recounted in the first story.

Dating prolems

As noted previously, this 14th chapter of *Genesis* is not part of any ongoing, if frequently broken, literary strand embedded in *Genesis*. As such, the placing of the events recounted in the 14th chapter of *Genesis* into a sequential understanding of Abraham's life cannot be done by following some flow of narration, through different installments of information, within a single literary strand. Instead, one must look for clues within the chapter itself. In that regard, the chapter mentions the names of a number of specific kings of the time, but none of these names can be positively identified with any known historical figures, whose presence in the story would allow for definitive dating.

However, there is one internal clue within the 14th chapter of *Genesis*, which is most helpful in providing a range of possibilities regarding the timing of occurrence of the events described in this chapter. *Genesis* 14: 12 specifically states that Lot was living in Sodom when these events took place. Assuming the accuracy of that statement, this places the events of the 14th chapter of *Genesis* between the time of Lot's separation from Abraham, and the time of the destruction of Sodom and Gomorrah.

As noted previously, Abraham and Lot were together throughout their sojourn in Egypt, and they did not separate until being together at Bethel during their second sojourn in Palestine. If it is assumed that Abraham was about 75 years old when he left Harran[659], that he spent at least two years in Palestine before going to Egypt[660], and that he spent five years more in Egypt[661], that would make Abraham about 82 or 83 years old when he and Lot return to Palestine, and head in stages to Bethel. One therefore, would assume that Abraham was about 83 years old when Lot separated from him. Now, Abraham was reported to have been 100 years old when Isaac was born[662], and the angels who subsequently destroyed Sodom and Gomorrah reportedly visited Abraham the year before Isaac was born, when Abraham was 99 years old. [663] Thus, the events recounted in *Genesis* 14 appear to have taken place any time between Abraham's 83rd and 99th year of life.

As will be seen in the following section on Events in Makkah II, Abraham's 99th year of life was crowded by many time consuming events, including a pilgrimage to Makkah that would have taken up at least four to six months of that year, and it thus becomes extremely doubtful that the events of *Genesis* 14 could also be fit into that year. As such, the most probable estimate is that the events of *Genesis* 14 occurred between Abraham's 83rd and 98th year of life.

However, before being satisfied with that estimate, one must acknowledge that *Jubilees* states that Lot and Abraham separated when Abraham was 88 years old, and that the events of *Genesis* 14 occurred during that same year.[664] However, during this period of Abraham's life, the usually precise dating of *Jubilees* becomes quite inconsistent, probably due to scribal errors in the transmission of the manuscript. For example, *Jubilees* simultaneously maintains that Ismael was born when Abraham was 86 and 89 years old.[665] If one assumes that the reference to when Lot and Abraham separated was an error, one could still accept the dating of the events of *Genesis* 14 to Abraham's 88th year of life, which falls within the earlier estimate of Abraham being 83 to 98 years old, and which falls between Events in Makkah-I and Events in Makkah-II. Whether or not one accepts the events of *Genesis* 14 as occurring when Abraham was 88 years old, it certainly appears probable that they occurred between Abraham's first two known excursions to Makkah.

Summary

After the above discussion, one can assign two events to Abraham's third sojourn in Palestine.

    1. Abraham rescues the captive Lot.
    2. Abraham meets with the king of Jerusalem.

Events in Makkah – II: The intended Sacrifice of Abraham's son

Introduction: There is probably no other event in Abraham's life, about which there is more disagreement between the Islamic and the Judaeo-Christian traditions, than the story of the sacrifice of Abraham's son. These disagreements center on two points of contention: who was the intended sacrificial victim, i.e., Ismael or Isaac; and what was the location of the intended sacrifice, i.e., Jerusalem or the vicinity of Makkah. The Judaeo-Christian tradition maintains that the intended sacrificial victim was Isaac, and that the location of the intended sacrifice was the land of Moriah, which is typically identified as being Temple Mount in Jerusalem. These identifications are made on the basis of the *E* strand of *Genesis*.[666]

The Islamic tradition has historically been less definitive in stating a position. Neither the *Qur'an*[667] nor *Sahih Ahadith* give a definitive and unambiguous answer to the question as to who was the intended sacrificial victim. Different individual narrations within the Islamic tradition have variously maintained that the intended sacrificial victim was Ismael, and that the intended victim was Isaac[668], although the rites of the *Hajj* pilgrimage would appear to imply that the victim was Ismael. If the sacrificial victim were Ismael, this would then identify the place of the sacrifice as being in the vicinity of Makkah, as Hagar and Ismael remained in Makkah after Abraham left them there.[669] If the sacrificial victim were Isaac, this would then identify the site as being Palestine, as there is no record of Isaac having ever gone to Makkah.

Still More Problems with the *E* Strand: Given the above discussion, and disregarding the personal preferences of later Muslim narrators, the identity of the sacrificial victim (Ismael vs. Isaac), and thus of the site of the intended sacrifice (Makkah vs. Jerusalem), must be primarily based on a reading of the eighth century BCE *E* strand of *Genesis* 22:1-14. This is a most unfortunate limitation, which raises some special concern and justifiable misgivings. Twice before, in fact the only two times that the *E* strand of *Genesis* has supplied any significant length of narrative material concerning the life of Abraham, the *E* strand material of *Genesis*, unlike that of either the *J* or *P* strands of *Genesis*, has been shown to be highly confabulated and contaminated.[670] As such, one needs to examine the *E* strand account of *Genesis* 22:1-14 with special thoroughness, in order to insure internal consistency in its narration.

In subjecting this *E* strand account to a critical reading, one's attention is immediately focused on the first two verses in this passage, which are quoted in full below:

> After these things God tested Abraham. He said to him, "Abraham!" And he said, "Here I am." He said, "Take your son, your only son, Isaac, whom you love, and go to the land of Moriah, and offer him there as a burnt offering on one of the mountains that I shall show you."[671]

There are two issues presented in this passage, each of which needs to be examined in turn, and each of which is vitally important in assessing the viability of the *E* strand account. These two issues are examined in reverse order of presentation.

Firstly, the description given of the land of Moriah specifically mentions that it includes mountains. This description would appear to exclude Jerusalem as the sacrificial site on two counts: (A) Jerusalem and its terrain do not conform to the specific requirement of a land containing several mountains; and (B) Jerusalem was already a settled city at the time of Abraham, and one would assume that the more exact identification of Jerusalem would be used, if, in fact, that were the site of the intended sacrfice.[672] In addition, the description of the sacrifice certainly does not sound like it is taking place within the walls of a city-state. Yet, that would definitely have been the case, if Jerusalem were the site of the intended sacrifice. These are rather obvious contraindications to the site of the sacrifice being Jerusalem, and they raise the question of how the land of Moriah ever got to be associated in Judaeo-Christian tradition with Temple Mount in Jerusalem. The answer to this question is to be found in *II Chronicles*, where Mount Moriah is specifically identified as being the site at which King Solomon began to build his temple to Allah.[673] Despite this identification, Biblical scholars have repeatedly stressed that the "land of Moriah" has to be considered unknown, and that the identification provided in *II Chronicles* is erroneous.[674] It must be taken note of that "Moriah" occurs in no other passages in the entire *Bible*[675], and the description of Moriah does fit that of Makkah, whose vicinity does have several mountains around it. Moreover, Makkah was only sparsely populated by the Jorahamites, and by Hagar and Ismael, at the time in question.[676]

So far, one has excluded Jerusalem, although not Palestine, as being the site of the intended sacrifice. In addition, as far as the meager description of the land of Moriah goes, Makkah fits that description, i.e., the vicinity of Makkah has the requisite mountains mentioned in the E strand of *Genesis* 22: 2. However, there is even more to link the land of Moriah with Makkah. The E strand of *Genesis* 22: 14 notes that after Allah had ransomed Abraham's son with a sacrificial ram, Abraham called the mountain on which he was standing Jeruel, meaning "Allah will provide". The place name "Jeruel" occurs only one other time in the entire *Bible* [677], where it is described as being in a wilderness and as lying just outside a valley.[678] As previously noted, Makkah lies inside a valley, and is surrounded by wilderness. Furthermore, the specific area around Makkah, which is typically associated with the intended sacrifice, is Mina. The Arabic word "Mina" implies the concept of a non-obligatory gift or provision. Thus, linguistically, one can associate Mina with Jeruel, further strengthening the association of the vicinity of Makkah with the site of the intended sacrifice.

Second, the E strand of *Genesis* 22: 2 specifically identifies both Ismael and Isaac as being the intended victim. Isaac is identified by name, while Ismael is definitively identified by description, i.e., "your only son".[679] Now, as far as can be determined by the historical record, there was only one time in Abraham's life when he could have had an "only son", i.e., after the birth of Ismael and before the birth of Isaac.[680] In short, there is no logical way in which the designation "your only son" can be applied to Isaac. Clearly, there is a major textual contamination in this verse.

Resolving the Problems in the E Strand: How does one resolve the problems apparent in the E strand account of the intended sacrifice of Abraham's son? Two options are open to the investigator. Firstly, one notes that the physical description of the land of Moriah is consistent with that of Makkah, but not with that of Jerusalem. This consideration is not definitive, because Isaac could have been sacrificed at some mountainous place in Palestine away from Jerusalem, but it does tend to tip the probabilities in favor of Ismael. Further, the suggested linguistic identification of Jeruel with Mina (actually, it would have probably been Minat Allah in its original form) adds even more to the probability that the vicinity of Makkah was the site of the intended sacrifice. Secondly, one has to address the issue of probable motivation for the contamination of equating Isaac with a description, i.e., Abraham's only son, which could only have been applied to Ismael, and then only during the first 14 years of Ismael's life.

One assumes that in its pristine and original form, the story, upon which the E strand account is based, did not contain the aforementioned contamination. In short, one assumes that the description of and the name of Abraham's son clearly identified the same person in the original story. As such, one has to ask which statement was altered, i.e., the description of "only son" or the name of that son. This leads immediately to the issue of motivation. Why was the E strand account altered? More specifically, why was this piece of Jewish scripture, identified as being part of the E strand, altered?

It seems rather incongruous and illogical that an eighth century BCE Jewish scribe or storyteller would have wished to alter what had been a clear designation of Isaac as being the intended sacrificial victim into an ambiguous statement, which raised the possibility that Ismael was the intended victim. However, this scribe or storyteller, who traced his ethnic and religious heritage through Isaac, not through Ismael, would have had a clear motivation to alter the identification of Ismael into an identification of Isaac. The easiest way to do this would have been to substitute the one name for the other. However, in so doing, this scribe or storyteller left an inadvertent clue to his alteration, i.e., he forgot to excise the statement identifying the sacrificial victim as being Abraham's "only son".

In short, considerations of physical terrain, considerations of geographical site names, and considerations of the motivation for the above noted contamination of the E strand verse, suggest that the intended sacrificial victim was Ismael. While these considerations are not totally conclusive, they provide strong circumstantial evidence, and heavily weigh the probabilities in terms of Ismael being the intended victim. As such, while noting the probabilistic nature of this identification, this book identifies Ismael as having been the "only son", whom Abraham was called upon to sacrifice.

The E Strand in Perspective: It is instructive that in all three cases in which the E strand has offered a lengthy narration about Abraham's life, there have been major problems with confabulation and/or contamination within the written narrative. In the current case, the identified contamination does not necessitate the total discard of the *E* strand material, but it does suggest that such material must be used cautiously, judiciously, only after every due deliberation, and only after every effort has been made to expunge contaminated material from the *E* strand account.

A Qur'anic Consideration: Having reached this point in the discussion, one additional consideration can be introduced. The story of the sacrifice of Abraham's son is told in the *Qur'an*[681], but without any clear identification of whether that son is Ismael or Isaac. However, if one closely examines the flow of associations in that Qur'anic account, one is confronted by the following sequence of events: (1) Allah promises Abraham that he will have a son; (2) the son is born, grows, and reaches the age of "serious work with him"; (3) Abraham is then called upon to sacrifice that son; (4) Allah substitutes a different sacrifice for the son; and (5) Allah gives Abraham "the good news of Isaac". Assuming that the "good news of Isaac" is a promise of the coming birth of Isaac to Abraham and Sarah, the flow of the Qur'anic story makes clear that the intended sacrificial victim was Ismael. For the reader's convenience, the sum total of the English translation of the meaning of this Qur'anic account is quoted below.

> He said: "I will go to my Lord! He will surely guide me! O my Lord! grant me a righteous (son)!" So We gave him the good news of a boy ready to suffer and forbear. Then, when (the son) reached (the age of serious) work with him, he said: "O my son! I see in a vision that I offer thee in sacrifice: now see what is thy view!" (The son) said: "O my father! Do as thou art commanded: thou will find me, if Allah so wills, one practicing patience and constancy!" So when they had both submitted their wills (to Allah), and he had laid him prostrate on his forehead (for sacrifice), We called out to him, "O Abraham! thou hast already fulfilled the vision!"—thus indeed do We reward those who do right. For this was obviously a trial— and We ransomed him with a momentous sacrifice: and We left (this blessing) for him among generations (to come) in later times: "peace and salutation to Abraham!" Thus indeed do We reward those who do right for he was one of our believing servants. And We gave him the good news of Isaac—a prophet—one of the righteous. We

blessed him and Isaac: but of their progeny are (some) that do right, and (some) that obviously do wrong, to their own souls.[682]

Dating the Sacrifice

The *Qur'an* states that the sacrifice took place when Abraham's son had reached the age of "serious work".[683] By this statement, one may assume that Ismael had reached his early adolescence. However, even more specific information is available from the *P* strand of *Genesis*, where it is stated that: (A) Abraham received the covenant from Allah, and received the promise of the birth of Isaac, when Abraham was 99 years old[684]; and (B) immediately thereafter, Abraham (age 99) and Ismael (age 13) upheld part of their end of the covenant by undergoing circumcision.[685] Now, it has already been established that Abraham left Hagar and Ismael in Makkah when Ismael was still a nursing infant, and that Hagar and Ismael then remained there.[686] As such, Abraham's receipt of the covenant from Allah, and Abraham's and Ismael's circumcisions took place in the vicinity of Makkah, when Abraham was 99 years old, and when Ismael was 13 years old.

Having already established that Ismael was in at least his early adolescence at the time of the intended sacrifice, and that Isaac was probably not yet born, it seems fairly illogical that Abraham would have made two lengthy trips to Makkah in close proximity to each other. As such, one assumes that Abraham made one trip to Makkah when he was 99 years old. If this assumption is correct, then in rapid sequence during his stay at Makkah, Abraham received his instructions to sacrifice Ismael, Allah released Ismael from the sacrifice, Allah entered into a covenant with Abraham, Allah promised Abraham the birth of Isaac, and Abraham and Ismael underwent circumcision.

So far, the sequencing holds together quite nicely. However, in an *Hadith* narrated by Abu Huraira, it is stated that Abraham underwent circumcision at age 80[687], which would have been six years before the birth of Ismael.[688] However, a more correct translation of one of these two *Ahadith* would read "after" the age of 80, but probably before the age of 90.[689] Given this slippage in the reported age of Abraham in these *Ahadith*, it seems reasonable to assume that the age reported should be taken in a general, as opposed to specific, sense. As such, within this book, Abraham's age at circumcision will be assumed to have been 99 years.

Summary

Given the sum total of the above discussion, one can identify the following events occurring in rapid sequence in Makkah during Abraham's 99th year of life.

1. Abraham receives a vision from Allah, in which Abraham is commanded to sacrifice Ismael to Allah.
2. Allah releases Ismael from the sacrifice, and informs Abraham that he and Ismael have passed this test of faith.
3. Allah enters into a covenant with Abraham.
4. Allah promises Abraham the coming birth of Isaac.
5. Abraham and Ismael undergo circumcision.

Events in Palestine – IV

Having returned from Makkah to Hebron, there were still several major events left to occur in Abraham's 99th year of life. The basic sequencing of these events is given in the *J* strand of *Genesis* and in *Jubilees*, and appears to have been quite rapid. *Jubilees* maintains that the following events all occurred within a two-month span of time during Abraham's 99th year of life[690]: (1) Allah talked to Abraham at Hebron, and announced the coming birth of Isaac—conforms to the angelic visit in *Genesis* and the *Qur'an*; (2) Sodom and Gomorrah were destroyed—conforms to *Genesis* and to the *Qur'an*; (3) Abraham moved deep into the Negeb, between Kadesh and Shur, near the mountains of Gerar[691] —conforms to the *E* strand of *Genesis* account of such a move by Abraham; (4) Abraham moved to Beersheba, which was only 18 miles (29 kilometers) southeast of Gerar—conforms to the *E* strand account of Abraham having dealings with Abimelech, the king of Gerar; and (5) Sarah conceived.[692] Having established the above sequence, one then can insert the following additional events into the timeline: (A) the angels announced the coming destruction of Sodom and Gomorrah, inserted between 1 and 2 above; (B) Isaac was born and circumcised, inserted after 5 above; (C) Abraham and Abimilech, the king of Gerar, resolved a dispute about a well at Beersheba, inserted after addition B in order to conform to the sequencing within the *J* strand of *Genesis*; and (D) Abraham celebrated Isaac being weaned, inserted after addition C.[693] As such, the following sequential steps are proposed for Abraham in Palestine – IV:

1. Angels visit Abraham at Hebron:
    A. Announcing the coming of Isaac; and
    B. Announcing the destruction of Sodom and Gomorrah.
2. Sodom and Gomorrah are destroyed.
3. Abraham moves to between Kadesh and Shur.
4. Abraham moves to Beersheba, which was near Gerar.
5. Sarah conceives.
6. Isaac is born and circumcised.
7. Abraham confronts King Abimelech about the well.
8. Isaac is weaned.

However, before leaving this discussion of the events transpiring during Abraham's fourth sojourn in Palestine, it should be noted that the various accounts in *Genesis* and in the *Qur'an* of the angelic visitation can appear upon superficial reading to be in significant conflict with each other. More specifically, these accounts may appear to disagree in respect to the sequential details involving: when Sarah laughed; and whether the birth of Isaac was predicted before or after the prediction of the destruction of Sodom and Gomorrah. As shown in Table 8, these apparent inconsistencies are resolved as soon as one places these passages next to each other in sequential format. Such a procedure demonstrates that: Sarah laughed at least twice, and for very different reasons each time; and the prediction of the destruction of Sodom and Gomorrah was given both before and after the prediction of the birth of Isaac.

Table 8:
Sequential Steps in the Angelic Visitation

J Strand (*Genesis* 18:1-33)	*Qur'an* 11: 69-76	*Qur'an* 51: 24-37	*Qur'an* 15: 51-60	*Qur'an* 29: 31-32
Angels arrive	Angels arrive	Angels arrive	Angels arrive	Angels arrive
Salutation	Salutation	Salutation "Unusual men"	Salutation	
Calf & food	Roasted calf	Roasted calf		
Angels ate	No eating	No eating		
	Abraham's fear	Abraham's fear		
	1st Sodom prediction			
	Sarah laughed			
Isaac prediction	Isaac prediction	Isaac prediction	Isaac prediction	
Sarah laughs		Sarah laughs [694]		
Sarah doubts	Sarah doubts	Sarah doubts		
	Discussion w. Sarah	Discussion w. Sarah		
			Disc. w. Abraham	
Sodom prediction		Sodom prediction	Sodom prediction	Sodom predictior
Abraham's plea	Abraham's plea	Abraham's plea	Abraham's plea	Abraham's plea

Events in Makkah – III

Sahih Ahadith report three trips made by Abraham to Makkah, after the death of Hagar, after the marriage of Ismael, and before the death of Sarah.[695] These associations with Hagar, Sarah, and Ismael allow these trips to be placed between Abraham's 106th and 137th year of life.[696] In addition, the *Qur'an* also refers to the third of these three trips that Abraham made to Makkah, at which time Abraham and Ismael built the Ka'ba.[697] It is noted that in neither of the first two trips is there any mention of Ismael having fathered any children. However, the Qur'anic account of the third trip implies that Ismael may have had children at the time of the building of the Ka'ba, as indicated by Abraham's prayer, in which he refers to "some of my offspring" residing in Makkah.[698]

Given the above, the following three sequential events are posited for Abraham in Makkah.

1. Abraham attempts to visit Ismael, finds him gone, and meets Ismael's first wife.
2. Abraham attempts to visit Ismael, finds him gone, and meets Ismael's second wife.
3. Abraham and Ismael build the Ka'ba.

Events in Palestine – V

The final chapter in the life of Abraham is represented by events placed by this author in Abraham's fifth sojourn in Palestine. By and large, one is dependent upon information provided by *Genesis* for the events occurring in this segment of Abraham's life, although *Jubilees* provides some dating information, and although one event finds mention only in *Al-Tabari*. For most of these events, precise dating is offered by the *P* strand of *Genesis* or by *Jubilees*. Thus, one notes that: (1) Abraham moved back to Hebron from Beersheba, when Abraham was 134 years old[699]; (2) Sarah died when Abraham was 137 years old[700]; (3) Isaac married Rebekah when Abraham was 140 years old[701]; (4) Isaac fathered Esau and Jacob, who were twins, when Abraham was 160 years old[702]; and (5) Abraham died when he was 175 years old.[703] However, for two other events, dating becomes a most precarious enterprise, and one is left with a wide range of possible dates for these two events. These two events are: (A) Abraham married Keturah (Qantura, the daughter of Maftur) and fathered Zimran, Jokshan, Medan, Midian, Ishbak, Shu'ah, and Basar[704]; and (B) Abraham married Hajur, the daughter of Arhir, and fathered Kaysan, Shawarukh, Amin, Lutan, and Nafis.[705]

Quite frankly, one is left to speculate about the dating of these last two events. In that regard, given Sarah's earlier conflict with Hagar, once Abraham had married Hagar, one suspects that Abraham did not marry Keturah or Hajur until after the death of Sarah. As such, these two marriages would appear to have occurred after Abraham's 137th year of life. Given that Abraham reportedly fathered at least seven children out of Keturah, and given that Abraham died at age 175, one suspects that Abraham married Keturah before his 168th year of life. In addition, given that Abraham reportedly fathered at least five children out of Hajur, and given that Abraham died at age 175, one suspects that Abraham married Hajur before his 170th year of life. These are, however, rather wide ranges for dating.

There may be an additional clue, which can help narrow down the range of possibilities. The *J* strand of *Genesis* implies that Abraham's sons out of Keturah, and by extension out of Hajur, although the *J* strand never mentions anything to do with this latter marriage, were old enough to have been sent out on their own before Abraham died.[706] This implication receives explicit support from *Jubilees*, where it is stated that Keturah's sons by Abraham were all old enough to have children of their own by the time of Abraham's death.[707] If one accepts this implication, and if one thus assumes that the youngest child from each of these two marriages must have been at least 20 years old at the time of Abraham's death, this narrows the range considerably. Given these considerations, Abraham appears to have married Keturah between his 138th and 148th year of life, and he appears to have married Hajur between his 138th and 150th year of life. As such, it would appear more likely than not that these two marriages transpired after Isaac married Rebekah, but before the birth of Jacob and Esau.

However, before being totally satisfied with those ranges of estimates, *Jubilees* provides some additional information. First, *Jubilees* states that Isaac married Rebekah before Abraham married Keturah.[708] (Unfortunately, like the *J* strand, *Jubilees* makes no mention of Hajur.) This refines the earlier estimate of when Abraham married Keturah to between Abraham's 140th and 148th year of life. However, *Jubilees* offers one additional piece of information regarding this marriage to

Keturah, when it notes that there was a 14 year range between the oldest
and youngest son produced by this marriage.[709] As the current estimate of
Abraham being 140 to 148 years of age at the time of marrying Keturah
was based on a range of seven years between oldest and youngest child,
this further constricts the estimate to Abraham being 140 to 141 years of
age. As it appears reasonable to assume that Abraham married Hajur after
he married Keturah, this marriage is placed after the one to Keturah.

In summary, the following sequential events are hypothesized for
Abraham's fifth sojourn in Palestine.

1. Abraham moves from Beersheba back to Hebron, when he is
   about 134 years old.
2. Sarah dies, when Abraham is 137 years old.
3. Abraham arranges for Isaac's marriage to Rebekah, when
   Abraham is 140 years old.
4. Abraham marries Keturah (probably between his 140th and 141st
   years of life), and fathers seven children out of her.
5. Abraham marries Hajur (probably between his 140th and 150th
   years of life), and fathers five children out of her.
6. Isaac fathers twin sons, Esau and Jacob, when Abraham is 160
   years old.
7. Abraham dies at age 175.

Summary of Sequential Events in Abraham's life

Table 9 presents a listing in chart form of the major events in Abraham's
life. Included in this chart is a listing of the estimated date at the time of
the event, Abraham's probable age at the time of the event, the location
of the event, and the event in question. Because the entries in this chart
have been discussed in some depth previously in this appendix, the
references that were previously given in this appendix are not needlessly
repeated here.

Table 9: Summary of Abraham's life

Date[710]	Age[711]	Location	Event
2,166	–	Ur, Iraq	Birth of Abraham, the son of Azar.
2,152	14	Ur, Iraq	Abraham uses natural observation to arrive at the truth of monotheism—start of his message to the people of Ur.

Date	Age	Location	Event
2,150	16	Ur, Iraq	Abraham destroys the temple idols,
2,150	16	Ur, Iraq	Abraham is tried by the emperor, Naram-Sin.
2,150	16	Ur, Iraq	Abraham is thrown into the fire.
2,150	16	Ur, Iraq	Lot converts.
2,117	49	Ur, Iraq	Abraham marries Sarah.
2,106	60	Ur, Iraq	Abraham burns the temple at Ur? Death of Lot's father, Haran II?
2,105	61	Ur, Iraq	Abraham, Sarah, Lot, Azar, Nahor II, and Milcah leave Ur.
2,105	61	Harran, Turkey	Abraham and his group arrive in Harran —start of Abraham's message to the people of Harran.
2,091	75	Harran, Turkey	Abraham's father threatens to kill Abraham.
2,091	75	Harran, Turkey	Abraham makes his final break from his father.
2,091	75	Harran, Turkey	Abraham, Sarah, and Lot leave Harran.
2,091	75	Syria & Jorden	Abraham, Sarah, and Lot pass through Syria and Jordan.
2,091	75	Palestine	Abraham, Sarah, and Lot enter Palestine.
2,091	75	Shechem, Palestine	Abraham builds an altar to Allah—start of his message to the people of Palestine.
2,091	75	Bethel, Palestine.	Abraham builds an altar to Allah.
2,091	75	Hebron, Palestine.	Abraham, Sarah, and Lot settle in Hebron for two years.
2,089	77	Bealoth, Palestine.	Abraham, Sarah, and Lot confront a famine.
2,089	77	Egypt	Abraham, Sarah, and Lot enter Egypt – start of Abraham's message to the people of Egypt.
2,089	77	Egypt	For the next five years, Abraham and Lot prosper and become wealthy.

Date	Age	Location	Event
2,084	82	Egypt	The pharaoh takes Sarah, and is afflicted by Allah.
2,084	82	Egypt	The pharaoh returns Sarah, and gives gifts of reparation, including Hagar.
2,084	82	Egypt	The pharaoh orders Abraham, Lot, Sarah, and Hagar out of Egypt.
2,084	82	Palestine	Abraham, Lot, Sarah, and Hagar enter Palestine —Abraham resumes his message to the people of Palestine.
2,084	82	Bethel, Palestine.	Abraham and Lot separate—Lot begins his message to the people of Sodom.
2,084	82	Hebron, Palestine.	Abraham, Sarah, and Hagar move to Hebron.
2,081	85	Hebron, Palestine.	Sarah gives Hagar to Abraham as a second wife.
2,081	85	Hebron, Palestine.	Hagar becomes pregnant by Abraham.
2,081	85	Hebron, Palestine.	Sarah deals harshly with Hagar.
2,081	85	Hebron, Palestine.	Hagar escapes from Sarah, gets to Kadesh on her way back to Egypt, is confronted by an angel, and then returns to Hebron.
2,080	86	Hebron, Palestine.	Ismael is born.
2,079	87	Hebron, Palestine.	Sarah orders the banishment of Hagar and Ismael.
2,079	87	Makkah, Saudi Arabia	Abraham leaves Hagar and Ismael in Makkah, where Gabriel intervenes to save them.
2,078	88	Hebron, Palestine.	Hebron receives word of Lot's capture.

Date	Age	Location	Event
2,078	88	Hebron, Palestine.	Abraham arms his 318 servants, enlists his allies (Mamre, Eshcol, and Aner), and gives pursuit.
2,078	88	Laish, Syria.	Abraham's forces defeat the five kings of Iraq and Iran.
2,078	88	Hobah, Syria.	Abraham's forces stop their pursuit of the routed armies of Iraq and Iran.
2,078	88	Shaveh, Palestine.	Abraham and his returning forces are greeted by King Melchizedek, Jerusalem, who blesses Abraham in the name of Allah.
2,078	88	Shaveh, Palestine.	Abraham returns the booty and people to Bera, the king of Sodom.
2,067	99	Makkah, Saudi Arabia.	Abraham's intended sacrifice of Ismael.
2,067	99	Makkah, Saudi Arabia.	Allah establishes his covenant with Abraham.
2,067	99	Makkah, Saudi Arabia.	The circumcision of Abraham and Ismael.
2,067	99	Hebron, Palestine.	Three angels visit Abraham, and predict the birth of Isaac and the destruction of Sodom and Gomorrah.
2,067	99	Siddim, Palestine.	Destruction of Sodom and Gomorrah, from which Lot escapes.
2,067	99	Sinai, Palestine.	Abraham moves to between Kadesh and Shur
2,067	99	Beersheba, Palestine.	Abraham moves to Beersheba.
2,066	100	Beersheba, Palestine.	Confrontation with King Abimelech of Gerar over a well.
2,066	100	Beersheba, Palestine.	Birth and circumcision of Isaac.
2,068	102	Beersheba, Palestine.	Weaning of Isaac.
?	? [712]	Makkah, Saudi Arabia.	Abraham attempts to visit Ismael, and finds only Ismael's wife.

Date	Age	Location	Event
?	? [713]	Makkah, Saudi Arabia.	Abraham's attempts to visit Ismael, and finds only Ismael's new wife.
?	? [714]	Makkah, Saudi Arabia.	Abraham and Ismael build the Ka'ba.
2,032	134	Hebron, Palestine.	Abraham moves from Beersheba to Hebron.
2,029	137	Hebron, Palestine.	Sarah dies and is buried at Hebron.
2,026	140	Harran, Turkey.	Abraham, remaining in Hebron in Palestine, arranges for Isaac's marriage to Rebekah from Harran, Turkey.
2,025	141	Hebron, Palestine.	Abraham marries Keturah, and fathers seven children by her.
?	? [715]	Hebron, Palestine.	Abraham marries Hajur, and fathers five children by her.
2,006	160	Palestine	Isaac fathers Esau and Jacob.
1,991	175	Hebron, Palestine.	The death and burial of Abraham at Hebron.

Appendix V
The Offspring of Abraham

The immediate offspring of Abraham, as mentioned in the various sources are numerous.[716] Table 10 presents some of this information for a few generations post Abraham. However, the reader should note that Table 10 is by no means an exhaustive listing of Abraham's offspring. Numbers have been included in the text of the table to allow the reader: to align easily the different generations of offspring of Abraham; and to determine quickly how many generations removed a particular descendant is from Abraham. The initials "pbuh" follow the names of individuals recognized within Islam as having been prophets of Allah.

Table 10
The Offspring of Abraham

Out of Hagar

Ismael (pbuh)

1 Nabaioth (Nabet), the eponymous ancestor of the Nabetaeans

1 Kedar (Qaydar) from which line Prophet Muhammad descended

1 Adbeel (Adabil or Adbal)

1 Mibsam (Mabasha or Mabasham)

1 Mishma (Masma')

1 Dumah (Duma or Dhuma)

1 Massa (Mas or Masa)

1 Hadad (Adad or Haddad)

1 Tema (Tuma or Taym)

1 Jetur (Yatur or Watur)

1 Naphish (Nafis)

1 Kedemah (Qaydaman or Qadaman)

1 Mahalath (Basemath or Basmah), wife of Esau, son of Isaac, son of Abraham

Out of Sarah Bt. Haran I

Isaac (pbuh)

1 Esau (Edom or Seir), the eponymous ancestor of the Edomites

1 2 Eliphaz

1 2 3 Teman

1 2 3 Omar

1 2 3 Zepho

1 2 3 Kenaz

1 2 3 Korah

1 2 3 Gatam

1 2 3 Amalek, the eponymous ancestor
           of the Amalekites?

1 2 Reuel or Al-Rum

1 2 3 Nahath

1 2 3 Zerah

1 2 3 Shammah

1 2 3 Mizzah

1 2 Jeush

1 2 Jalam

1 2 Korah

1 2 Razih or Raghwil

1 2 3 Maws or Mawas

1 2 3 4 Job (Ayyub, pbuh)

1 Jacob (pbuh), Israel – the eponymous ancestor of the 12 tribes
   of Israel

1 2 Reuben, the eponymous ancestor of the Israelite tribe
         of Reuben

1 2 3 Hanoch

1 2 3 Pallu

1 2 3 Hezron

1 2 3 Carmi

1 2 Simeon, the eponymous ancestor of the Israelite tribe
         of Simeon

1 2 3   Jemuel (Nemuel)

1 2 3   Jamin

1 2 3   Ohad

1 2 3   Jachin

1 2 3   Zohar (Zerah)

1 2 3   Shaul

1 2   Levi, the eponymous ancestor of the Israelite tribe
    of Levi (Levites)

1 2 3   Gershon

1 2 3   Kohath

1 2 3   Merari

1 2   Judah, the eponymous ancestor of the Israelite tribe
    of Judah (Jews)

1 2 3   Er

1 2 3   Onan

1 2 3   Shelah

1 2 3   Perez

1 2 3 4   Hezron

1 2 3 4   Hamul

1 2 3   Zerah

1 2   Dan, the eponymous ancestor of the Israelite tribe of Dan

1 2 3   Hashum (Hushim or Shuham)

1 2   Naphtali, the eponymous ancestor of the Israelite tribe
    of Naphtali

1 2 3   Jahzeel

1 2 3   Guni

1 2 3   Jezer

1 2 3   Shillem

1 2   Gad, the eponymous ancestor of the Israelite tribe of Gad

1 2 3   Ziphion (Zephon)

1 2 3   Haggi

1 2 3   Shuni

1 2 3   Ezbon (Ozni)

1 2 3 Eri

1 2 3 Arodi (Arod)

1 2 3 Areli

1 2 Asher, the eponymous ancestor of the Israelite tribe
     of Asher

1 2 3 Imnah

1 2 3 Ishvah

1 2 3 Ishvi

1 2 3 Beriah

1 2 3 4 Heber

1 2 3 4 Malchiel

1 2 3 Serah

1 2 Issachar, the eponymous ancestor of the Israelite tribe
     of Issachar

1 2 3 Tola

1 2 3 Puvah

1 2 3 Jashub

1 2 3 Shimron

1 2 Zebulun, the eponymous ancestor of the Israelite tribe
     of Zebulun

1 2 3 Sered

1 2 3 Elon

1 2 3 Jahleel

1 2 Dinah, possibly the wife of Job b Maws b
     Razih b Esau b Isaac

1 2 Joseph (pbuh), the eponymous ancestor of the
     Israelite tribe of Joseph

1 2 3 Manasseh, the eponymous ancestor
       of the tribe of Manasseh

1 2 3 4 Machir

1 2 3 4 5 Gilead

1 2 3 Ephraim, the eponymous ancestor of the tribe
       of Ephraim

1 2 Benjamin, the eponymous ancestor of the Israelite tribe
     of Benjamin

1 2 3 Bela

1 2 3 Becher

1 2 3 Ashbel

1 2 3 Gera

1 2 3 Naaman [717]

1 2 3 Ehi

1 2 3 Rosh

1 2 3 Muppim

1 2 3 Huppim (Hupham)

1 2 3 Ard [718]

Out of Keturah (Qantura Bt. Maftur or Qaturah Bt. Yaqtan)

Zimran

Jokshan

1 Sheba

1 Dedan, the eponymous ancestor of the Dedanites

1 2 Asshurim

1 2 Letushim

1 2 Leummim

Medan

Midian, the eponymous ancestor of the Midianites

1 Ephah

1 Epher

1 Hanoch

1 Abida

1 Elda'ah

1 Thabit

1 2 'Anqa

1 2 3 Safyun

1 2 3 4 Shu'ayb (pbuh)

Ishbak

Shu'ah

Basar

Out of Hajur Bt. Arhir

Kaysan
Shawarukh
Amin
Lutan
Nafis

Notes

Notes

Chapter 1: Introduction

1. It is customary for Muslims to use the phrase "peace be upon him" after the mention of one of the prophets recognized by Islam. However, for non-Muslim readers, this practice frequently becomes an irritant and a hindrance in reading. As such, in the current book, the phrase "peace be upon him" will be used after the first use of a prophet's name within the main text, and will then be discontinued for subsequent reiterations of that prophet's name.

2. The Jewish tradition recognizes a prior, limited covenant between Allah and Noah, but this pre-dates the tracing of the Hebrew people through Eber.

3. *Qur'an* 16: 120-123.

4. *Qur'an* 6: 83-90; 19: 41.

5. *Qur'an* 53:36-37; 87:18-19. The Islamic tradition maintains that this book of revelation has subsequently been lost.

6. Eighth century BCE or later book of *Isaiah* 41:8.

7. Fourth century BCE book of *II Chronicles* 20:7.

8. First century CE book of *James* 2:23.

9. *Qur'an* 4: 125.

10. See, for example, the following. Ginzberg L (1909-1936).

11. *Al-Bukhari* 4: 667.

Chapter 2: The Birth and Family of Abraham

12. See Appendix II (Chronology) for the reasoning behind the author's determination of the time of Abraham.

13. (A) Tenth century BCE *J* strand of *Genesis* 11: 29; 12:1, 6-7,9-10, 14, 16-18; 13: 1-2, 4-5, 7-8, 14, 18; 15: 1,3,11-12,18; 16: 2, 5-6. (B) Eighth century BCE *E* strand of *Genesis* 15:2,13. (C) Sixth or fifth century BCE *P* strand of *Genesis* 11: 26-27,31; 12: 4-5; 13: 12; 16: 1,3, 15-16; 17: 1, 3, 5. (D) Undated and unknown strand of *Genesis* 14: 12-14, 19-23.

14. Marks JH (1971).

15. Sixth or fifth century BCE *P* strand of *Genesis* 17: 5.

16. Marks JH (1971).

17. *Qur'an* 6: 74.

18. *Al-Bukhari* 4: 569.

19. Sixth or fifth century BCE *P* strand of *Genesis* 5: 3-32; 11: 10-26.

20. Sixth or fifth century BCE *P* strand of *Genesis* 11:26-27.

21. *Al-Tabari* (1987).

22. Third or second century BCE book of *Jubilees* 8:1-6.

23. Third or second century BCE book of *Jubilees* 11:14-15.

24. (A) Eighth century BCE *E* strand of *Exodus* 3:1. (B) Tenth century BCE *J* strand of *Exodus* 2:18. (C) Tenth century BCE *J* strand of *Numbers* 10: 29.

25. (A) Seventh century BCE book of *Deuteronomy* 26: 5-10. (B) Sixth or fifth century BCE *P* strand of *Genesis* 28: 5

26. Sixth or fifth century BCE *P* strand of *Genesis* 10: 22.

27. Sixth or fifth century BCE *P* strand of *Genesis* 11: 10-26.

28. (A) Tenth century BCE *J* strand of *Genesis* 22:20-23. (B) Sixth or fifth century BCE *P* strand of *Genesis* 10:22-23.

29. (A) Sixth or fifth century BCE *P* strand of *Genesis* 11: 31; 12: 4. (B) Tenth century BCE *J* strand of *Genesis* 24: 10.

30. (A) Sixth or fifth century BCE *P* strand of *Genesis* 5:6-26. (B) Tenth century BCE *J* strand of *Genesis* 4: 17-19.

31. Robinson TH (1929a).

32. *Qur'an* 6:74.

33. *Al-Bukhari* 4:569.

34. The identification of Terah as the father of Abraham is also found in *Joshua* 24: 2. While not in the *Torah*, *Joshua* is part of the Jewish scriptures and this particular verse appears to be from the eighth century BCE *E* strand. See Smith RH (1971a).

35. (A) *Al-Tabari* (1987) variously states that: Azar is merely the Arabic rendering of Terah (page 15); and Terah was the actual name of Abraham's father, while Azar was a name later given to Terah by Nimrod (page 22). (B) Hughes TP (1994).

36. (A) Wright GE (1960), (B) Marks JH (1971), (C) Robinson TH (1929b).

37. The construction of this family tree is based on synthesizing the following information. (A) Sixth or fifth century BCE *P* strand of *Genesis* 11: 10-27; 25: 20. (B) *Al-Tabari* (1987), pages 15 and 22. (C) Third or second century BCE book of *Jubilees* 8: 1-6. (D) *Qur'an* 6: 74. (E) *Al-Bukhari* 4: 569. (F) Tenth century BCE *J* strand of Genesis 22: 20-23; 24: 67. (G) Eighth century BCE *E* strand of *Genesis* 29: 16-23,25-28.

38. Eighth century BCE *E* strand of *Genesis* 20: 11-12.

39. Third or second century BCE book of *Jubilees* 12: 9-10.

40. The Mosaic Law prohibiting marriage between paternal half-siblings can be found in the sixth or fifth century BCE *P* strand of *Leviticus* 18: 9; 20: 17.

41. For references concerning the necessarily incestuous marriages of the sons and daughters of Adam and Eve, see the following sources. (A) Third or second century BCE book of *Jubilees* 4: 9-15. (B) *Al-Tabari* (1989).

42. *Al-Tabari* (1987), page 129.

43. *Al-Tabari* (1987), page 111.

44. Sixth or fifth century BCE *P* strand of *Genesis* 17: 17.

45. *Al-Tabari* (1987), pages 61-62.

46. Tenth century BCE *J* strand of *Genesis* 11: 28-30.

47. Josephus F (1988, 1999). Of note, Josephus may well have had access to a more ancient version of the *Torah* than exists today (Rohl DM (1995)), and, if so, that version may have made clear that Sarah was the daughter of a Haran.

48. Sixth or fifth century BCE *P* strand of *Genesis* 11:31.

49. Sixth of fifth century BCE *P* strand of *Genesis* 11:31.

50. (A) *Qur'an* 6: 74. (B) *Al-Bukhari* 4:569.

51. Terah may or may not have been identical with Azar.

52. Sixth or fifth century BCE *P* strand of *Genesis* 11:10-26.

53. See Appendix II (Chronology) for a discussion of these issues.

Chapter 3: Abraham in Ur

54. (A) Eighth century BCE or later editorial insertion into the 10th century BCE *J* strand of *Genesis* 11: 28-30; 15: 7. (B) Fourth century BCE book of *Nehemiah* 9: 7. (C) Sixth or fifth century BCE *P* strand of *Genesis* 11:31.

(D) Sixth or fifth century BCE *P* strand of *Genesis* 11: 31; 12: 4-5. (E) Tenth century BCE *J* strand of *Genesis* 24:1-10,15,50. (F) Given *E,* then also see the eighth century BCE combined *JE* strand of *Genesis* 27: 42-45 and the sixth and fifth century BCE *P* strand of *Genesis* 28: 1-2. (G) See discussion in Appendix II (Chronology: The *Torah* and Biblical References: Abraham's Initial Residence).

55. Sixth or fifth century BCE *P* strand of *Genesis* 11:26-27,31.

56. *Qur'an* 6:74; 9:113-114; 19:41-46; 21:51-57; 26:70-71; 37:83-93; 43:26.

57. The hypothesis that Azar kept idols within the family home finds indirect support in the eighth century BCE *E* strand of *Genesis* 31:19, where it is noted that Rachel stole the household idols from her father's house. By combining the 10th century BCE *J* strand information of *Genesis* 22: 20; 24: 29; and 29: 10, one identifies Rachel as the daughter of Laban, the son of Bethuel, the son of Nahor II, the brother of Abraham.

58. See Appendix IV (Sequential Events in Abraham's Life: Events in Ur) for the reasoning behind the dating of this event to Abraham's early teenage years.

59. Third or second century BCE book of *Jubilees* 11:15-16.

60. *Qur'an* 6: 75-79. 'Ali has suggested that these verses be interpreted as an allegory. This is an option rejected by the current author, as it was precisely the moon, sun, and evening star that were the primary focus of worship in Ur during the third millennium BCE, an archaeological discovery not made until the 20th century CE, i.e., approximately 13 centuries after the revelation of the above *Ayat*! For those who have any doubt about the divine nature of the revelation of the *Qur'an*, the above consideration is worthy of contemplation. 'Ali 'AY (1992a), notes # 898-901.

61. Some commentators on the *Qur'an* interpret the above quoted Qur'anic verses as being examples of Abraham's arguments to his people against astral polytheism, as opposed to being a process of naturalistic observation whereby Abraham reasoned to intellectual monotheism. This interpretation finds some support in *Qur'an* 6: 83: "That was the reasoning about Us, which We gave to Abraham (to use) against his people". However, in this author's opinion, the two interpretations, i.e., naturalistic observation vs. rhetorical argument, are neither mutually contradictory nor mutually exclusive. Nonetheless, as in all cases, Allah knows best.

62. Josephus F (1999).

63. *Qur'an* 2: 130.

64. *Qur'an* 6: 83, 87-88. Material within square brackets is the author's editorial insertion.

65. *Qur'an* 16: 120-121.

66. *Qur'an* 38: 45-47.

67. *Qur'an* 19: 41; 37: 84; 21: 51.

68. *Qur'an* 19: 41; 16: 120; 60: 4.

69. *Qur'an* 16: 121.

70. *Qur'an* 2: 130-131.

71. *Da'wa* may be translated as "preaching" or "religious exhortation".

72. While the above statement is based solely on what appears to the author to have been probable. It is noted the proposed sequence of events has important parallels in the *Da'wa* of Prophet Muhammad. Muhammad began his *Da'wa* with his wife, Khadijah, then with his close relatives and friends, then with his clan, and then with the Quraish tribe as a whole. (A) Al-Mubarakpuri S (1996). (B) Haykal MK (1976). (C) Lings M (1983). (D) Siddiqui AH (1991).

73. *Qur'an* 6: 74.

74. Third or second century BCE book of *Jubilees* 12: 1-5.

75. This hypothesis is based on the eighth century BCE *E* strand of *Genesis* 31: 19, where it is recounted that Rachel stole her father's household idols from her father. Rachel's father is identified as Laban, the son of Bethuel, the son of Nahor II, the brother of Abraham by combining the information in the 10th century BCE *J* strand of *Genesis* 29: 10; 22: 20; 24: 29.

76. This hypothesis is based on the third or second century BCE book of *Jubilees* 12: 12-14.

77. *Qur'an* 29: 16-18.

78. *Qur'an* 26: 70-102.

79. *Qur'an* 6: 80-82.

80. Consider for example, Jesus driving the money changers from the temple in Jerusalem (*Matthew* 21:12-13; *Mark* 11:15-19; *Luke* 19:45-48) and Muhammad destroying the idols in the Ka'ba, as referenced in: (A) Al-Mubarakpuri S (1996). (B) Siddiqui AH (1991). (C) Lings M (1983). (D) Haykal MH (1976).

81. (A) *Al-Tabari* (1987). (B) Al-Kisa'i (1978). (C) Al-Tha'labi AM (---). (D) Hatun HA (1996).

82. *Qur'an* 21: 51-57.

83. *Al-Bukhari* 4: 578.

84. *Qur'an* 37: 88-90.

85. *Qur'an* 37: 91-92.

86. *Qur'an* 37: 93.

87. *Qur'an* 21: 58.

88. *Qur'an* 37: 94-96.

89. *Qur'an* 37: 97.

90. *Qur'an* 21: 59-67.

91. *Al-Bukhari* 4: 578.

92. In so doing, the teenage Abraham's actions were foreshadowing an alleged event from the life of Prophet Jesus. See *Luke* 2: 41-51.

93. *Qur'an* 2: 258.

94. *Qur'an* 21: 68; 37: 97.

95. *Qur'an* 26: 90-95.

96. *Al-Tabari* (1987), page 68.

97. *Al-Bukhari* 6: 86, 87. These words of Abraham were reiterated by Prophet Muhammad, when he was confronted by a large army opposing him. See *Qur'an* 3: 173.

98. *Qur'an* 21: 68-69.

99. *Qur'an* 29: 24.

100. *Qur'an* 21: 70.

101. *Qur'an* 37: 98.

102. (A) Josephus F (1988, 1999). (B) Sixth of fifth century BCE *P* strand of *Genesis* 11: 31; 12: 5. (C) Tenth century BCE *J* strand of *Genesis* 11: 27-28.

103. *Qur'an* 29: 24-26.

104. Josephus F (1988, 1999).

105. *Al-Tabari* (1987), page 61.

106. (A) Tenth century BCE *J* strand of *Genesis* 11: 29; 12: 11, 17; 16: 2, 5-6, 8. (B) Sixth or fifth century BCE *P* strand of *Genesis* 11: 31; 12:5; 16: 1, 3; 17: 15.

107. Sixth or fifth century BCE *P* strand of *Genesis* 17: 15.

108. Marks JH (1971).

109. Sixth or fifth century BCE *P* strand of *Genesis* 17: 17.

110. Third or second century BCE book of *Jubilees* 11: 14-15; 12: 9-10.

111. Third or second century BCE book of *Jubilees* 11: 14-15; 12: 12-15.

112. See footnote # 75.

113. Third or second century BCE book of *Jubilees* 12: 12-14.

Chapter 4: Abraham in Harran

114. Third or second century BCE book of *Jubilees* 11: 14-15; 12: 12-15.

115. Sixth or fifth century BCE *P* strand of *Genesis* 11: 31.

116. Tenth century BCE *J* strand of *Genesis* 24: 10.

117. The third or second century BCE book of *Jubilees* 12: 31 states that Nahor II was living in Harran by the time Abraham left Harran.

118. (A) *Qur'an* 9: 113-114; 19: 41-49. (B) Epstein I (1966).

119. See footnote # 75.

120. Eighth century BCE or later editorial gloss of or editorial insertion into the *J* strand of *Genesis* 11:28.

121. Josephus F (1988, 1999).

122. *Qur'an* 29:26.

123. For information on the pilgrimage of Prophet Muhammad, see the following sources. (A) Al-Mubarakpuri S (1996). (B) Lings M (1983). (C) Haykal MH (1976). (D) Siddiqui AH (1991)

124. Third or second century BCE book of *Jubilees* 12: 12-13.

125. Third or second century BCE book of *Jubilees* 12: 14.

126. Eighth century BCE or later editorial gloss of or editorial insertion into the 10th century *J* strand of *Genesis* 11:28.

127. Josephus F (1988, 1999).

128. Third or second century BCE book of *Jubilees* 12: 9-15.

129. *Qur'an* 19: 41-45.

130. *Qur'an* 19: 46.

131. *Qur'an* 19: 47-48.

132. It is unclear exactly when Abraham made this final prayer for Allah to forgive and guide Azar, although it appears from *Qur'an* 14: 35-41 that this prayer was made many years after the separation from Azar, and after Abraham and Ismael built the Ka'ba at Makkah.

133. *Qur'an* 9: 113-114.

134. *Qur'an* 60: 4.

135. *Qur'an* 60: 4-6.

136. Tenth century BCE *J* strand of *Genesis* 12:1-4a.

137. Third or second century BCE book of *Jubilees* 12: 15-16.

138. Third or second century BCE book of *Jubilees* 11:16; 12: 12-15.

139. Third or second century BCE book of *Jubilees* 11: 14-15; 12: 12-15.

140. Sixth or fifth century BCE *P* strand of *Genesis* 12: 4b.

141. Sixth or fifth century BCE *P* strand of *Genesis* 17: 17.

142. Sixth or fifth century BCE *P* strand of *Genesis* 11: 32 followed by the 10th century BCE *J* strand of *Genesis* 12: 1.

143. *Qur'an* 9: 113-114; 19: 41-48; 60: 4.

144. Sixth or fifth century BCE *P* strand of *Genesis* 11: 26,32; 12: 4b.

Chapter 5: Abraham in Palestine I

145. (A) Sixth or fifth century BCE *P* strand of *Genesis* 12: 4b. (B) Third or second century BCE book of *Jubilees* 12: 12-16.

146. Sixth or fifth century BCE *P* strand of *Genesis* 12: 4b; 17: 17.

147. Sixth or fifth century BCE *P* strand of *Genesis* 12: 5.

148. Josephus F (1988, 1999).

149. Tenth century BCE *J* strand of *Genesis* 12: 6.

150. Tenth century BCE *J* strand of *Genesis* 12: 8.

151. Tenth century BCE *J* strand of *Genesis* 12: 6.

152. Tenth century BCE *J* strand of *Genesis* 12: 6.

153. Tenth century BCE *J* strand of *Genesis* 12: 7.

154. Tenth century BCE *J* strand of *Genesis* 12: 7.

155. (A) Tenth century BCE *J* strand of *Genesis* 12: 8. (B) Third or second century BCE book of *Jubilees* 13: 5.

156. (A) Tenth century BCE *J* strand of *Genesis* 12: 8. (B) Third or second century BCE book of *Jubilees* 13: 5.

157. (A) Third or second century BCE book of *Jubilees* 13: 9. (B) Tenth century BCE *J* strand of *Genesis* 12: 8.

158. Tenth century BCE *J* strand of *Genesis* 12: 9.

159. Third or second century BCE book of *Jubilees* 13: 10.

160. (A) Tenth century BCE *J* strand of *Genesis* 13: 18; 18: 1. (B) Unidentified and undated strand of *Genesis* 14: 13. (C) Sixth or fifth century BCE *P* strand of *Genesis* 23: 17-20.

161. Third or second century BCE book of *Jubilees* 13: 10.

162. Third or second century BCE book of *Jubilees* 13: 10.

163. (A) Seventh or sixth century BCE book of *Joshua* 15: 24. (B) Sixth century BCE book of *I Kings* 4: 16.

164. (A) Tenth century BCE *J* strand of *Genesis* 12: 9-10. (B) Third or second century BCE book of *Jubilees* 13: 10-11.

165. (A) Sixth or fifth century BCE *P* strand of *Genesis* 12:4b. (B) Third or second century BCE book of *Jubilees* 12: 12-16.

166. Third or second century BCE book of *Jubilees* 13: 10.

167. Sixth or fifth century BCE *P* strand of *Genesis* 17: 17.

Chapter 6: Abraham in Egypt

168. (A) Tenth century BCE *J* strand of *Genesis* 12: 9-10. (B) Third or second century BCE book of *Jubilees* 13: 10-11.

169. See Appendix II (Chronology).

170. (A) Third or second century BCE book of *Jubilees* 12: 12-16; 13: 10-12. (B) Sixth of fifth century BCE *P* strand of *Genesis* 12: 4b.

171. Rohl DM (1995).

172. Rohl DM (1995).

173. Baines JR (1998b).

174. Budge EAW (1995).

175. Third or second century BCE book of *Jubilees* 13: 11.

176. Tenth century BCE *J* strand of *Genesis* 12: 16. This source also lists camels as among Abraham's possessions, but this would appear to be an anachronism, as camels were not domesticated until almost a millennia after this event took place, as noted in the following sources. (A) Edzard DO, von Soden WT, Frye RN (1998). (B) Marks JH (1971).

177. Third or second century BCE book of *Jubilees* 13: 14.

178. Second or third century BCE *Genesis Apocryphon* 20: 34.

179. Rohl DM (1995).

180. Josephus F (1988, 1999).

181. See Chapter V: Abraham in Palestine I: Postscript to Abraham in Palestine I.

182. (A) Tenth century BCE *J* strand of *Genesis* 12: 11. (B) *Al-Bukhari* 3: 420; 4:578.

183. (A) Tenth century BCE *J* strand of *Genesis* 12: 15. (B) *Al-Bukhari* 3: 420; 4: 578.

184. *Al-Bukhari* 3: 420; 4: 578.

185. *Al-Bukhari* 3: 420; 4: 578.

186. *Al-Bukhari* 3: 420; 3: 803; 4: 578; 7: 21; 9: 82.

187. Tenth century BCE *J* strand of *Genesis* 12: 11-12.

188. Tenth century BCE *J* strand of *Genesis* 12: 16.

189. *Al-Bukhari* 3: 420; 3: 803; 4:578; 7: 21.

190. Eighth century BCE *E* strand of *Genesis* 20:10-13. The *E* strand of *Genesis* 20 is a rather obvious confabulation of the 10th century BCE *J* strand of *Genesis* 12: 10-20 and 26: 6-11, the former *J* strand narrative concerning Abraham and the latter *J* strand narrative concerning Isaac. See Appendix IV (Sequential Events in Abraham's Life: Events in Egypt).

191. Eighth century BCE *E* strand of *Genesis* 20: 11.

192. *Al-Bukhari* 4: 578.

193. *Al-Bukhari* 3: 420; 4: 578.

194. (A) Tenth century BCE *J* strand of *Genesis* 12: 15. (B) *Al-Bukhari* 3: 420; 4: 578.

195. (A) Eighth century BCE *E* strand of *Genesis* 20: 13. (B) Tenth century BCE *J* strand of *Genesis* 12: 12-13. (C) *Al-Bukhari* 3: 420; 4: 578.

196. *Al-Bukhari* 3: 420; 4: 578; 9: 82.

197. *Al-Bukhari* 3: 420; 4: 578.

198. (A) Third or second century BCE book of *Jubilees* 13: 13. (B) Tenth century BCE *J* strand of *Genesis* 12: 17.

199. Eighth century BCE *E* strand of *Genesis* 20: 3, 17-18.

200. *Al-Bukhari* 4: 578.

201. *Al-Bukhari* 3:420; 3:803.

202. Eighth century BCE *E* strand of *Genesis* 20:16.

203. (A) *Al-Bukhari* 3: 420; 3: 803; 4: 578; 7: 21. (B) Second or third century BCE *Genesis Apocryphon* 20: 31-32.

204. (A) Tenth century BCE *J* strand of *Genesis* 12:20. (B) Late second century BCE book of *Jubilees* 13: 15.

205. This age estimate for Sarah is based upon combining the information from the following sources. (A) Sixth or fifth century BCE *P* strand of *Genesis* 12: 4b; 17: 17. (B) Third or second century BCE book of *Jubilees* 12: 12-16; 13: 10-12.

206. Sixth or fifth century BCE *P* strand of *Genesis* 11: 22-25, 32; 23:1; 25: 7.

207. (A) Rohl DM (1995). (B) Baines JR (1998b).

208. *Malik* (1985). *Hadith* 1647.

209. Second or third century BCE *Genesis Apocryphon* 20: 17-18.

Chapter 7: Abraham in Palestine II

210. This estimate is based on a combination of sources. (A) Sixth or fifth century BCE *P* strand of *Genesis* 12: 4b; 17:17. (B) Third or second century book of *Jubilees* 12:12-16; 13:10-12.

211. Eighth century BCE *E* strand of *Genesis* 20:16.

212. (A) Tenth century BCE *J* strand of *Genesis* 12:16; 13:2. (B) Third or second century BCE book of *Jubilees* 13:14 (C) Eighth century BCE *E* strand of *Genesis* 20:14.

213. *Al-Bukhari* 3: 420; 3: 803; 4: 578; 7: 21.

214. Third or second century BCE book of *Jubilees* 13: 14-15.

215. Second or third century BCE *Genesis Apocryphon* 20: 34.

216. Tenth century BCE *J* strand of *Genesis* 13: 1,3.

217. (A) Tenth century BCE *J* strand of *Genesis* 12: 6-8. (B) Third or second century BCE book of *Jubilees* 13: 5, 8-12.

218. Sixth or fifth century BCE *P* strand of *Genesis* 13: 6.

219. Tenth century BCE *J* strand of *Genesis* 13: 7.

220. Josephus F (1988, 1999).

221. Third or second century BCE book of *Jubilees* 12: 12-16; 13: 10-12.

222. Tenth century BCE *J* strand of *Genesis* 13: 8-9.

223. Tenth century BCE *J* strand of *Genesis* 13: 10.

224. Tenth century BCE *J* strand of *Genesis* 13: 10-11. This passage implies that Lot's motivation was based only upon economic and agricultural potential. However, as the various strands comprising *Genesis* frequently attribute rather base motivations to the actions of the prophets, one must look at such statements with a bit of a jaundiced eye.

225. Tenth century BCE *J* strand of *Genesis* 13: 12. This verse indicates that both Abraham and Lot were continuing to live a nomadic, tent-dwelling existence as of this time.

226. Tenth century BCE *J* strand of *Genesis* 13: 12; 19: 1-11.

227. Tenth century BCE *J* strand of *Genesis* 13: 14-17.

228. Tenth century BCE *J* strand of *Genesis* 12: 1-4a.

229. Tenth century BCE *J* strand of *Genesis* 12: 7.

230. Tenth century BCE *J* strand of *Genesis* 13: 18.

231. Tenth century BCE *J* strand of *Genesis* 12: 7.

232. Tenth century BCE *J* strand of *Genesis* 12: 8.

233. Identification of this site with El is based upon linguistic considerations, i.e., Bethel means "house of El".

234. Tenth century BCE *J* strand of *Genesis* 13: 18.

235. Tenth century BCE *J* strand of *Genesis* 15: 1.

236. Eighth century BCE *E* strand of *Genesis* 15: 2,5-6 and tenth century BCE *J* strand of *Genesis* 15: 3-4.

237. Tenth century BCE *J* strand of *Genesis* 15: 7-11.

238. *Qur'an* 2: 260.

239. Tenth century BCE *J* strand of *Genesis* 15: 17-20.

240. *Al-Bukhari* 3: 420; 3: 803; 4: 578; 7: 21.

241. (A) Tenth century BCE *J* strand of *Genesis* 12:20. (B) Third or second century BCE book of *Jubilees* 13: 15.

242. Ages of Abraham and Sarah are based on the combined information within the following sources. (A) Sixth or fifth century BCE *P* strand of *Genesis* 12:4b; 17:17. (B) Third or second century book of *Jubilees* 12: 12-16; 13: 10-12.

243. This time frame can be established by noting Abraham's age when re-entering Palestine, by comparing that age with the information found in the sixth or fifth century BCE *P* strand of *Genesis* 16: 16, which states that Abraham was 86 years old when Hagar gave birth to Ismael, and by allowing a normal nine month gestation for Ismael.

244. Tenth century BCE *J* strand of *Genesis* 16:1b-2,4-6 and sixth or fifth century BCE *P* strand of *Genesis* 16: 3. The last cited verse suggests that Sarah gave Hagar to Abraham as a second wife after Abraham had lived in Palestine for 10 years, thus throwing off all other dating about this event. However, if this verse is read as referring to 10 years having gone by since Abraham first entered Palestine, all the dating immediately lines up again.

245. The figure of 36 years of childless marriage is based upon: (A) the third or second century BCE book of *Jubilees* 11: 14-15; 12: 9-10 where it indicates that Abraham was 49 years old when he married Sarah; (B) the sixth or fifth century BCE *P* strand of *Genesis* 16: 16 where it states that Abraham was 86 years old when Ismael was born; and (C) allowing a normal nine month gestation for Ismael.

246. Tenth century BCE *J* strand of *Genesis* 16: 5-6.

247. Tenth century BCE *J* strand of *Genesis* 16: 5-6.

248. *Al-Bukhari* 4: 584.

249. Tenth century BCE *J* strand of *Genesis* 16: 5.

250. Tenth century BCE *J* strand of *Genesis* 16: 6.

251. Tenth century BCE *J* strand of *Genesis* 16: 6-7, 14.

252. *Al-Bukhari* 4: 583. This *Hadith* prefaces the account of Abraham taking Hagar and the infant Ismael to Makkah, by noting that Hagar was the first person to use a girdle, and that she had used that girdle to cover her tracks from Sarah. This statement about the use of her girdle would make no sense in the context of Hagar and Ismael accompanying Abraham to Makkah, is not

mentioned in the account of Abraham, Hagar, and Ismael going to Makkah in *Al-Bukhari* 4: 584, and most likely refers back to Hagar fleeing from Sarah as recounted in *Genesis*.

253. Tenth century BCE *J* strand of *Genesis* 16: 7, 14.

254. Tenth century BCE *J* strand of *Genesis* 16: 7.

255. (A) Tenth century BCE *J* strand of *Genesis* 12: 20. (B) Third or second century BCE book of *Jubilees* 13: 15.

256. Tenth century BCE *J* strand of *Genesis* 16: 7-8, 11-14.

257. Undated editorial gloss of or editorial insertion into the *J* strand narrative, as found in *Genesis* 16: 10.

258. Sixth or fifth century BCE *P* strand of *Genesis* 16: 15-16.

259. *Al-Bukhari* 4: 583-584.

260. *Al-Bukhari* 3: 420, 803; 4: 578; 7:21.

261. (A) Tenth century BCE *J* strand of *Genesis* 12:20; 16:2,6. (B) Third or second century BCE book of *Jubilees* 13:15. (C) Sixth or fifth century BCE *P* strand of *Genesis* 16: 3.

262. Marks JH (1971).

263. (A) Tenth century BCE *J* strand of *Genesis* 16: 7,11,14. (B) Sixth or fifth century *P* strand of *Genesis* 16: 15-16.

264. This end dating is determined by reference to the story recounted in *Al-Bukhari* 4: 582-584, where it is noted that Ismael was still nursing on Hagar at the time.

265. *Al-Bukhari* 4: 583-584.

266. Tenth century BCE *J* strand of *Genesis* 16: 13, which is quoted in the following. "So she named the Lord who spoke to her, 'You are Elroi'; for she said "Have I really seen God and remained alive after seeing him?'" (See translation footnote explaining the meaning of the name of Elroi.) As this *J* strand verse is currently translated, Hagar appears to be addressing the angel of Allah with the name of Elroi, i.e., "God Who sees". However, as noted elsewhere (Marks JH (1971)) the Hebrew of this verse is badly garbled and difficult to translate. As such, it appears likely to this author that the Hebrew original of this verse contained a statement of Hagar's acceptance of and submission to Allah, in which she acknowledged that Allah had seen her plight.

Chapter 8: Abraham in Makkah I

267. For a detailed analysis of the confabulated nature of the *E* strand narrative of *Genesis* 21:8-21, see Appendix IV (Sequential Events in Abraham's Life: Events in Makkah I).

268. *Al-Bukhari* 4: 584.

269. *Al-Bukhari* 4: 584.

270. One assumes that this is the historical event, which lies behind the contaminated rendition of the eighth century BCE *E* strand of *Genesis* 21: 9: "But Sarah saw the son of Hagar, whom she had borne to Abraham, playing with her son Isaac". The third or second century BCE book of *Jubilees* 17: 1-13 basically follows the *E* strand account of *Genesis* 21: 8-21. However, *Jubilees* 17: 4, which parallels the *E* strand of *Genesis* 21: 9 reads: "And Sarah saw Ishmael playing and dancing, and Abraham rejoicing with great joy, and she became jealous of Ishamel..." For a discussion of the *E* strand account of *Genesis* 21: 8-21 and of how it is a confabulation of the *J* strand account of *Genesis* 16: 5-8,11-14 with the story told in *Al-Bukhari* 4: 582-584, see Appendix IV: Sequential Events in Abraham's Life: Events in Makkah I.

271. Third or second century BCE book of *Jubilees* 17: 4.

272. Tenth century BCE *J* strand of *Genesis* 16: 6.

273. Eighth century BCE *E* strand of *Genesis* 21: 10-11.

274. Eighth century BCE *E* strand of *Genesis* 21: 12-13.

275. Eighth century BCE *E* strand of *Genesis* 21: 14.

276. *Al-Bukhari* 4: 583-584.

277. Lings M (1983).

278. Toombs LE (1971).

279. Lings M (1983).

280. (A) Edzard DO, von Soden WT, Frye RN (1998). (B) Marks JH (1971).

281. It is inferred that Hagar did not yet know the eventual purpose of this journey, given her questions to Abraham when Abraham later left Hagar and Ismael at Bakka. See *Al-Bukhari* 4: 583-584.

282. *Al-Bukhari* 4: 583-584.

283. *Al-Bukhari* 4: 583.

284. *Al-Bukhari* 4: 584.

285. *Al-Bukhari* 4: 583-584.

286. *Al-Bukhari* 4: 583. This *Hadith* then goes on to quote *Qur'an* 14: 37 as the text of Abraham's prayer delivered at this time. There are several reasons to question exactly when Abraham said this prayer. First, Abraham's prayer encompasses *Qur'an* 14: 35-41, and verse 35 refers to Makkah as being a city, but the development of the city of Makkah did not begin until after the Jorhamites joined Hagar and Ismael at Makkah. Second, verse 35 refers to Abraham having sons, not a son, and this would appear to date the prayer to after the birth of Isaac. Third, verse 37 reiterates that Abraham has more than one offspring at the time of the prayer, again suggesting that the prayer was said after the birth of Isaac. Fourth, verse 37 refers to "Thy sacred house", i.e., the Ka'ba, which was not built until many years later by Abraham and Ismael. Fifth, verse 39 specifically refers to both Ismael and Issac having already been born. For all of these reasons, the specific detail of the *Hadith* that links *Qur'an* 14: 37 to the prayer Abraham said as he initially left Hagar and Ismael in Makkah might be questioned, although the fact that Abraham prayed for Hagar and for Ismael would seem rather certain, given the context. Much of this same reasoning is presented in *Ibn Kathir* (1998, pages 238-239), although it is there hypothesized that the prayer, or parts of the prayer, may have been repeated by Abraham on several occasions.

287. Average daily high temperature readings in Makkah are currently about 81 degrees Fahrenheit (27.4 degrees Celsius) during the coolest month, i.e., January, and about 103 degrees Fahrenheit (39.2 degrees Celsius) during the warmest month, i.e., August. Mohamed MN (1996).

288. *Al-Bukhari* 4: 583-584.

289. *Al-Bukhari* 4: 583-584.

290. *Al-Bukhari* 4: 583-584.

291. *Al-Bukhari* 4: 583-584.

292. *Al-Bukhari* 4: 584.

293. *Al-Bukhari* 4: 583.

294. *Al-Bukhari* 4: 582-584.

295. *Al-Bukhari* 4: 583.

296. *Al-Bukhari* 4: 583.

297. *Al-Tabari* (1987).

298. (A) *Al-Bukhari* 4: 583. (B) Josephus F (1999), the Jewish historian of the first century CE, also reports that Hagar and Ismael were befriended by a band of shepherds, although he appears to follow the Biblical account of Ismael being at least 14 years old at the time.

299. This estimate of the continuing length of the marriage of Abraham and Sarah is based upon the following. (A) Abraham was 86 years old when Ismael was born (sixth or fifth century BCE *P* strand of *Genesis* 16: 16). (B) Abraham was 10 years Sarah's senior (sixth or fifth century BCE *P* strand of *Genesis* 17: 17). (C) Abraham left Hagar and Ismael at Makkah, when Ismael was still nursing on Hagar (*Al-Bukhari* 4: 583-584), suggesting that Ismael was not yet two years old. (D) Sarah died at 127 years of age (sixth or fifth century BCE *P* strand of *Genesis* 23: 1), suggesting that Sarah lived for 49 years after Abraham left Hagar and Ismael at Makkah.

300. Undated psalm from *Psalms* 84: 5-7.

Chapter 9: Abraham in Palestine III

301. Unidentified and undated strand of *Genesis* 14: 1-4.

302. Unidentified and undated strand of *Genesis* 14: 1.

303. Unidentified and undated strand of *Genesis* 14: 5.

304. The term "Amalekites" may well be anachronistic, as the Amalekites reportedly descended from Amalek, the son of Eliphaz, the son of Esau, the son of Isaac, the son of Abraham. (See the sixth or fifth century BCE *P* strand of *Genesis* 36: 15-16.)

305. (A) Unidentified and undated strand of *Genesis* 14: 5-7. (B) Marks JH (1971).

306. (A) Unidentified and undated strand of *Genesis* 14: 8-12,16. (B) Third or second century BCE book of *Jubilees* 13:21-23.

307. (A) Unidentified and undated strand of *Genesis* 14: 13-14. (B) Third or second century BCE book of *Jubilees* 13: 24-25.

308. Unidentified and undated strand of *Genesis* 14: 13,24.

309. Unidentified and undated strand of *Genesis* 14: 14.

310. Unidentified and undated strand of *Genesis* 14: 14.

311. Josephus F (1988, 1999).

312. Unidentified and undated strand of *Genesis* 14: 15.

313. (A) Unidentified and undated strand of *Genesis* 14: 15. (B) Josephus F (1988, 1999).

314. Unidentified and undated strand of *Genesis* 14: 15.

315. Unidentified and undated strand of *Genesis* 14: 5-7.

316. This is a rather direct paraphrase of the summation of the battle given several days later by King Melchizedek of Jerusalem. See unidentified and undated strand of *Genesis* 14: 20.

317. Unidentified and undated strand of *Genesis* 14: 16.

318. The return back south would have gone through the hill country of Palestine, as opposed to going through western Jordan, because Abraham and his band were greeted along the way by the King of Jerusalem (unidentified and undated strand of *Genesis* 14: 18).

319. Unidentified and undated strand of *Genesis* 14: 17.

320. (A) Unidentified and undated strand of *Genesis* 14: 18. (B) Undated book of *Psalms* 110:4. (C) First century CE *Letter to the Hebrews* 5: 6,10; 6: 20; 7: 1, 10, 11, 15, 17, which is part of the Christian canon of scripture. Dating of the *Letter to the Hebrews* is based on Quanbeck WA (1971).

321. (A) Unidentified and undated strand of *Genesis* 14: 18. (B) Josephus F (1999).

322. Unidentified and undated strand of *Genesis* 14: 19-20.

323. Unidentified and undated strand of *Genesis* 14: 20.

324. Unidentified and undated strand of *Genesis* 14: 22-24.

325. Third or second century BCE book of *Jubilees* 13: 17-19.

326. Third or second century BCE book of *Jubilees* 11: 15-16.

Chapter 10: Abraham in Makkah II

327. The eighth century BCE *E* strand of *Genesis* 22: 1-14. See Appendix IV (Sequential Events in Abraham's Life: Events in Makkah II: The Intended Sacrifice of Abraham's Son) for additional information about the need for a reconstruction of this narration.

328. Dating of Abraham's age at this point in his life is based upon the sixth to fifth century BCE *P* strand of *Genesis* 17: 24-25 account of the age of Abraham and of Ismael at the time of their circumcision.

329. Eighth century BCE *E* strand of *Genesis* 22: 3.

330. (A) Unidentified and undated strand of *Genesis* 14: 14. (B) Tenth century BCE *J* strand of *Genesis* 12: 16. (C) Third or second century BCE book of *Jubilees* 13: 14-15.

331. *Al-Bukhari* 4: 583-584.

332. *Al-Bukhari* 4: 583-584.

333. *Qur'an* 37: 102.

334. Eighth century BCE *E* strand of *Genesis* 21: 12.

335. Dating is based upon two considerations: (A) *Al-Bukhari* 4: 583-584, which indicate that Ismael was still nursing at the time of the separation between Abraham and Ismael, thus implying that Ismael was not yet two years old; and (B) the sixth or fifth century BCE *P* strand of *Genesis* 17: 25, which indicates that Ismael was 13 years old at the time of his circumcision.

336. Sixth or fifth century BCE *P* strand of *Genesis* 17: 25.

337. *Qur'an* 37: 102.

338. *Qur'an* 37: 101-102.

339. The 8th century BCE *E* strand of *Genesis* 22: 2 is quite specific that the sacrifice was to be a burnt offering, and there is nothing known to the author in the *Qur'an* or *Sahih Ahadith* that would specifically contradict this proposition. Nonetheless, it is noted that Islam prohibits the burning of a corpse, and specifies burial as the proper procedure for dealing with a corpse. Likewise, Islam prohibits human sacrifice. However, in this trial of Abraham, we are dealing with a special situation, ordered by Allah, and nothing in the actions or behavior of Abraham should be interpreted as being contrary to Islam. Further, it should be noted that no human sacrifice or burning of a human corpse actually took place, as Allah ransomed Ismael.

340. Reconstruction of the eighth century BCE *E* strand of *Genesis* 22: 3, 5-6, 9.

341. Reconstruction of the eighth century BCE *E* strand of *Genesis* 22: 9.

342. *Qur'an* 37: 103.

343. *Qur'an* 37: 103.

344. *Qur'an* 37: 103-111.

345. Reconstruction of the eighth century BCE *E* strand of *Genesis* 22:13-14.

346. Fourth century BCE book of *II Chronicles* 20: 16.

347. Sixth or fifth century BCE *P* strand of *Genesis* 17: 1-22.

348. Sixth or fifth century BCE *P* strand of *Genesis* 17: 1-22.

349. Sixth or fifth century BCE *P* strand of *Genesis* 17: 24-26.

350. Eighth century BCE *E* strand of *Genesis* 22: 3.

351. *Al-Bukhari* 4: 575; 8: 313. For those readers of these *Ahadith* who have often wondered why Abraham would have used a hatchet to perform circumcision, the synthesis of the Judaeo-Chrisitian and Islamic literature has provided a sequence of events, which offers a plausible explanation.

352. Sixth or fifth century BCE *P* strand of *Genesis* 17: 10-14.

353. (A) Sixth century BCE *I Kings* 16:34. (B) Sixth century BCE *II Kings* 3: 27; 16: 3; 17: 17; 21: 6. (C) Seventh or sixth century BCE *Judges* 11: 29-40. (D) Eighth century BCE or later *Isaiah* 57: 5. (E) Sixth century BCE *Jeremiah* 7: 31; 19: 4-5. (F) Sixth century BCE or later book of *Ezekiel* 16: 20-21.

354. *Qur'an* 37: 106.

355. Eighth century BCE *E* strand of *Genesis* 22: 12.

356. *Qur'an* 37: 102.

357. Eighth century BCE *E* strand of *Genesis* 22: 7-8.

358. *Qur'an* 37: 103.

359. Eighth century BCE *E* strand of *Genesis* 22: 9.

360. Technically, Judaism recognizes a primitive covenant with Noah, the covenant with Abraham, and the revision of the Abrahamic covenant with Moses.

361. Sixth or fifth century BCE *P* strand of *Genesis* 17: 4-8.

362. Sixth or fifth century BCE *P* strand of *Genesis* 17: 9-14.

363. Sixth or fifth century BCE *P* strand of *Genesis* 17: 14.

364. Sixth or fifth century BCE *P* strand of *Genesis* 17: 15-16, 18-21.

365. Sixth or fifth century BCE *P* strand of *Genesis* 17: 25-26.

366. Sixth or fifth century BCE *P* strand of *Genesis* 17: 17.

367. Tenth century BCE *J* strand of *Genesis* 18: 10-15.

368. (A) Marks JH (1971): The book of *Genesis*. In Interpreter's. (B) Robinson TH (1929a). (C) Josephus F (1988, 1999).

369. *Qur'an* 3: 81.

370. *Qur'an* 33: 7.

371. *Qur'an* 2: 40, 63, 83, 92-32, 125; 4: 153-155; 5: 12-14, 70; 20: 80-93, 115; 33: 7; 43: 46-49.

372. The following list of specific obligations to Allah under prior covenants is based upon *Qur'an* 2: 41, 43, 4583; 4: 154; 5: 12; 20: 81.

373. The following list of specific obligations to self and others under prior covenants is based upon *Qur'an* 2: 42-44, 83-84; 5: 12.

374. *Qur'an* 2: 27; 5: 13-14; 7: 169; 13: 25; 20: 81; 33: 15-17.

375. Given that the origins of the Hebrew or Habiru people were mixed, and the early Hebrews did not represent a group of common ethnic descent, some common denominator was needed to provide them with a sense of shared identity. (A) Appendix III (The People or Tribe of Abraham: The Hebrew Hypothesis: Hebrew as a Non-Ethnic Term). (B) McKenzie JL (1971).

376. Third or second century BCE book of *Jubilees* 16: 16-18. Note that all of the descendants of Abraham are to be considered Gentiles, except for the "holy seed" of one of the two sons of Isaac, i.e., Jacob, aka. Israel. The descendants of Jacob, aka Israel, are to be considered an actual "portion of" Allah, and are to be considered as being superior to ("above all") other people.

377. See, for example the seventh or sixth century BCE book of *Joshua* 6: 17, 21; 8: 2, 21-26; 10: 28-43; 11: 1-14, 16-21.

378. *Qur'an* 10: 47; 14: 4; 16: 84; 17: 71.

379. *Qur'an* 34: 28.

Chapter 11: Abraham in Palestine IV

380. *Malik* (1985). *Hadith* 1647.

381. Tenth century BCE *J* strand of *Genesis* 18: 1-2.

382. *Qur'an* 11: 69; 15: 57; 29: 31; 51: 31. The tenth century BCE *J* strand account of *Genesis* 18: 1-33 and 19: 1 presents the story as though Allah Himself were one of the three visitors, the other two being angels of Allah. This is a rather crude and primitive anthropomorphism, in which Allah is portrayed as taking on a human-like body, and as descending to earth in bodily form, not unlike the Greek gods of mythology, in their occasional descent from Mt. Olympus to interact with men.

383. *Qur'an* 51: 25.

384. (A) Tenth century BCE *J* strand of *Genesis* 18: 2-7. (B) *Qur'an* 11: 69 and 51: 26 also notes Abraham's haste to serve his guests. (C) *Qur'an* 11: 69; 15: 52; 51: 25 note that Abraham and his guests exchanged the greeting of "peace".

385. (A) Tenth century BCE *J* strand of *Genesis* 18: 8. (B) *Qur'an* 11: 69 and 51: 26 specifically mentions the roasted calf, but the *Qur'an* makes no mention of the cakes, curds, and milk.

386. *Qur'an* 11: 70; 51: 26-28. In contrast, the tenth century BCE *J* strand of *Genesis* 18: 8 maintains that the three of them, reportedly Allah and His two angels, ate, thus continuing the crudely anthropomorphic portrayal of Allah.

387. *Qur'an* 11: 70; 15: 52; 51: 26-28.

388. *Qur'an* 11: 70-71a.

389. *Qur'an* 15: 52.

390. *Qur'an* 15: 53.

391. Tenth century BCE *J* strand of *Genesis* 18: 10-12.

392. *Qur'an* 51: 29. Not all translators of and commentators on this Qur'anic verse agree that the implication is that Sarah laughed out loud at this point.

393. Tenth century BCE *J* strand of *Genesis* 18: 12.

394. *Qur'an* 15: 54.

395. *Qur'an* 15: 55

396. *Qur'an* 11: 71.

397. *Qur'an* 51: 30.

398. *Qur'an* 11: 57; 51: 31.

399. *Qur'an* 15: 56.

400. *Qur'an* 11: 72.

401. *Qur'an* 11: 73.

402. Tenth century BCE *J* strand of *Genesis* 18: 15.

403. *Qur'an* 15: 57; 51: 31.

404. (A) *Qur'an* 11: 70; 15: 58-60; 29: 31-35; 51: 32-34. (B) Unidentified and undated insertion into the tenth century BCE *J* strand of *Genesis* 18: 17-21.

405. *Qur'an* 11: 74; 29: 32.

406. *Qur'an* 15: 59-60; 29: 32.

407. *Qur'an* 11: 76.

408. *Qur'an* 11: 69-76.

409. *Qur'an* 15: 51-60.

410. *Qur'an* 29: 31-32.

411. *Qur'an* 51: 24-34.

412. *Qur'an* 11: 74-75.

413. *Qur'an* 29: 32.

414. Tenth century BCE *J* strand of *Genesis* 18: 23-33.

415. Tenth century BCE *J* strand of *Genesis* 19: 1-3.

416. *Qur'an* 7: 80-81; 15: 58-60; 21: 74; 26: 160-169; 27: 54-56; 29: 28-30, 33; 51: 35-36.

417. *Qur'an* 7: 80-81.

418. *Qur'an* 7: 82; 54: 33,36.

419. *Qur'an* 27: 54-56.

420. *Qur'an* 26: 160-169.

421. *Qur'an* 29: 28-30.

422. *Qur'an* 15: 62.

423. *Qur'an* 7: 80-84; 11: 77-83; 15: 57-77; 21: 74-75; 26: 160-175; 27:54-58; 29: 28-35; 37: 133-138; 51: 31-37; 54: 33-39.

424. *Qur'an* 11: 77-83.

425. *Qur'an* 15: 61-74.

426. (A) *Qur'an* 7: 83; 11: 81; 15: 59-60, 65; 26: 170-171; 27: 57: 29: 33; 37: 133-135; 54: 34. (B) Tenth century BCE *J* strand of *Genesis* 19: 15-16, 26.

427. Unidentified and undated insertion into the tenth century BCE *J* strand of *Genesis* 19: 17-22.

428. Tenth century BCE *J* strand of *Genesis* 19: 4-16, 23-28.

429. (A) *Qur'an* 15: 72; 54: 37. (B) Tenth century BCE *J* strand of *Genesis* 19: 11.

430. (A) *Qur'an* 11: 81; 15: 65; 54: 34. (B) Tenth century BCE *J* strand of *Genesis* 19: 15-16.

431. (A) *Qur'an* 7: 83; 11: 81; 15: 59-60; 26: 171; 27: 57; 29: 33; 37: 133-135. (B) Tenth century BCE *J* strand of *Genesis* 19: 26.

432. (A) *Qur'an* 7: 84; 11: 82; 15: 74; 26: 173; 27: 58; 51: 32-33; 54: 34. (B) Tenth century BCE *J* strand of *Genesis* 19: 24.

433. Tenth century BCE *J* strand of *Genesis* 19: 8-10.

434. Tenth century BCE *J* strand of *Genesis* 19: 12-15. Of note, the *J* strand needed to maintain that these prospective sons-in-law of Lot did not accompany Lot and his daughters out of Sodom, in order to justify the slanderous story about Lot that the *J* strand imparts in *Genesis* 19: 30b-38, where it is maintained that Lot's daughters believed there were no more men left on earth, and thus committed incest with their father, thus giving birth to the tribes of the 'Ammonites and Moabites. However, the *J* strand had previously (*Genesis* 19: 23) stated that Lot and his daughters had gone to the city of Zoar after leaving Sodom, so the daughters of Lot knew full well there were other men left on earth. In short, the *J* strand story of Lot's incestuous relationship with his daughters is riddled with inconsistency, and was fabricated, probably in order to justify the Israelite people dealing with the 'Ammonites and Moabites in a prejudicial and bigoted manner.

435. Contrast *Qur'an* 15: 59, 61; 29: 33; and 37: 134 with 51: 36-37. The former verses refer to the "adherents" or "followers" of Lot, which would be a somewhat strange way of stating things if the only "adherents" and "followers" were Lot's two daughters. Yet, the latter verses state that the angels did not find any just persons, except in one, i.e., Lot's, house. Thus, the prospective sons-in-law become explanatory, assuming that they were present in Lot's house that evening to help entertain Lot's guests. In short, Lot's adherents or followers, i.e., those who believed in and submitted to Allah, probably included Lot, Lot's two daughters, and the two prospective sons-in-law of Lot.

436. Tenth century BCE *J* strand of *Genesis* 19: 23-28.

437. Tenth century BCE *J* strand of *Genesis* 19: 27-28.

438. Tenth century BCE *J* strand of *Genesis* 13: 10.

439. Unidentified and undated strand of *Genesis* 14: 10.

440. (A) Tenth century BCE *J* strand of *Genesis* 19: 24-25, 28. (B) Sixth or fifth century *P* strand of *Genesis* 19: 29.

441. *Qur'an* 7: 84; 11: 82; 15: 74; 26: 173; 27: 58; 51: 33-34.

442. *Al-Tabari* (1987) pages 119-120.

443. For justification of this dating, see Appendix II (Chronology) and Appendix IV (Sequential Events in Abraham's Life).

444. Third or second century BCE book of *Jubilees* 16: 5-10. Support for this move is also found in the eighth century BCE *E* strand of *Genesis* 20: 1, although this source refers to the move being to Gerar, and although there is no dating available from that source.

445. Third or second century BCE book of *Jubilees* 16: 11.

446. Third or second century BCE book of *Jubilees* 16: 11-12.

447. Tenth century BCE *J* strand of *Genesis* 18: 11.

448. Third or second century BCE book of *Jubilees* 16: 12-13.

449. Sixth or fifth century BCE *P* strand of *Genesis* 17: 17; 21:5.

450. Eighth century BCE *E* strand of *Genesis* 21: 6a.

451. Tenth century BCE *J* strand of *Genesis* 18: 11-15.

452. Sixth or fifth century BCE *P* strand of *Genesis* 21: 4.

453. The story of Abraham and the Well of the Oath is told in the tenth century BCE *J* strand of *Genesis* 21: 25-26, 28-30, 32-33 and in the eighth century BCE *E* strand of *Genesis* 21: 22-24, 27, 31, 34. It has rather remarkable parallels with the story of Isaac and his sojourn in Gerar, as told in the tenth century BCE *J* strand of *Genesis* 26: 17-33. It is certainly possible that the compiler of the *J* strand was confronted with two different oral traditions, one of which attributed the events in question to Abraham, and one of which attributed the events to Isaac. Perhaps, unable to make a determination as to which of these prophets of Allah was actually involved, the compiler of *J* simply told the story twice, once for each prophet. However, the fact that the compiler of *E* also attributed the events in question to Abraham tends to strengthen the association with Abraham, rather than with Isaac. However, the reader should keep the above caution in mind when considering the story of Abraham and the Well of the Oath.

454. (A) Tenth century BCE *J* strand of *Genesis* 21: 25-26, 28-30, 32-33; 26: 1, 8, 17-33. (B) Eighth century BCE *E* strand of *Genesis* 20: 2; 21: 22-24, 31, 34.

455. (A) Tenth century BCE *J* strand of *Genesis* 21: 32; 26: 1, 814-15, 18. (B) Eighth century BCE *E* strand of *Genesis* 21: 34.

456. Marks JH (1971).

457. Eighth century BCE *E* strand of *Genesis* 21: 22-24, 27.

458. (A) Tenth century BCE *J* strand of *Genesis* 21: 25-26, 28-30, 32-33; 26: 18. (B) Eighth century BCE *E* strand of *Genesis* 21: 27, 31, 34.

459. Tenth century BCE *J* strand of *Genesis* 21: 25-26, 28-30, 32-33.

460. (A) Asimov I (1968). (B) Marks JH (1971). (C) Robinson TH (1929a).

461. Eighth century BCE *E* strand of *Genesis* 21: 8. While there is no reason to doubt that Abraham celebrated and gave thanks to Allah for Isaac having achieved this milestone in his early life, the subsequent verses of the *E* strand account of *Genesis* 21: 9-21 appear to be a confabulated merging of the *J* strand account of *Genesis* 16: 5-8, 11-14 and the material recorded in *Al-Bukhari* 4: 583-584.

462. *Al-Bukhari* 4: 590.

Chapter 12: Abraham in Makkah III

463. Dating is based upon the following considerations. (A) *Al-Bukhari* 4: 584 states that Sarah was still living at the time of the third and fourth trips. (B) *Al-Bukhari* 4: 583-584 state that Ismael had already married, indicating an age for Ismael of maybe 20 years or more at the time of the third trip, although it is noted that *Al-Bukhari* 4: 583 states that this marriage took place after Ismael reached the age of puberty. Unfortunately, one doesn't know how long after the age of puberty. (C) According to the sixth or fifth century BCE *P* strand of *Genesis* 16:16, Abraham was 86 years old when Ismael was born. (D) According to the sixth or fifth century BCE *P* strand of *Genesis* 17: 17, Abraham was 10 years older than Sarah. (E) According to the sixth or fifth century BCE *P* strand of *Genesis* 23: 1, Sarah died at age 127. (F) If Ismael were at least 20 years old at the time of the third trip, then Abraham would have been at least 106 years old. (G) Allowing one year between the third and fourth trips, and given that Sarah was still alive at the time of both trips, Sarah could not have been more than 126 years old at the time of the third trip, making Abraham not more than 136 years old. (H) Finally, the sixth or fifth century BCE *P* strand of *Genesis* 17: 24-25 states that Abraham was 99 years old and that Ismael was 13 years old at the time of their circumcisions, which information dates Abraham's second trip to Makkah.

464. *Al-Bukhari* 4: 583-584.

465. *Al-Bukhari* 4: 583-584.

466. *Al-Bukhari* 4: 583-584. The eighth century BCE *E* strand of *Genesis* 21: 21 identifies Ismael's wife as having been an Egyptian.

467. *Al-Bukhari* 4: 583-584.

468. *Al-Bukhari* 4: 583-584.

469. (A) *Al-Tabari* (1987). (B) Al-Mubarakpuri S (1996).

470. Al-Mubarakpuri S (1996).

471. *Al-Bukhari* 4: 584.

472. *Al-Bukhari* 4: 583-584.

473. *Al-Bukhari* 4: 583.

474. *Al-Bukhari* 4: 583.

475. (A) *Al-Tabari* (1987). (B) Sixth or fifth century BCE *P* strand of *Genesis* 25: 12-17; 28: 9; 36: 1-3. (C) There is some significant confusion about the name of Ismael's daughter. *Al-Tabari* names Ismael's daughter as being Basmah, and identifies her as having married Esau. However, the sixth or fifth century BCE *P* strand of *Genesis* 26: 34 identifies two Hittite wives of Esau, one being Judith bint Beeri and the other being Basemath bint Elon. According to the sixth or fifth century BCE *P* strand of *Genesis* 28: 9, Esau later took Mahalath bint Ismael as a wife. However, the sixth or fifth century BCE *P* strand of *Genesis* 36: 1-3 identifies Esau's wife, who was the daughter of Ismael, as being named Basemath. The current author notes the confusion, but has no explanation for it.

476. *Al-Bukhari* 4: 583-584.

477. *Al-Bukhari* 4: 583-584.

478. (A) *Al-Bukhari* 4: 583-584. (B) Eighth century BCE *E* strand of *Genesis* 21: 20.

479. The possibility that Ismael and Al-Sayyidah already had at least one child is suggested by *Qur'an* 14: 37, in which Abraham refers to leaving "some of my offspring" in Makkah, presumably upon leaving Makkah at the end of this trip, implying that more than one of Abraham's descendants were being left behind.

480. *Al-Bukhari* 4: 583-584.

481. *Al-Bukhari* 4: 583-584.

482. *Al-Bukhari* 4: 583-584.

483. (A) *Qur'an* 2: 127. (B) *Al-Bukhari* 4: 583-584.

484. *Al-Tirmidhi, Hadith* 2577.

485. *Al-Bukhari* 4: 583-584.

486. (A) *Qur'an* 2:127. (B) *Al-Bukhari* 4: 583-584.

487. *Qur'an* 2: 124-129.

488. *Qur'an* 3: 95-97.

489. *Qur'an* 22: 26.

490. This aspect of Abraham's prayer has been mentioned in numerous *Sahih Ahadith*, including the following. (A) *Al-Bukhari* 3: 339; 4: 139, 143, 586; 5:410; 7:336; 8:374; 9:433. (B) *Muslim* (1971?). *Hadith* 3150 3151, 3153, 3157, 3170, 3172, 3176. (C) *Malik* (1985). *Hadith* 1573.

491. One assumes that this asking for forgiveness, by Abraham, for his parents is the prayer referred to in *Qur'an* 19: 47-48, 113-114; 60: 4.

492. *Qur'an* 14: 35-41. See footnote #286 for additional detail regarding the temporal placement of this prayer of Abraham.

493. *Qur'an* 3: 97.

494. *Qur'an* 22: 27-33.

495. (A) *Al-Bukhari* 2: 653-656; 4: 587. (B) *Malik* (1985). *Hadith* 794. (C) *Muslim* (1971?). *Hadith* 3078-3088. (D) *Abu Dawud* (1990). *Hadith* 1870, 2023. (E) Al-Mubarakpuri S (1996). (F) Lings M (1983). (G) Haykal MH (1976).

496. (A) *Al-Bukhari* 2: 653-656; 4: 583-584,587. (B) *Muslim* (1971?). *Hadith* 3078-3088. (C) *Malik* (1985). *Hadith* 794. (D) *Abu Dawud* (1990). *Hadith* 1870, 2023. (E) Lings M (1983). (F) Haykal MH (1976). (G) Al-Mubarakpuri S (1996).

497. *Qur'an* 22: 27.

Chapter 13: Abraham in Palestine V

498. (A) Third or second century BCE book of *Jubilees* 16: 11. (B) Eighth century BCE *E* strand of *Genesis* 20: 1. (C) For additional information, see Appendix IV (Sequential Events in Abraham's Life: Events in Palestine IV).

499. This estimate is based on a combination of sources, including the following. (A) Sixth or fifth century BCE *P* strand of *Genesis* 12: 4b; 17: 17. (B) Third or second century BCE book of *Jubilees* 11: 15; 12: 12-16; 13: 10-12; 19: 1.

500. Third or second century BCE book of *Jubilees* 11: 15; 19: 1.

501. Sixth or fifth century BCE *P* strand of *Genesis* 23: 1-2.

502. This estimate is based on a combination of sources, including the following. (A) Sixth or fifth century BCE *P* strand of *Genesis* 17: 17; 23: 1-2. (B) Third or second century BCE book of *Jubilees* 11: 15; 12: 9-10.

503. This estimate is based on the sixth or fifth century BCE *P* strand of *Genesis* 17: 17; 21:5; 23: 1-2.

504. Sixth or fifth century BCE *P* strand of *Genesis* 23: 2.

505. Sixth or fifth century BCE *P* strand of *Genesis* 23: 3-9,17. These verses identify the local population as being Hittites, which is probably anachronistic, as it is doubtful that Hittites were already in this area at this time. Marks JH (1971).

506. Sixth or fifth century BCE *P* strand of *Genesis* 23: 10-16, 19.

507. Tenth century BCE *J* strand of *Genesis* 22: 20-24.

508. Dating based on the sixth or fifth century BCE *P* strand of *Genesis* 17: 17; 21: 5; 23: 1-2; 25: 20.

509. Tenth century BCE *J* strand of *Genesis* 24: 62.

510. Tenth century BCE *J* strand of *Genesis* 16: 4-8, 11-14.

511. Tenth century BCE *J* strand of Genesis 24: 2-4.

512. Tenth century BCE *J* strand of *Genesis* 24: 1-10, 22, 53.

513. The tenth century BCE *J* strand of *Genesis* 24: 10-11, 14, 19-20, 22, 30-32, 35, 44, 46, 61, 63-65 consistently states that the caravan consisted of camels. This is an evident anachronism, as the camel was not domesticated until almost a millennium after the event in question. (A) Marks JH (1971). (B) Edzard DO, von Soden WT, Frye RN (1998). As such, the author has substituted "donkeys" for "camels".

514. Tenth century BCE *J* strand of *Genesis* 24: 32.

515. Tenth century BCE *J* strand of *Genesis* 24: 11.

516. Dating based on the following sources. Sixth or fifth century BCE *P* strand of *Genesis* 12: 4; 21: 5; 25: 20.

517. Tenth century BCE *J* strand of *Genesis* 24: 12-14. In this quotation from *J,* the author has substituted the word "donkeys" for "camels".

518. Tenth century BCE *J* strand of *Genesis* 24: 15-21.

519. Tenth century BCE *J* strand of *Genesis* 24: 22-28.

520. Tenth century BCE *J* strand of *Genesis* 24: 28-32.

521. Tenth century BCE *J* strand of *Genesis* 24: 33-49.

522. Tenth century BCE *J* strand of *Genesis* 24: 50. This is the only time Bethuel is mentioned in the entire narrative. Given this fact, given the earlier reference to Rebekah's "mother's household" (*J* strand of *Genesis* 24: 28), given that gifts are only given to Rebekah, to Laban, and to their mother (*J* strand of *Genesis* 24: 53), and given that only Laban and his mother see Rebekah off the next day (*J* strand of *Genesis* 24: 55-60), it is possible that this single reference to Bethuel is incorrect, and that Bethuel had previously died by this time. In this regard, it should be noted that Josephus directly states that Bethuel had died by this time. Josephus F (1999).

523. Tenth century BCE *J* strand of *Genesis* 24: 50-54.

524. Tenth century BCE *J* strand of *Genesis* 24: 54-61.

525. Tenth century BCE *J* strand of *Genesis* 24: 62-67.

526. See Appendix IV (Sequential Events in Abraham's Life: Events in Palestine V) for an in-depth discussion of the evidence, which suggests that Abraham married Keturah within about a year following Isaac's marriage to Rebekah, and at about Abraham's 141st year of life.

527. (A) Tenth century BCE *J* strand of *Genesis* 25: 1-4. (B) Third or second century BCE book of *Jubilees* 19: 11-12. (C) *Al-Tabari* (1987), pages 127, 129, & 143.

528. *Al-Tabari* (1987), page 129.

529. (A) Sixth or fifth century BCE *P* strand of *Genesis* 25: 20, 26b. (B) Tenth century BCE *J* strand of *Genesis* 25: 21-26a. (C) Marks JH (1971).

530. Sixth or fifth century BCE *P* strand of *Genesis* 21: 5; 25: 26b.

531. Third or second century BCE book of *Jubilees* 22: 1-3.

532. (A) Tenth century BCE *J* strand of *Genesis* 25: 5-6. (B) Sixth or fifth century BCE *P* strand of *Genesis* 25: 7-10.

533. Tenth century BCE *J* strand of *Genesis* 25:5-6.

534. Sixth or fifth century BCE *P* strand of *Genesis* 16:3.

535. Tenth century BCE *J* strand of *Genesis* 25:1.

536. *Qur'an* 2: 124.

537. (A) *Qur'an* 4: 125. (B) Eighth century BCE or later book of *Isaiah* 41: 8. (C) Fourth century BCE book of *II Chronicles* 20: 7. (D) First century CE book of *James* 2: 23.

Appendix I: Sources of Information

538. (A) Marks JH (1971). On page 2 of this reference, there is a simple to use chart providing a complete breakdown of *Genesis* into *J, E,* and *P* sources. (B) Robinson TH (1929a). (C) Hyatt JP (1971). (D) Duncan GB (1971a). (E) Eiselen FC (1929).

539. A) Duncan GB (1971a). (B) Gottwald NK (1971). (C) Eiselen FC (1929).

540. (A) Duncan GB (1971a). (B) Leslie EA (1929). (C) Hyatt JP (1971).

541. See the following for a fuller discussion of these issues than presented in the text of this book. Reumann J (1971). Unless otherwise specifically referenced, all information in this section is from the Reumann article.

542. Sarna NM (1998).

543. Sarna NM (1998).

544. As previously noted, utilizing their names and divisions as found in the Christian *Old Testament*, the books comprising the *Torah* include: *Genesis*; *Exodus; Leviticus; Numbers;* and *Deuteronomy.*

545. Utilizing their names and divisions as found in the Christian *Old Testament*, the books of the *Nevi'im* include: *Joshua*; *Judges*; *I Samuel*; *II Samuel; I Kings; II Kings; Isaiah; Jeremiah; Ezekiel; Hosea; Joel; Amos; Obadiah; Jonah; Micah; Nahum; Habakkuk; Zephaniah; Haggai; Zechariah; and Malachi.*

546. Utilizing their names and divisions as found in the Christian *Old Testament*, the books of the *Ketuvim* include: *Psalms*; *Proverbs; Job; Song of Solomon; Ruth; Lamentations; Ecclesiastes; Esther; Daniel; Ezra; Nehemiah; I Chronicles; and II Chronicles.*

547. (A) Brownlee WH (1971). (B) Duncan GB (1971a).

548. Duncan GB (1971a).

549. Frost SB (1971).

550. (A) Smith RH (1971a). (B) Duncan GB (1971a).

551. Smith RH (1971b).

552. Dahlberg BT (1971).

553. (A) Fritsch CT (1971). (B) Duncan GB (1971a).

554. The book of *Psalms*, also known as *The Psalter*, is a collection of 150 individual psalms. While most of these psalms appear to date to prior to the Jewish exile to Babylon in 586 BCE, and while some may well date to the tenth century BCE or even earlier, many others simply cannot be dated with precision. The final collection of these individual psalms into a single book probably occurred between 400 and 200 BCE. Toombs LE (1971).

555. (A) Fritsch CT (1971). (B) Duncan GB (1971a).

556. (A) Fritsch CT (1971). (B) Duncan GB (1971a).

557. Wevers JW (1971a).

558. Wevers JW (1971a).

559. Wevers JW (1971b).

560. Stegemann H (1998).

561. Stegemann H (1998).

Appendix II: Chronology

562. *Qur'an* 2:258.

563. (A) Ibn Hymayd from Salamah from Muhammad b. Ishaq; and (B) Musa b. Harun from 'Amr b. Hammad from Asbat from Al-Suddi from Abu Salih from Abu Malik from Ibn 'Abbas and Murrah Al-Hamdani.

564. (A) *Al-Tabari* (1987). (B) 'Ali 'AY (1992), notes # 303, 1565, 2725, and 6055. (C) Hatun HA (1996). (D) Hendel RS (1993). (E) Asimov I (1968).

565. Tenth century BCE *J* strand of *Genesis* 10: 8-12. While these verses contain some anachronisms, e.g., Nineveh was not built until many centuries after the time being discussed in these verses, it is assumed that such geographical references refer to earlier cities on the sites of later cities.

566. The fourth century BCE book of *I Chronicles* 1: 10.

567. Eighth to sixth century BCE book of *Micah* 5: 6. This verse appears to be part of a sixth century BCE insertion (chapters 4-7) into the eighth century BCE book of *Micah*. Dahlberg BT (1971).

568. Eighth century BCE or later editorial gloss of or insertion into the 10th century BCE *J* strand of *Genesis* 11: 28-30.

569. Sixth or fifth century BCE *P* strand of *Genesis* 11: 31.

570. The fourth century BCE book of *Nehemiah* 9: 7.

571. Marks JH (1971).

572. Sixth century BCE book of *I Kings* 6: 1.

573. Sixth or fifth century BCE *P* strand of *Exodus* 12: 40.

574. (A) Eighth century BCE *E* strand of *Genesis* 45: 6. (B) Sixth or fifth century BCE *P* strand of *Genesis* 21: 5; 25: 26; 41: 46; 47: 28.

575. (A) Robinson TH (1929b). (B) Asimov I (1968).

576. (A) Leslie EA (1929). (B) Edzard DO, von Soden WT, Frye RN (1998). (C) Duncan GB (1971a). (D) Asimov I (1968). (E) Rohl DM (1995).

577. Edzard DO, von Soden WT, Frye RN (1998).

578. Rohl DM (1995).

579. Sixth or fifth century BCE *P* strand of *Genesis* 11: 16-26.

580. *Al-Tabari* (1987).

581. (A) *Al-Tabari* (1987). (B) 'Ali 'AY (1992), notes # 303, 1565, 2725, and 6055. (C) Hatun HA (1996). (D) Asimov I (1968).

582. Enheduanna (1999).

583. *Qur'an* 6: 75-79.

584. While this author arrived at the identification of Nimrod with Naram-Sin through an independent line of inquiry, it has subsequently come to the author's attention that this identification had been previously suggested. Hallo WW (1993).

585. North CR (1929).

Appendix III: The People or Tribe of Abraham

586. Unidentified and undated strand of *Genesis* 14:13.

587. (A) May HG (1971). (B) Asimov I (1968). (C) Josephus F (1988, 1999).

588. Tenth century BCE *J* strand of *Genesis* 10: 24-26 and sixth or fifth century BCE *P* strand of *Genesis* 11: 14-16.

589. Sixth or fifth century BCE *P* strand of *Genesis* 11: 16-26.

590. Diakonoff IM (1998).

591. Tenth century BCE *J* strand of *Genesis* 10: 25.

592. Tenth century BCE *J* strand of *Genesis* 10: 26-29.

593. (A) Lewis B (1967). (B) Epstein I (1966).

594. Tenth century BCE *J* strand of *Genesis* 43: 32. See the sixth century BCE book of *I Samuel* 4: 9 and the 10th century BCE *J* strand of *Genesis* 39: 14 for additional examples.

595. (A) Appendix II: Chronology (The *Torah* and Biblical References: Abraham's Initial Residence). (B) Tenth century BCE *J* strand of *Genesis* 24:10. (C) Sixth or fifth century BCE *P* strand of *Genesis* 25: 20 and 28: 2. (D) Sixth or fifth century BCE editorial insertion combining *E* and *P* strand material in *Genesis* 48: 7.

596. Seventh century BCE book of *Deuteronomy* 26: 5.

597. Sixth or fifth century BCE *P* strand of *Genesis* 25: 20.

598. Sixth or fifth century BCE *P* strand of *Genesis* 28: 5.

599. Tenth century BCE *J* strand of *Genesis* 22: 20-23.

600. Diakonoff IM (1998)

601. Sixth or fifth century BCE *P* strand of *Genesis* 10: 21-22.

602. Sixth or fifth century BCE *P* strand of *Genesis* 10: 21; 11: 10-26.

603. Tenth century BCE *J* strand of *Genesis* 22: 20-21.

604. (A) Al-Hanbly QA (15th century). (B) Al-Mubarakpuri S (1996).

605. Tenth century BCE *J* strand of *Genesis* 25: 1-4.

606. Tenth century BCE *J* strand of *Genesis* 25: 1-4.

607. Tenth century BCE *J* strand of *Genesis* 25: 21-25 in combination with the sixth or fifth century BCE *P* strand of *Genesis* 36: 9-12.

608. Lewis B (1966), pages 10-11.

609. Lewis B (1966).

610. Lewis B (1966).

611. Kohlenberger III JR (1991).

612. (A) Fourth century BCE book of *Nehemiah* 2: 19; 4: 7; 6:1; (B) fourth century BCE book of *II Chronicles* 17: 11; 21: 16; 22: 1; 26: 7; (C) late seventh or early sixth century BCE book of *Joshua* 15: 52; and (D) eighth century BCE or later book of *Isaiah* 13:20.

613. Kohlenberger III JR (1991).

614. (A) Fourth century BCE book of *II Chronicles* 9: 14; (B) sixth century BCE or later book of *Ezekiel* 27: 21; 30:5; (C) sixth century BCE book of *I Kings* 10: 15; and (D) sixth century BCE book of *Jeremiah* 25: 24.

615. Mansfield P (1986).

616. Diakonoff IM (1998).

617. (A) *Al-Tabari* (1987). (B) Haykal MH (1976). (C) Al-Mubarakpuri S (1996).

618. Dirks JF, Dirks DL (1998).

619. Sixth or fifth century BCE *P* strand of *Genesis* 11: 16-26.

620. Tenth century BCE *J* strand of *Genesis* 10: 25-29.

621. *Qur'an* 3:65,67.

622. 'Ali 'AY (1992), note # 402.

Appendix IV: Sequential Events in Abraham's Life

623. (A) Eighth century BCE or later editorial gloss of or editorial insertion into 10th century BCE *J* strand of *Genesis* 11: 28-30; 15: 7. (B) Sixth or fifth century BCE *P* strand of *Genesis* 11:31. (C) Fourth century BCE book of *Nehemiah* 9: 7.

624. Sixth or fifth century BCE *P* strand of *Genesis* 11: 31.

625. *Qur'an* 21: 51-60. Note use of the word "*Fta*" in verse 60.

626. *Qur'an* 6: 75-79.

627. Third or second century BCE book of *Jubilees* 11: 15-16.

628. *Qur'an* 6: 75-82. Note that Abraham's announcement to his people of his monotheistic belief in verse 78 comes immediately upon his realization of the Oneness of Allah.

629. (A) Robinson TH (1929b). (B) Epstein I (1966). (C) Parrot A (1998).

630. Edzard DO, von Soden WT, Frye RN (1998).

631. *Qur'an* 21: 68-69; 29: 24-26; 37: 83-98.

632. *Al-Tabari* (1987).

633. *Qur'an* 29: 24-26.

634. Third or second century BCE book of *Jubilees* 11: 15; 12: 9-10.

635. Sixth or fifth century BCE *P* strand of *Genesis* 11: 31.

636. Third or second century BCE book of *Jubilees* 12: 12-16.

637. Sixth of fifth century BCE *P* strand of *Genesis* 11: 31.

638. Tenth century BCE *J* strand of *Genesis* 24: 10.

639. Third or second century BCE book of *Jubilees* 12: 12-16.

640. (A) Tenth century BCE *J* strand of *Genesis* 12: 1. (B) *Qur'an* 19: 47-48; 60: 4.

641. (A) Third or second century BCE book of *Jubilees* 12: 15-16. (B) Sixth or fifth century BCE *P* strand of *Genesis* 12: 4.

642. (A) Tenth century BCE *J* strand of *Genesis* 12: 6-10. (B) Third or second century BCE book of *Jubilees* 13: 10.

643. (A) Third or second century BCE book of *Jubilees* 13: 14-15. (B) Tenth century BCE *J* strand of *Genesis* 12: 16.

644. Second or third century BCE *Genesis Apocryphon* 20: 34.

645. Josephus F (1988, 1999).

646. Third or second century BCE book of *Jubilees* 13: 11-12.

647. Eighth century BCE *E* strand of *Genesis* 20: 3b.

648. Eighth century BCE *E* strand of *Genesis* 20: 16.

649. *Al-Bukhari* 3: 420; 3: 803; 4: 578; 7: 21.

650. (A) Tenth century BCE *J* strand of *Genesis* 12: 19-20. (B) Third or second century BCE book of *Jubilees* 13: 15.

651. Tenth century BCE *J* strand of *Genesis* 13: 3, 5, 7-11a, 12b-18; 15: 1, 3-4, 7-12, 17-18; 16: 1b-2, 4-8, 11-14.

652. Sixth or fifth century BCE *P* strand of *Genesis* 16: 15-16.

653. *Al-Bukhari* 4: 582; 4: 584.

654. Sixth or fifth century BCE *P* strand of *Genesis* 16: 16.

655. *Al-Bukhari* 4: 583-584.

656. Eighth century BCE *E* strand of *Genesis* 21: 8-21.

657. This dating of Ismael being about 16 years old is based on the following. (A) Abraham was 86 years old when Ismael was born, according to the sixth or fifth century BCE *P* strand of *Genesis* 16: 16. (B) Abraham was 100 years old when Isaac was born, according to the sixth or fifth century BCE *P* strand of *Genesis* 17: 17; 21: 5. (C) The banishment of Hagar and Ismael took place immediately after the weaning of Isaac, according to the eighth century BCE *E* strand of *Genesis* 21: 8-14. (D) If Isaac were about two years old when he was weaned, and if Ismael were 14 years older than Isaac, then Ismael would have been about 16 years old at the time of Isaac's weaning.

658. Dating based on the combined information presented in: (A) the sixth or fifth century BCE *P* strand of *Genesis* 16: 16; 17: 17; and (B) the eighth century BCE *E* strand of *Genesis* 21: 8-14.

659. (A) Sixth of fifth century BCE *P* strand of *Genesis* 12: 4. (B) Third or second century BCE book of *Jubilees* 12: 12-15.

660. Third or second century BCE book of *Jubilees* 13: 10.

661. Third or second century BCE book of *Jubilees* 13: 11.

662. Sixth or fifth century BCE *P* strand of *Genesis* 21: 5.

663. Tenth century BCE *J* strand of *Genesis* 18: 1-16, in combination with the sixth or fifth century BCE *P* strand of *Genesis* 17: 1, 17.

664. Third or second century BCE book of *Jubilees* 11: 15; 13: 17-19.

665. Third or second century BCE book of *Jubilees* 11: 15; 14: 24.

666. Eighth century BCE *E* strand of *Genesis* 22: 1-14.

667. *Qur'an* 37: 99-111.

668. *Al-Tabari* (1987).

669. *Al-Bukhari* 4: 583-584.

670. (A) As shown previously in this appendix (Events in Egypt), the eighth century BCE *E* strand of *Genesis* 20: 1-17 is a confabulated merging of: the tenth century BCE *J* strand of *Genesis* 26: 6-11, which is a story involving Isaac in Gerar; and the tenth century BCE *J* strand of *Genesis* 12: 10-20, which is a story involving Abraham in Egypt. (B) As shown previously in this appendix (Events in Makkah I), the eighth century BCE *E* strand of *Genesis* 21: 8-21 is a confabulated merging of: the tenth century BCE *J* strand of *Genesis* 16: 5-8, 11-14, which concerns Hagar's flight from Sarah; and the story recounted in *Al-Bukhari* 4: 583-584, which concerns Abraham leaving Hagar and Ismael in Makkah.

671. Eighth century BCE *E* strand of *Genesis* 22: 1-2.

672. Marks JH (1971).

673. Fourth century BCE book of *II Chronicles* 3: 1.

674. (A) Marks JH (1971). (B) Robinson TH (1929a).

675. Kohlenberger III JR (1991).

676. *Al-Bukhari* 4: 583-584.

677. Kohlenberger III JR (1991).

678. Fourth century BCE book of *II Chronicles* 20: 16.

679. (A) The name "Isaac" is used in three other places in the eighth century BCE *E* strand account of the sacrifice of Abraham's son, i.e., *Genesis* 22:6,7,9. (B) The designation of "only son" is used in one other place in this *E* strand account, i.e., *Genesis* 22: 12.

680. This point cannot be avoided by resorting to hypotheses on the order of Ismael having died, because the sixth to fifth century BCE *P* strand of *Genesis* 24: 9 specifically states that Ismael and Isaac jointly buried their father, Abraham.

681. *Qur'an* 37: 99-113.

682. *Qur'an* 37: 99-113.

683. *Qur'an* 37: 102.

684. Sixth or fifth century BCE *P* strand of *Genesis* 17: 1-19.

685. Sixth or fifth century BCE *P* strand of *Genesis* 17: 23-27.

686. *Al-Bukhari* 4: 583-584.

687. *Al-Bukhari* 4: 575; 8: 313.

688. Sixth or fifth century BCE *P* strand of *Genesis* 16:16.

689. (A) *Al-Bukhari* 8: 303. (B) The Arabic of 8: 303 uses "*Al-Thamaneen*", while 4: 575 uses "*Thamaneen*", thus creating the difference in the two statements. 'Awad WH (1999).

690. Third or second century BCE book of *Jubilees* 16: 1-13.

691. This identification of an area between Kadesh and Shur being by the mountains of Gerar is apparently an error. Gerar was a city-state located about 60 miles (97 kilometers) northeast of the area between Kadesh and Shur.

692. A *Qur'an* 7: 80-84; 11: 69-73, 77-83; 15: 51-56, 61-74; 26: 160-173; 27: 54-58; 29: 28-35; 37: 133-136; 51: 24-30, 35-37; 54: 33-39. (B) Tenth century BCE *J* strand of *Genesis* 18: 1-15; 19: 1-16, 20-28. (C) Sixth or fifth century BCE *P* strand of *Genesis* 19: 29. (D) Eighth century BCE *E* strand of *Genesis* 20: 1. The remainder of this *E* strand narrative, i.e., verses 2-17, is an obvious confabulated merging of two tenth century BCE *J* strand stories (see *Genesis* 12: 10-20 and 26: 1-16).

693. (A) *Qur'an* 11: 70, 74-76; 15: 57-60; 29: 31-32; 51: 31-34. (B) Tenth century BCE *J* strand of *Genesis* 18: 16, 20-33; 21: 1a, 2a, 6b-7, 25-26, 28-30, 32-33. (C) Sixth of fifth century BCE *P* strand of *Genesis* 21: 1b, 2b-5.

(D) Eighth century BCE *E* strand of *Genesis* 21: 8, 22-24, 27, 3, 34.

694. Not all translators of and commentators on the *Qur'an* agree that 51: 29 implies that Sarah laughed.

695. *Al-Bukhari* 4: 583-584.

696. Dating is based on the following considerations. (A) *Al-Bukhari* 4: 584 states that Sarah was still living. (B) *Al-Bukhari* 4: 583-584 state that Ismael had already married, indicating an age for Ismael of maybe 20 years or more, although it is noted that *Al-Bukhari* 4: 583 states that Ismael married for the first time after reaching puberty. Unfortunately, one doesn't know what is meant by the age of puberty at a time when life spans were about two to three times the length of what they are now, and one doesn't know how long after the age of puberty. (C) According to the sixth or fifth century BCE *P* strand of *Genesis* 16: 16, Abraham was 86 years old when Ismael was born. If Ismael were 20 or more years old, Abraham would have been 106 or more years old. (D) According to the sixth or fifth century BCE *P* strand of *Genesis* 17: 17, Abraham was 10 years older than Sarah. (E) According to the sixth or fifth century BCE *P* strand of *Genesis* 23: 1, Sarah died at age 127. If Sarah were still living when Abraham made these two trips, then it would appear that Abraham was not older than 137 years of age.

697. *Qur'an* 2: 124-129; 3: 95-97; 14: 35-41; 22: 26-33.

698. *Qur'an* 14: 37.

699. Third or second century BCE book of *Jubilees* 11: 15; 19: 1.

700. Sixth or fifth century BCE *P* strand of *Genesis* 17:17; 23: 1. The former verse establishes that Abraham was 10 years older than Sarah, while the latter verse documents that Sarah died at age 127.

701. Sixth or fifth century BCE *P* strand of *Genesis* 21: 5; 25: 20. The former verse establishes that Abraham was 100 years old when Isaac was born, while the latter verse documents that Isaac was 40 years old when he married Rebekah.

702. Sixth or fifth century BCE *P* strand of *Genesis* 21: 5; 25: 26b. The former verse establishes that Abraham was 100 years old when Isaac was born, while the latter verse documents that Isaac was 60 years old when Esau and Jacob were born.

703. Tenth century BCE *P* strand of *Genesis* 25: 7-8.

704. (A) Tenth century BCE *J* strand of *Genesis* 25: 1-2. (B) *Al-Tabari* (1987). The former reference does not include Basar, while the latter does.

705. *Al-Tabari* (1987), page 129.

706. Tenth century BCE *J* strand of *Genesis* 25: 1-6.

707. Third or second century BCE book of *Jubilees* 20: 1-2.

708. Third or second century BCE book of *Jubilees* 19: 10-12.

709. Third or second century BCE book of *Jubilees* 19: 11-12.

710. All dates given are BCE, and are approximates.

711. All ages given are approximates.

712. This event would have been after Ismael had reached the age of marriage, and at least a year before Sarah died, so Abraham would have been approximately 106 to 136 years old.

713. This event would have been after the prior event, and before Sarah died, so Abraham would have been approximately 107 to 137 years old.

714. This event would have been after the prior event, and before Sarah died, so Abraham would have been approximately 108 to 137 years old.

715. This event appears to have been between Abraham's 141st and 150th year of life.

Appendix V: The Offspring of Abraham

716. Sources utilized include: *Genesis*; *Numbers*; *Al-Tabari* (1987); and Al-Mubarakpuri (1996).

717. Sixth or fifth century BCE *P* strand of *Genesis* 46: 21. However, the sixth or fifth century BCE *P* strand of *Numbers* 26: 40 lists Naaman as being the son of Bela, the son of Benjamin.

718. Sixth or fifth century BCE *P* strand of *Genesis* 46: 21. However, the sixth or fifth century BCE *P* strand of *Numbers* 26: 40 lists Ard as being the son of Bela, the son of Benjamin.

Bibliography

Bibliography

The following bibliography represents all sources consulted, whether actually cited in the text or not. For the reader's ease in locating references, the bibliography has been divided into sections: the *Bible*; non-canonical Jewish scripture; Qur'anic and *Ahadith* books; references with attributed authorship; and references with unattributed authorship.

Books of the *Bible*

Deuteronomy. In ---: *The Holy Bible: New Revised Standard Version*. Nashville, Thomas Nelson, Inc., 1989.

Exodus. In ---: *The Holy Bible: New Revised Standard Version*. Nashville, Thomas Nelson, Inc., 1989.

Ezekiel. In ---: *The Holy Bible: New Revised Standard Version*. Nashville, Thomas Nelson, Inc., 1989.

Genesis. In ---: *The Holy Bible: New Revised Standard Version*. Nashville, Thomas Nelson, Inc., 1989.

Isaiah. In ---: *The Holy Bible: New Revised Standard Version*. Nashville, Thomas Nelson, Inc., 1989.

James. In ---: *The Holy Bible: New Revised Standard Version*. Nashville, Thomas Nelson, Inc., 1989.

Jeremiah. In ---: *The Holy Bible: New Revised Standard Version*. Nashville, Thomas Nelson, Inc., 1989.

Joshua. In ---: *The Holy Bible: New Revised Standard Version*. Nashville, Thomas Nelson, Inc., 1989.

Judges. In ---: *The Holy Bible: New Revised Standard Version*. Nashville, Thomas Nelson, Inc., 1989.

Letter to the Hebrews. In ---: *The Holy Bible: New Revised Standard Version*. Nashville, Thomas Nelson, Inc., 1989.

Leviticus. In ---: *The Holy Bible: New Revised Standard Version*. Nashville, Thomas Nelson, Inc., 1989.

Luke. In ---: *The Holy Bible: New Revised Standard Version*. Nashville, Thomas Nelson, Inc., 1989.

Mark. In ---: *The Holy Bible: New Revised Standard Version.* Nashville, Thomas Nelson, Inc., 1989.

Matthew. In ---: *The Holy Bible: New Revised Standard Version.* Nashville, Thomas Nelson, Inc., 1989.

Micah. In ---: *The Holy Bible: New Revised Standard Version.* Nashville, Thomas Nelson, Inc., 1989.

Nehemiah. In ---:*The Holy Bible: New Revised Standard Version.* Nashville, Thomas Nelson, Inc., 1989.

Numbers. In ---: *The Holy Bible: New Revised Standard Version.* Nashville, Thomas Nelson, Inc., 1989.

Psalms. In ---: *The Holy Bible: New Revised Standard Version.* Nashville, Thomas Nelson, Inc., 1989.

I Chronicles. In ---: *The Holy Bible: New Revised Standard Version.* Nashville, Thomas Nelson, Inc., 1989.

II Chronicles. In ---: *The Holy Bible: New Revised Standard Version.* Nashville, Thomas Nelson, Inc., 1989.

I Kings. In ---: *The Holy Bible: New Revised Standard Version.* Nashville, Thomas Nelson, Inc., 1989.

II Kings. In ---: *The Holy Bible: New Revised Standard Version.* Nashville, Thomas Nelson, Inc., 1989.

I Samuel. In ---: *The Holy Bible: New Revised Standard Version.* Nashville, Thomas Nelson, Inc., 1989.

Non-Canonical Jewish Scripture

---: *Genesis Apocryphon.* In Dupont-Sommer A: *Les Ecrits esseniens decouverts pre de la mer Morte.* In Vermes G (trans.): *The Essene Writings from Qumran.* Cleveland, The World Publishing Company, 1967.

---: *Jubilees.* In Charles RH (trans.): The book of *Jubilees.* In Charles RH (ed.): *The Apocrypha and Pseudepigrapha of the Old Testament in English: Volume II. Pseudepigrapha.* Oxford, Oxford University Press, 1969.

Qur'anic and *Ahadith* Books
Qur'an and Commentaries

'Ali 'AY: Commentary. In 'Ali 'AY: *The Meaning of the Holy Qur'an.* Brentwood, Amana Corporation, 1992a.

'Ali 'AY: *The Meaning of The Holy Qur'an.* Brentwood, Amana Corporation, 1992b.

Arberry AJ: *The Koran Interpreted.* New York, Macmillan Company, ---.

Hilali MT, Khan MM: *Interpretation of the Meanings of The Noble Qur'an: A Summarized Version of Al-Tabari, Al-Qurtubi, and Ibn Kathir with Comments from Sahih Al-Bukhari in English Language: Volumes 1-9.* Lahore, Kazi Publications, 1989.

Ibn Kathir IA:*Tafsir ibn Kathir.* In Ar-Rafa'i MN (trans.): *Tafsir ibn Kathir: Part I.* London, Al-Firdous Ltd., 1998.

Pickthall MM: *The Meaning of the Glorious Koran.* New York, New American Library, ---.

Saheeh International: *The Qur'an: Arabic Text with Corresponding English Meanings.* Jeddah, Abul-Qasim Publishing House, 1997.

Usmani MSA: *Tafseer –'E-Usmani.* In Ahmad MA (trans.): *The Noble Qur'an: Tafsser-'E-Usmani: Volumes 1-3.* New Delhi, Idara Isha'at–E–Diniyat (P) Ltd., 1992.

Ahadith

Al-Asbahi MA (*Malik*): *Al-Muwatta.* In Rahimuddin M (trans.): *Muwatta Imam Malik.* Lahore, Sh. Muhammad Ashraf, 1985.

Al-Azdi SA (*Abu Dawud*): *Kitab Al-Sunan.* In Hasan A (trans.): *Sunan Abu Dawud.* New Delhi, Kitab Bhavan, 1990.

Al-Bukhari MI: *Kitab Al-Jami' Al-Sahih.* In Khan MM (trans.): *The Translation of the Meanings of Sahih Al-Bukhari.* Madinah, ---, undated.

Al-Bukhari MI: *Sahih Al-Bukhari.* In --- (trans.): *Alim Multimedia CD Rom.* ---, ISL Software Corporation, ---.

Al-Qushayri MH (*Muslim*): *Al-Jami' Al-Sahih.* In Siddiqi 'AH (trans.): *Sahih Muslim.* ---, ---, 1971(?).

Al-Tirmidhi MI: *Sahih Al-Tirmidhi.* In --- (trans.): *Alim Multimedia CD Rom.*

---, ISL Software Corporation, ---.

Miscellaneous References with Attributed Authorship

Abdo AS: Mecca and Medina: Mecca. In ---: *Encyclopaedia Britannica CD 98.* ---, ---, 1998.

Al-Hanbly QA: *Al-Uns Al-Jaleel Betarykh Al-Quds Wa Al-Khaleel.* ---, --, 15th century.

Al-Kisa'i: *The Tales of the Prophets.* In Thackston WM (trans.): *The Tales of the Prophets.* Boston, Twayne Publishers, 1978.

Al-Mubarakpuri S: *Al-Raheeq Al-Makhtum.* In ---: *The Sealed Nectar: Biography of the Noble Prophet.* Riyadh, Dar-us-Salam Publications, 1996.

Al-Tabari MH: *Ta'rikh Al-Rusul Wa Al-Muluk.* In Brinner WM (trans.): *The History of al-Tabari: Volume II. Prophets and Patriarchs.* Albany, State University of New York Press, 1987.

Al-Tabari MH: *Ta'rikh Al-Rusul Wa Al-Muluk.* In Rosenthal F (trans.): *The History of al-Tabari: Volume I. General Introduction and From the Creation to the Flood.* Albany, State University of New York Press, 1989.

Al-Tha'labi AM: *Qisas Al-Anbiya', Al-Musamma 'Ara'is Al-Majalis.* Beirut, Al-Matba'ah Al-Thaqafiyah, ---.

Asimov I: *Asimov's Guide to the Bible: Volume I. The Old Testament.* New York, Avon Books, 1968.

'Awad, WH: Personal communication of 10/22/1999.

Baines JR: Ancient Middle Eastern religions: A survey of ancient Middle Eastern religions: Egyptian religion. In ---: *Encyclopaedia Britannica CD 98.* ---, ---, 1998a.

Baines JR: Egypt: History: The predynastic and early dynastic periods. In ---: *Encyclopaedia Britannica CD 98.* ---, ---, 1998b.

Beck HF: The history of Israel: Part I. From the beginnings to the exile. In Laymon CM (ed.): *The Interpreter's One-Volume Commentary on the Bible.* Nashville, Abingdon Press, 1971.

Bourbon F: *Petra: Art, History and Itineraries in the Nabatean Capital.* In Fisher B (trans.): *Petra: Art, History and Itineraries in the Nabatean Capital.* Vercelli, White Star, 1999.

Brownlee WH: The book of *Ezekiel*. In Laymon CM (ed.): *The Interpreter's One-Volume Commentary on the Bible*. Nashville, Abingdon Press, 1971.

Budge EAW (trans.): *The Book of the Dead: The Hieroglyphic Transcript and English Translation of the Papyrus of Ani*. Avenel, Gramercy Books, 1995.

Charles RH: Introduction. In Charles RH (trans.): The book of *Jubilees*. In Charles RH (ed.): *The Apocrypha and Pseudepigrapha of the Old Testament in English: Volume II. Pseudepigrapha*. Oxford, Oxford University Press, 1969a.

Charles RH (ed.): *The Apocrypha and Pseudepigrapha of the Old Testament in English: Volume I. Apocrypha*. Oxford, Oxford University Press, 1969b.

Charles RH (ed.): *The Apocrypha and Pseudepigrapha of the Old Testament in English: Volume II. Pseudepigrapha*. Oxford, Oxford University Press, 1969c.

Dahlberg BT: The book of *Micah*. In Laymon CM (ed.):*The Interpreter's One-Volume Commentary on the Bible*. Nashville, Abingdon Press, 1971.

Dalley SM: Sargon. In ---: *Encyclopaedia Britannica CD 98.* ---, ---, 1998.

de Vaux R: *Ancient Israel: Volume I. Social Institutions*. New York, McGraw-Hill, 1965a.

de Vaux R: *Ancient Israel: Volume II. Religious Institutions*. New York, McGraw-Hill, 1965b.

Diakonoff IM: Languages of the world: Afro-Asiatic (Hamito-Semitic) languages. In ---: *Encyclopaedia Britannica CD 98.* ---, ---, 1998.

Dirks JF, Dirks DL: *The Lineage of the Bedouin Horsebreeding Tribes: Relationships to Biblical Tribes and Individuals and to Key Individuals in Arabic and Islamic History*. Kiowa, Bani Sham Association, 1998.

Duncan GB: Chronology. In Laymon CM (ed.): *The Interpreter's One-Volume Commentary on the Bible*. Nashville, Abingdon Press, 1971a.

Duncan GB: Measures and money. In Laymon CM (ed.): *The Interpreter's One-Volume Commentary on the Bible*. Nashville, Abingdon Press, 1971b.

Edzard DO, von Soden WT, Frye RN: The history of ancient Mesopotamia. In ---: *Encyclopaedia Britannica CD 98.* ---, ---, 1998.

Enheduanna: *Nin-Me-Sar-Ra*. In --- (trans.): The Mistress of all Divine Codes. In Fakhoury R: Poster celebrates Iraq's women, ancient history with homage to ancient poetess. *Jordan Times*. November 7, 1999. Page 2.

Epstein I: *Judaism*. Baltimore, Penguin Books, 1966.

Eiselen FC: The *Pentateuch*—Its origin and development. In Eiselen FC, Lewis E, Downey DG (eds.): *The Abingdon Bible Commentary*. New York, Abingdon-Cokesbury Press, 1929.

Fakhoury R: Poster celebrates Iraq's women, ancient history with homage to Ancient poetess. *Jordan Times*. November 7, 1999. Page 2.

Finegan J: *The Archaeology of World Religions: Volume III*. Princeton, Princeton U. Press, 1952.

Fritsch CT: The book of *Ezra*. In Laymon CM (ed.): *The Interpreter's One-Volume Commentary on the Bible*. Nashville, Abingdon Press, 1971.

Frost SB: The book of *Jeremiah*. In Laymon CM (ed.): *The Interpreter's One-Volume Commentary on the Bible*. Nashville, Abingdon Press, 1971.

Ginzberg L: *The Legends of the Jews: Volumes 1-7*. Philadelphia, Jewish Publication Society, 1909-1936.

Gottwald NK: The book of *Deuteronomy*. In Laymon CM (ed.): *The Interpreter's One-Volume Commentary on the Bible*. Nashville, Abingdon Press, 1971.

Gray J: The book of *Exodus*. In Laymon CM (ed.): *The Interpreter's One-Volume Commentary on the Bible*. Nashville, Abingdon Press, 1971.

Guthrie HH: The book of *Numbers*. In Laymon CM (ed.): *The Interpreter's One-Volume Commentary on the Bible*. Nashville, Abingdon Press, 1971.

Hallo WW: Sumer. In Metzger BM, Coogan MD (eds.): *The Oxford Companion to the Bible*. Oxford, Oxford University Press, 1993.

Hatun HA: *Lore of Light: Stories from the Lives of the Prophets*. In Shakrullah R (trans.): *Lore of Light: Stories from the Lives of the Prophets: Volume I*. Kuala Lumpur, AS Noordeen, 1996.

Haykal MK: *Hayat Muhammad*. In Al-Faruqi IR (trans.): *The Life of Muhammad*. Plainfield, American Trust Publications, 1976.

Hebert G: *The Old Testament from Within*. London, Oxford University Press, 1965.

Hendel RS: Nimrod. In Metzger BM, Coogan MD (ed.): *The Oxford Companion to the Bible*. Oxford, Oxford University Press, 1993.

Hitti PK: *History of the Arabs: Tenth Edition*. London, Macmillan, 1990.

Hughes TP: *Dictionary of Islam*. Chicago, Kazi Publications, 1994.

Hyatt JP: The compiling of Israel's story. In Laymon CM (ed.): *The Interpreter's One-Volume Commentary on the Bible*. Nashville, Abingdon Press, 1971.

Jacobsen T: Ancient Middle Eastern religions: A survey of ancient Middle Eastern religions: Mesopotamian religions. In ---: *Encyclopaedia Britannica CD 98*. ---, ---, 1998.

James TGH: Ancient Egyptian arts and architecture. In ---: *Encyclopaedia Britannica CD 98*. ---, ---, 1998.

Josephus F: *Jewish Antiquities*. In Maier PL (trans.): *Josephus: The Essential Writings: A Condensation of Jewish Antiquities and The Jewish War*. Grand Rapids, Kregel Publications, 1988.

Josephus F: *Jewish Antiquities*. In Whiston W (trans.): *The New Complete Works of Josephus*. Grand Rapids, Kregel Publications, 1999.

Khayyata MW: *Haleb Fi Al-Tarikh*. In Muslim M (trans.): *Aleppo in History*. ---, ---, ---

Kohlenberg III JR: *The NRSV Concordance: Unabridged: Including the Apocryphal/Deuterocanonical Books*. Grand Rapids, Zondervan Publishing House, 1991.

Leslie EA: The chronology of the *Old Testament*. In Eiselen FC, Lewis E, Downey DG (eds.): *The Abingdon Bible Commentary*. New York, Abingdon-Cokesbury Press, 1929.

Lewis B: *The Arabs in History*. New York, Harper Torchbooks, 1967.

Lings M: *Muhammad: His Life Based on the Earliest Sources*. Rochester, Inner Traditions International, Ltd., 1983.

Longacre LB: *Numbers*. In Eiselen FC, Lewis E, Downey DG (eds.): *The Abingdon Bible Commentary*. New York, Abingdon-Cokesbury Press, 1929.

Mansfield P: *The Arabs*. Middlesex, Penguin Books, 1986.

Marks JH: The book of *Genesis*. In Laymon CM (ed.): *The Interpreter's One-Volume Commentary on the Bible*. Nashville, Abingdon Press, 1971.

Matthews AD: *A Guide for Hajj and 'Umra.* Lahore, Kazi Publications, 1979.

May HG: The people of the *Old Testament* world. In Laymon CM (ed.): *The Interpreter's One-Volume Commentary on the Bible.* Nashville, Abingdon Press, 1971.

McEvedy C, Jones R: *Atlas of World Population History.* London, Allen & Unwin, 1978.

McKenzie JL: The Hebrew community and the *Old Testament.* In Laymon CM (ed.): *The Interpreter's One-Volume Commentary on the Bible.* Nashville, Abingdon Press, 1971.

Mohamed MN: *Hajj and 'Umrah from A to Z.* ---, ---, 1996.

Muir W: *The Life of Mahomet.* As quoted in Haykal MH: Hayat Muhammad. In Al-Faruqi IR (trans.): *The Life of Muhammad.* Plainfield, American Trust Publications, 1995.

North CR: The *Old Testament* in the light of archaeology. In Eiselen FC, Lewis E, Downey DG (eds.): *The Abingdon Bible Commentary.* New York, Abingdon-Cokesbury Press, 1929.

Noth M: *The History of Israel.* New York, Harper & Row, 1960.

Parker SB: Ancient Middle Eastern religions: A survey of ancient Middle Eastern religions: Syrian and Palestinian religion. In ---:*Encyclopaedia Britannica CD 98.* ---, ---, 1998.

Parrot A: Abraham. In ---: *Encyclopaedia Britannica CD 98.* ---, ---, 1998.

Quanbeck WA: The *Letter to the Hebrews.* In Laymon CM (ed.): *The Interpreter's One-Volume Commentary on the Bible.* Nashville, Abingdon Press, 1971.

Rasmussen WD, Mellanby K: The history of agriculture: Early agricultural societies: Sumer. In ---: *Encyclopaedia Britannica CD 98.* ---, ---, 1998.

Reumann J: The transmission of the Biblical text. In Laymon CM (ed.): *The Interpreter's One-Volume Commentary on the Bible.* Nashville, Abingdon Press, 1971.

Robinson TH: *Genesis.* In Eiselen FC, Lewis E, Downey DG (eds.): *The Abingdon Bible Commentary.* New York, Abingdon-Cokesbury Press, 1929a.

Robinson TH: History of the Hebrew and Jewish people. In Eiselen FC, Lewis E, Downey DG (eds.): *The Abingdon Bible Commentary.* New York, Abingdon-Cokesbury Press, 1929b.

Rohl DM: *Pharaohs and Kings: A Biblical Quest.* New York, Crown Publishers, 1995.

Sarna NM: Biblical literature and its critical interpretation: *Old Testament* canon, texts, and versions. In ---: *Encyclopaedia Britannica CD 98.* ---, --, 1998.

Sha'ath S: *The Citadel of Aleppo: An Archaeological and Historical Guide.* In Azraq M (trans.): *The Citadel of Aleppo:An Archaeological and Historical Guide.* ---, ---, 1993.

Shabbir M: *The Authority and Authenticity of Hadith as a Source of Islamic Law.* New Delhi, Kitab Bhavan, 1982.

Siddiqui AH: *Life of Muhammad.* Des Plaines, Library of Islam, 1991.

Silberman LH: The making of the *Old Testament* canon. In Laymon CM (ed.): *The Interpreter's One-Volume Commentary on the Bible.* Nashville, Abingdon Press, 1971.

Simpson DC: *First* and *Second Kings.* In Eiselen FC, Lewis E, Downey DG (eds.): *The Abingdon Bible Commentary.* New York, Abingdon-Cokesbury Press, 1929.

Smith RH: The book of *Joshua.* In Laymon CM (ed.): *The Interpreter's One-Volume Commentary on the Bible.* Nashville, Abingdon Press, 1971a.

Smith RH: The book of *Judges.* In Laymon CM (ed.): *The Interpreter's One-Volume Commentary on the Bible.* Nashville, Abingdon Press, 1971b.

Stegemann H: *Die Essener, Qumran, Johannes der Taufer und Jesus.* In --- (trans.): *The Library of Qumran: On the Essenes, Qumran, John the Baptist, and Jesus.* Grand Rapids, William B. Eerdmans Publishing Company, 1998.

Terrien S: *The Golden Bible Atlas.* New york, Golden Press, 1964.

Toombs LE: The *Psalms.* In Laymon CM (ed.):*The Interpreter's One-Volume Commentary on the Bible.* Nashville, Abingdon Press, 1971.

Voigt EE: The land of Palestine. In Eiselen FC, Lewis E, Downey DG: *The Abingdon Bible Commentary.* New York, Abingdon-Cokesbury Press, 1929.

Wevers JW: The first book of the *Kings*. In Laymon CM (ed.): *The Interpreter's One-Volume Commentary on the Bible*. Nashville, Abingdon Press, 1971a.

Wevers JW: The first book of *Samuel*. In Laymon CM (ed.): *The Interpreter's One-Volume Commentary on the Bible*. Nashville, Abingdon Press, 1971b.

Whitelam KW: *The Invention of Ancient Israel: The Silencing of Palestinian History*. London, Routledge, 1996.

Woolley L, et al: Ur. In ---: *Encyclopaedia Britannica CD 98*. ---, ---, 1998.

Wright GE: *Biblical Archaeology*. Philadelphia, Westminister Press, 1960.

Yarwood DY: Dress and adornment:The history of Middle Eastern and Western dress: Mesopotamia. In ---: *Encyclopaedia Britannica CD 98*. --, ---, 1998.

Miscellaneous References with Unattributed Authorship

---: Amorite. In ---: *Encyclopaedia Britannica CD 98*. ---, ---, 1998.

---: Anath. In ---: *Encyclopaedia Britannica CD 98*. ---, ---, 1998.

---: Anu. In ---: *Encyclopaedia Britannica CD 98*. ---, ---, 1998.

---: Asherah. In ---: *Encyclopaedia Britannica CD 98*. ---, ---, 1998.

---: Baal. In ---: *Encyclopaedia Britannica CD 98*. ---, ---, 1998.

---: Bel. In ---: *Encyclopaedia Britannica CD 98*. ---, ---, 1998.

---: Black Stone of Mecca. In ---: *Encyclopaedia Britannica CD 98*. ---, ---, 1998.

---: Canaanite languages. In ---: *Encyclopaedia Britannica CD 98*. ---, ---, 1998.

---: Dagan. In ---: *Encyclopaedia Britannica CD 98*. ---, ---, 1998.

---: Dead Sea. In ---: *Encyclopaedia Britannica CD 98*. ---, ---, 1998.

---: Ea. In ---: *Encyclopaedia Britannica CD 98*. ---, ---, 1998.

---: East African Rift System. In ---: *Encyclopaedia Britannica CD 98*. ---, ---, 1998.

---: El. In ---: *Encyclopaedia Britannica CD 98*. ---, ---, 1998.

---: Geb. In ---: *Encyclopaedia Britannica CD 98*. ---, ---, 1998.

---: Harran. In ---: *Encyclopaedia Britannica CD 98*. ---, ---, 1998.

---: Hawran. In ---: *Encyclopaedia Britannica CD 98.* ---, ---, 1998.

---: Hebrew. In ---: *Encyclopaedia Britannica CD 98.* ---, ---, 1998.

---: Horus. In ---: *Encyclopaedia Britannica CD 98.* ---, ---, 1998.

---: Ishtar. In ---: *Encyclopaedia Britannica CD 98.* ---, ---, 1998.

---: Isis. In ---: *Encyclopaedia Britannica CD 98.* ---, ---, 1998.

---: Ka'bah. In ---: *Encyclopaedia Britannica CD 98.* ---, ---, 1998.

---: Malik ibn Anas. In ---: *Encyclopaedia Britannica CD 98.* ---, ---, 1998.

---: Maps. In Laymon CM (ed.): *The Interpreter's One-Volume Commentary on the Bible.* Nashville, Abingdon Press, 1971.

---: Mot. In ---: *Encyclopaedia Britannica CD 98.* ---, ---, 1998.

---: Nimrod. In ---: *Encyclopaedia Britannica CD 98.* ---, ---, 1998.

---: Nut. In ---: *Encyclopaedia Britannica CD 98.* ---, ---, 1998.

---: Osiris. In ---: *Encyclopaedia Britannica CD 98.* ---, ---, 1998.

---: Pyramid. In ---: *Encyclopaedia Britannica CD 98.* ---, ---, 1998.

---: Pyramids of Giza. In ---:*Encyclopaedia Britannica CD 98.* ---, ---, 1998.

---: Rift valley. In ---: *Encyclopaedia Britannica CD 98.* ---, ---, 1998.

---: Seth. In ---: *Encyclopaedia Britannica CD 98.* ---, ---, 1998.

---: Shamash. In ---: *Encyclopaedia Britannica CD 98.* ---, ---, 1998.

---: Shu. In ---: *Encyclopaedia Britannica CD 98.* ---, ---, 1998.

---: Sin. In ---: *Encyclopaedia Britannica CD 98.* ---, ---, 1998.

---: Sodom and Gomorrah. In ---: *Encyclopaedia Britannica CD 98.* ---, ---, 1998.

---: Sphinx. In ---: *Encyclopaedia Britannica CD 98.* ---, ---, 1998.

---:*Student Map Manual: Historical Geography of the Bible Lands.* Jerusalem, Pictorial Archive (Near Eastern History) Est., 1983.

---: Sumer. In ---: *Encyclopaedia Britannica CD 98.* ---, ---, 1998.

---: *Syria.* Damascus, Ministry of Tourism in the Syrian Arab Republic, 1989.

---: Tefnut. In ---: *Encyclopaedia Britannica CD 98.* ---, ---, 1998.

---: Tirmidhi, at-. In ---: *Encyclopaedia Britannica CD 98.* ---, ---, 1998.

---: Yamm. In ---: *Encyclopaedia Britannica CD 98.* ---, ---, 1998.